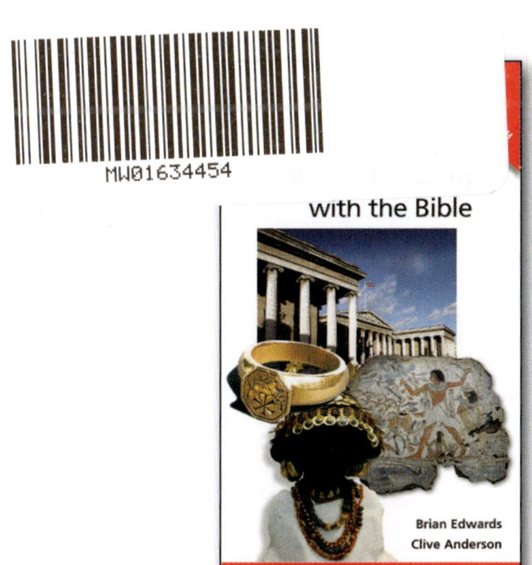

Series Editor: Brian H Edwards

Day One

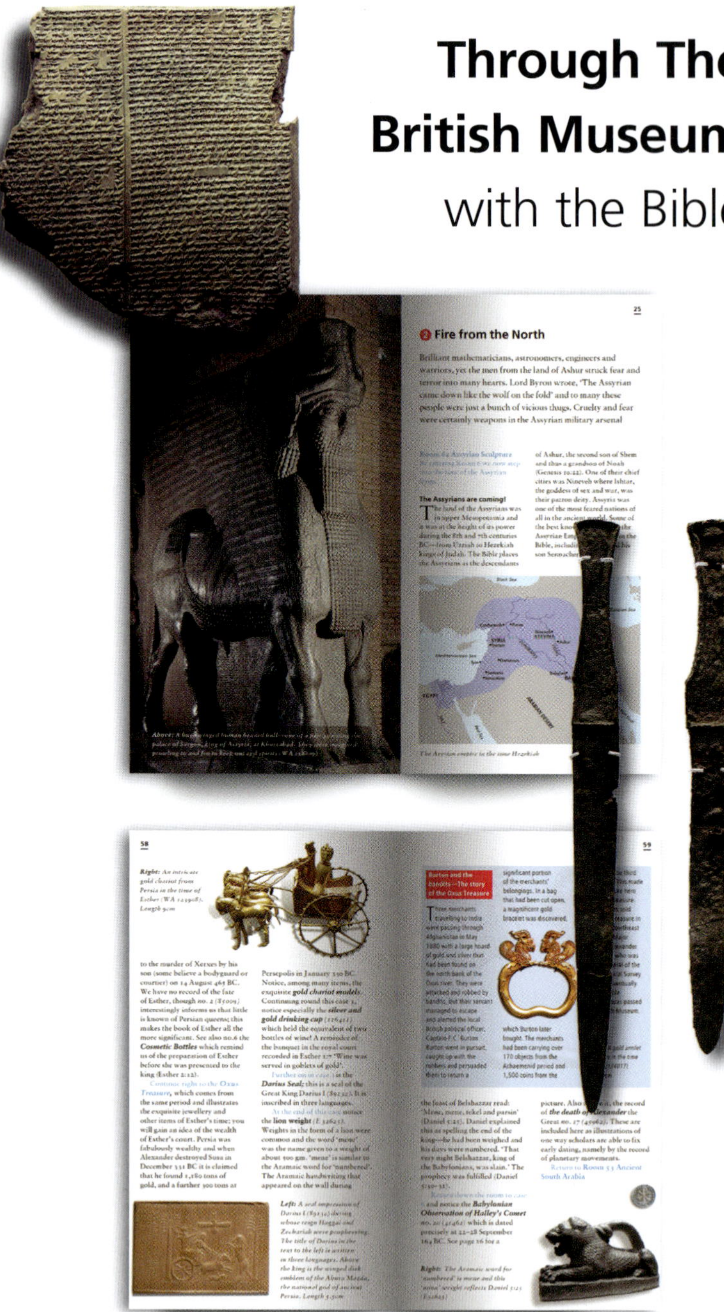

Through The British Museum
with the Bible

Above: *Two bronze Assyrian swords.* With swords like these Sennacherib was murdered by two of his sons (2 Chronicles 32:21)

CONTENTS

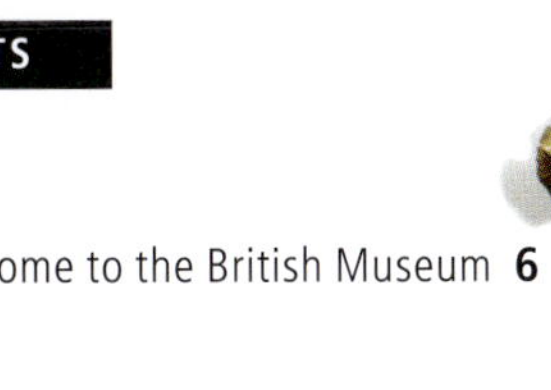
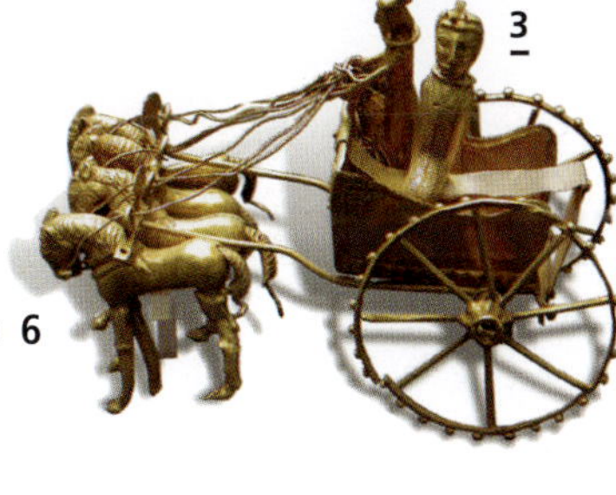

© Day One Publications 2004 Revised and updated 2008, 2011, 2013, 2015 and this edition 2019

All Scripture quotations are taken from the New International Version

A CIP record is held at The British Library   ISBN 978-1-84625-124-5

Published by Day One Publications Ryelands Road, Leominster, HR6 8NZ

☎ 01568 613 740 FAX 01568 611 473   email: sales@dayone.co.uk   www.dayone.co.uk   All rights reserved

Design: Steve Devane and Kathryn Chedgzoy (k-c-design.co.uk)   Printed by Polskabook, UK

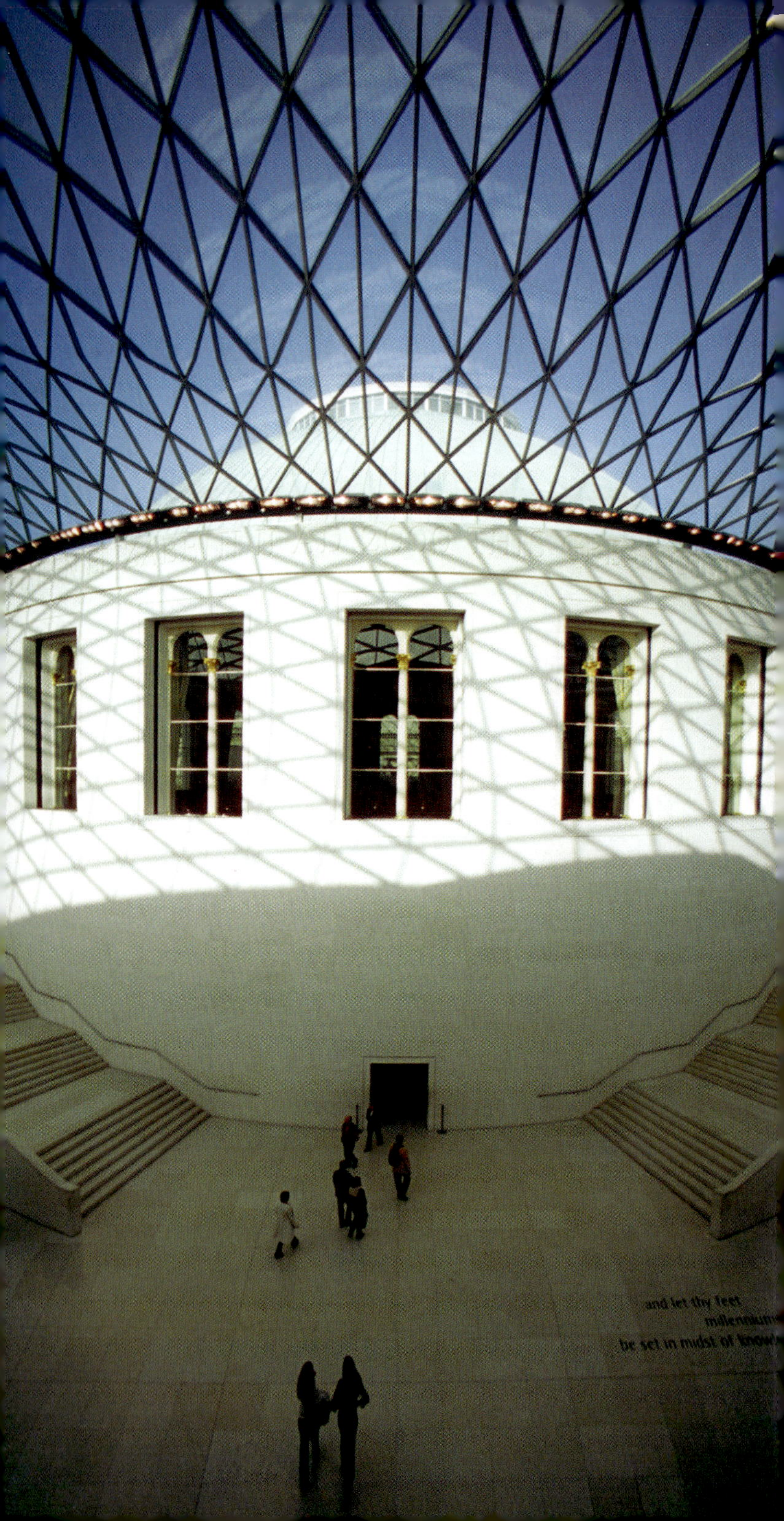
and let thy feet
millennium
be set in midst of knowl

Through the British Museum— footprints of the Bible

'And let thy feet, millenniums hence, be set in the midst of knowledge' is an appropriate text from Alfred Lord Tennyson's *The Two Voices* to greet visitors who enter the British Museum. Or, as one young mother was overheard encouraging her toddler as she released him from his buggy between the Ionic columns of the entrance: 'This is the most exciting place in the world'.

First opened in 1759, the Museum was accessible for just three hours a day for those who applied in writing stating why they wished to visit. The British Museum was the first public museum in the world. Today, the visitor can spend all day here and browse at leisure without appointment and at no charge. Almost eight million visitors take up this invitation each year; it is the most popular tourist attraction in the whole of the United Kingdom.

The British Museum is one of the finest Museums in the world and home to sixteen million objects, with around seventy thousand of them on display in one hundred galleries. There are exhibits from every continent and covering the whole of the history of civilization. And all are in a secure environment for the world to enjoy. The visitor can inspect one of Europe's finest collections of Japanese art, or study the three-quarters of a million coins from the time of Daniel to the present day. Or they may wander around the mummies of Egypt, examine the beautiful sculpture of Ancient Greece, delve into the history of Africa and the Americas, or research the story of the Romans and Anglo Saxons in Britain.

However, in this guide we have one object in mind: we will focus on those items that will help us in our understanding of the Bible. Some exhibits will point to the accuracy of the biblical records whilst others will simply throw light on Bible events and customs.

So, in a fascinating walk through Bible times we follow in the steps of Abraham right up to the time of Paul, and take in the great empires of Egypt, Assyria, Babylonia, Persia, Greece and Rome. We will wander through these powerful kingdoms and close with the 'People of the Way'.

Facing page: The Magnificent Great Court, with three thousand three hundred and twelve panes of glass each uniquely cut to size. It is the area of a football field and the roof contains 800 tons of glass and steel

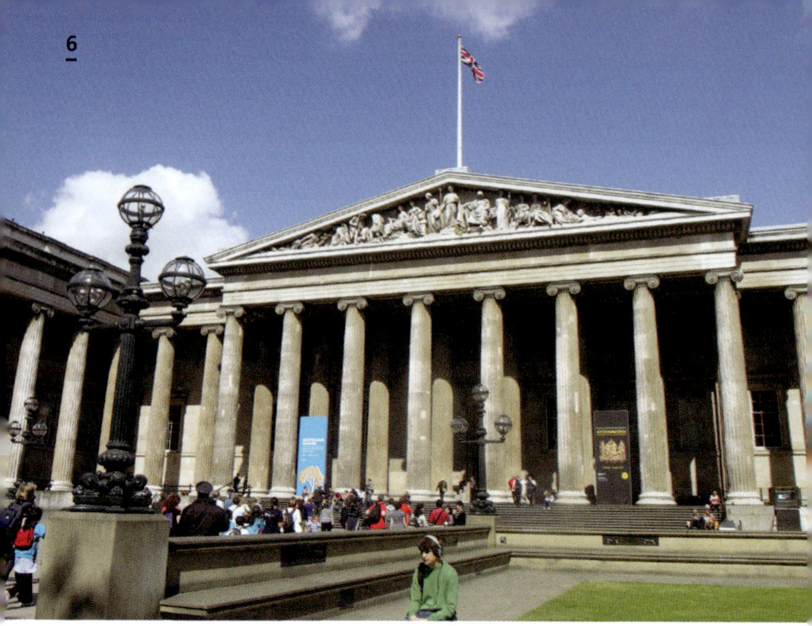

Welcome to the British Museum

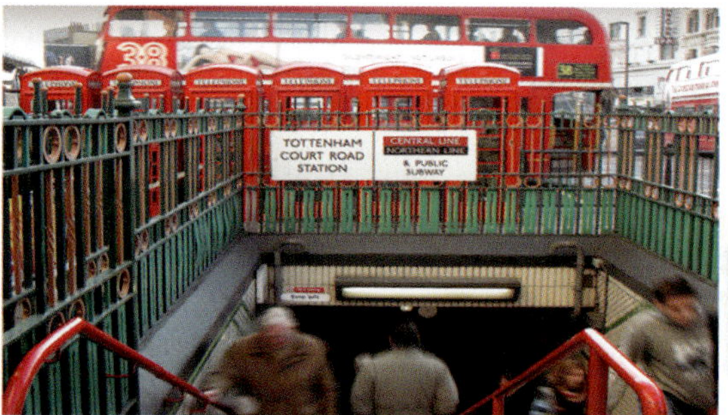

Left: Tottenham Court Road Underground Station

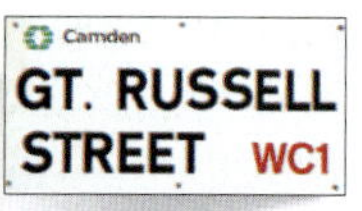

TRAVEL AND MUSEUM DIRECTIONS

The British Museum
Great Russell Street
London WC1 3DG
Telephone: ☎ +44(0) 20 7323 8000
www.thebritishmuseum.ac.uk

The best route to the Museum is to take the London Underground Northern Line to Tottenham Court Road. When you come out of this station look for Exit 3 and the signs to the British Museum; walk straight ahead and turn right at Great Russell Street. It is a ten minute walk to the Museum. It can also be reached from Holborn and Russell Square Underground stations but you will have a longer walk! Alternatively buses from Euston or Waterloo will take you to Theobold Road at the other end of Great Russell Street (nos. 59, 68, 168, 188).

Please be advised that there is a bag security check to enter the Museum and queues can be lengthy and in the open! Large bags and suitcases are not allowed in the Museum.

There is **no admission charge**, though the Museum Trustees do request a donation of approximately £4 per person. Any currency is accepted. Alternatively you may wish to consider becoming a **Friend of the British Museum,** the benefits of which include a quarterly magazine and a reduction on all purchases in the museum shops.

The Museum website

The website address is: www.thebritishmuseum.ac.uk. To search for an item click the 'Explore' tab. We advise you to check opening hours from the website.

Shopping in the Museum

There is an excellent **book room**, plus a **souvenir shop** and **children's shop** in the Great Court. If you can afford something special, you should visit the **Grenville shop** with its array of replica jewellery, sculptures and silks.

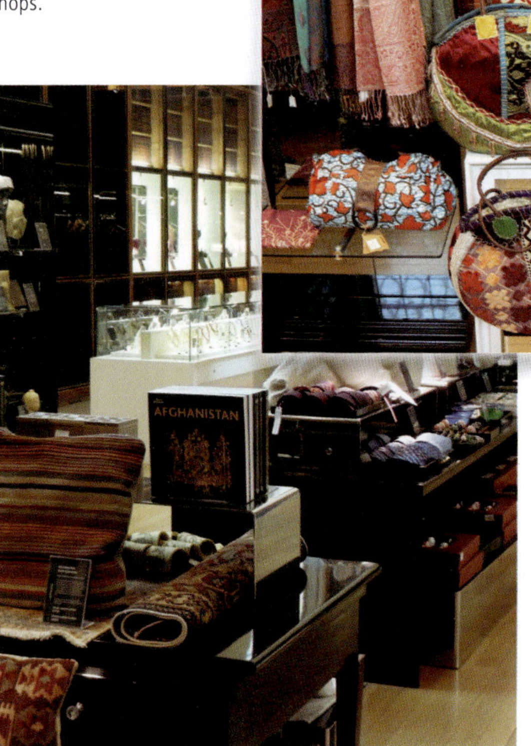

Left: The Grenville shop in the Museum—offering superb replicas, silks and other quality items for sale

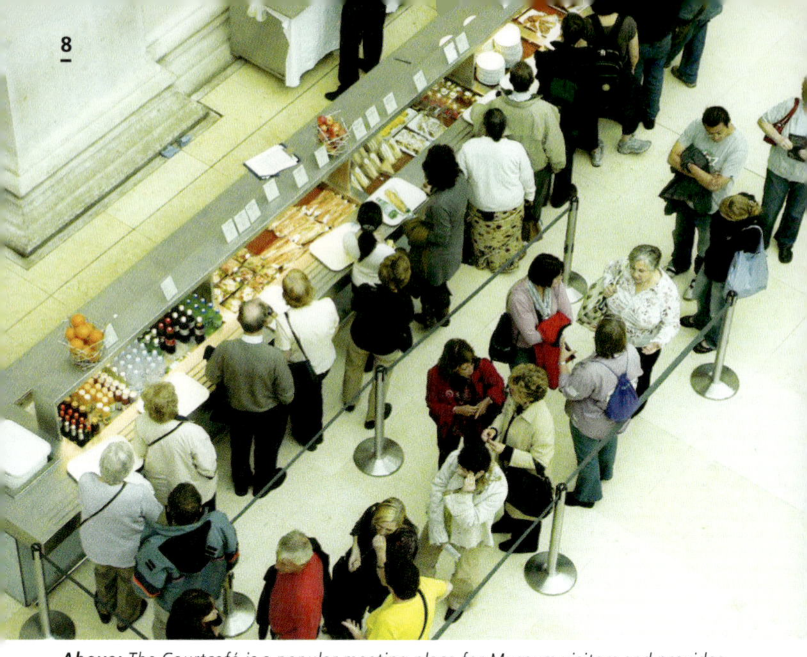

Above: The Courtcafé is a popular meeting place for Museum visitors and provides excellent food and drink

Refreshments in the Museum

The **Courtcafé,** situated in the Great Court with two serving points, provides hot drinks and light refreshments. If you take your lunch break outside the 'rush hour' of 1300 to 1400 hrs you will find a seat more easily. For something a little more substantial the **Pizzeria** is comfortable and not often as overcrowded. Or you can try the more expensive **Court Restaurant** just above the Great Court. **Light refreshments** are also available on the landing above the main staircase (Room 37)

You may prefer to bring a packed lunch; you can eat this in the Great Court away from the Courtcafé. You must not eat or drink in the galleries (exhibition rooms)—and this includes chewing gum!

At weekends and during school holidays, families with children are welcome to use the Ford Centre for Young Visitors as a picnic-style eating area. It has high chairs, water fountains and vending machines for treats.

General information

School visits. Visits to the Museum are free but you must book for any group of 10 or more. Booking enables the Museum to provide schools with a range of facilities and services to make your visit beneficial and enjoyable. Schools will be interested in the two activity books that twin with this guide. See pages 126-127 for details.

Travel light around the museum, as there is a lot of walking. Light portable stools are available in the Great Court. These are free of charge but must be returned before you exit the museum. This guide is all that you really need unless you want a notebook and pencil for your own notes. You may also wish to have a small copy of the Bible with you. You can check any bags into the cloakroom for a small charge or keep a rucksack on your back, taking care that any valuables are not vulnerable to pickpockets.

For **security** reasons, large bags and suitcases are not allowed into the Museum.

The Museum is accessible for **disabled visitors**, and a limited supply of wheelchairs is available (phone to reserve on 020 7323 8299); lifts are available for the upper galleries. Guide dogs are welcome in the Museum, and there are facilities for the blind.

Toilet and nappy changing facilities are available off the Great Court and toilets are also located in other areas of the museum.

You are allowed to take **photographs and videos,** but you must not use a tripod. However, remember that a flash will normally flash-back from a glass case. Please note that you may not use your pictures for anything other than personal use; publication of your own pictures is forbidden under copyright law.

You may use a **mobile phone** only in the Great Court area.

Throughout the tour **you must not touch exhibits or lean on the glass display cases.** Visitors are advised that CCTV is in operation.

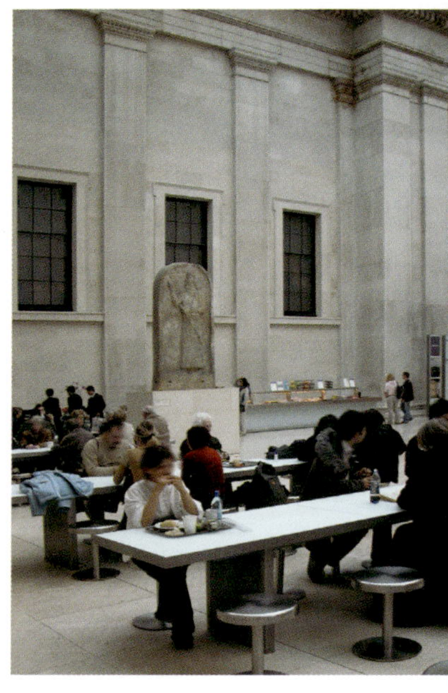

Above: *The Great Court*

Below: *The well-stocked Bookshop has a wide range of informative books including Day One publications*

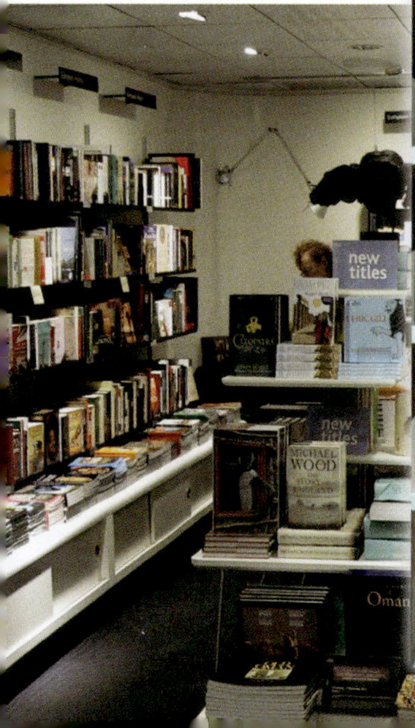

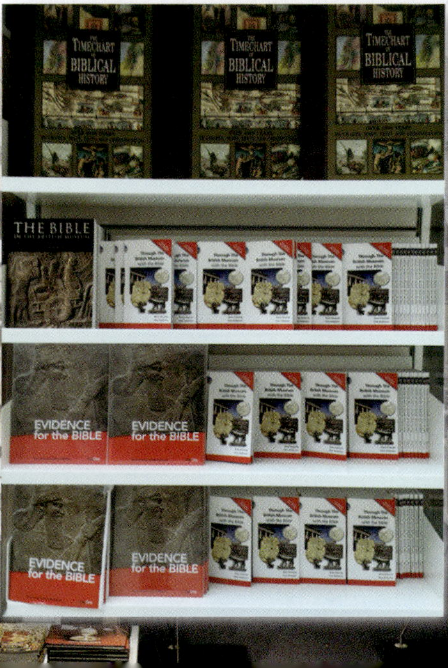

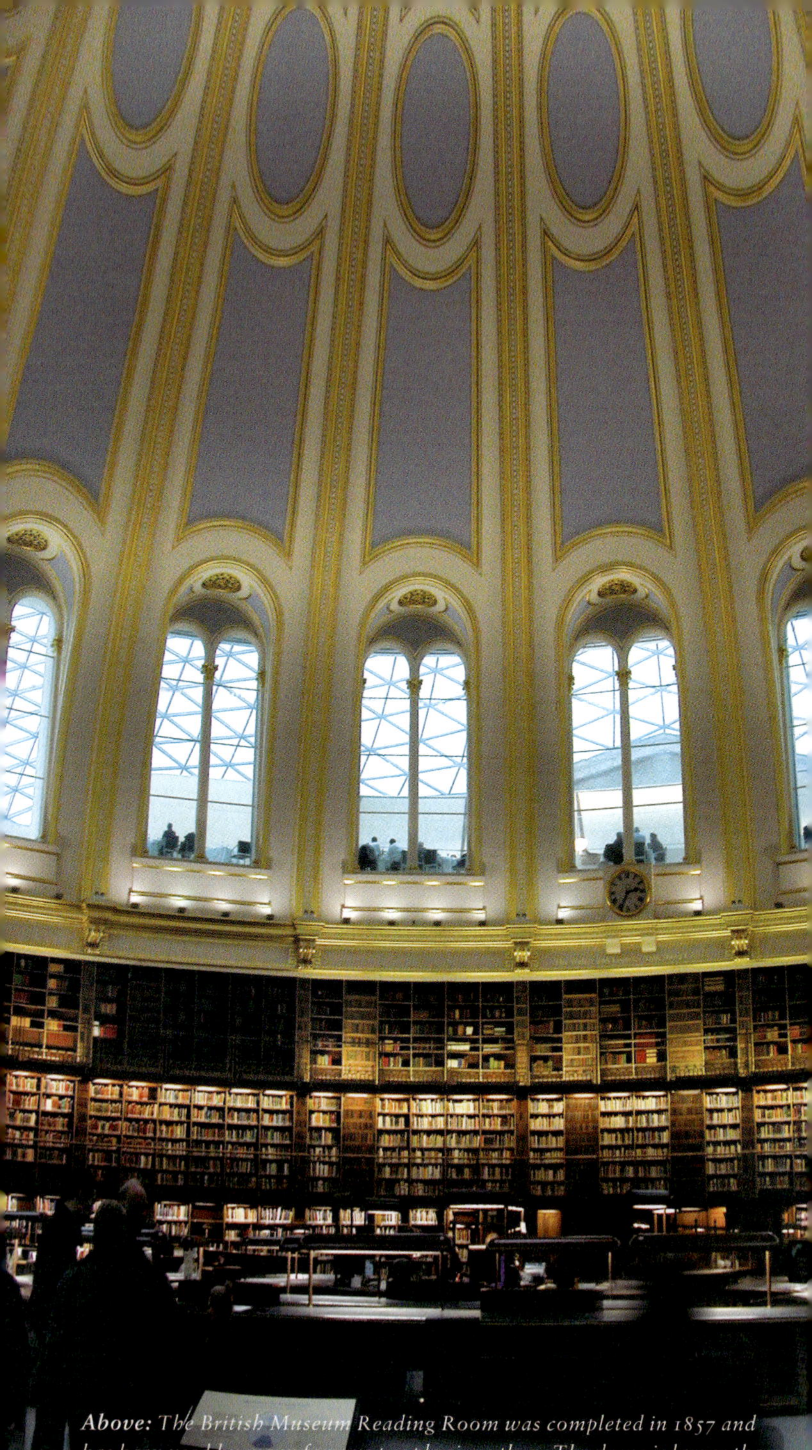

Above: *The British Museum Reading Room was completed in 1857 and has been used by many famous people since then. The dome is larger than the dome of St Paul's Cathedral*

❶ Starting your tour

Household waste and the spoils of war, along with apparently unexciting trash, are an archaeologist's dream. Alongside monuments, inscriptions and statues, these commonplace items help to bring the dead past to life

The British Museum Act of 1753 authorised the building of 'one general repository' to house the collections of Sir Hans Sloane, the Harley and Cotton families, 'and of the additions thereto'. On 15 January 1759 the museum was first opened to the public, and during the eighteenth and nineteenth centuries books, manuscripts, pottery, statues, coins, medals, botanical and zoological specimens, poured into the collection from statesmen and explorers, from both private and company collections. Soon the building was inadequate to house the fascinating collection and in 1823 an extensive rebuilding programme began. By 1887 the natural history collection had to be moved to South Kensington (now the Natural History Museum), and in 1997 the books and manuscripts went to the British Library at St Pancras.

The building you enter, with its fine Greek Ionic columns, was completed in 1842 and is now a Grade I listed building.

The Museum is owned by the nation and is governed by a Board of Trustees which is responsible to the British Parliament. The first popular guide to the Museum was published in 1808.

Whenever you see a **room number** it refers to the room you are in—not the one you are about to enter. Every item in the Museum has its own **accession number** and we have noted these for you so that you can be sure you are looking at the correct exhibit. The initial letters will indicate the gallery represented: for example EA refers to Egyptian Antiquity, WA to Western Asiatic (or ME Middle East), and GR to Greece and Rome—though this initial letter is increasingly omitted and only the number is used. The **case numbers,** which we use to guide you to an object, are often indistinct—generally

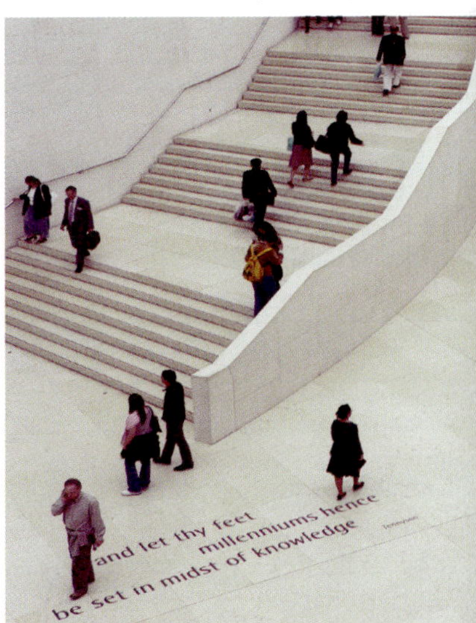

The generally accepted Archaeological Timeline

	BC	Period in the Bible
Neolithic (the age of stone implements)	From creation	
Chalcolithic (the use of copper and stone)	4500–3300	
Early Bronze Age (the use of bronze)	3300–2400	
Early Bronze Age II	2400–2000	Before Abraham
Middle Bronze Age	2000–1550	Abraham to Moses
Late Bronze Age	1550–1200	Exodus, Joshua, Judges
Iron Age I (the use of iron)	1200–1000	The monarchy of Saul and David
Iron Age II	1000–586	The Kings and prophets
Babylonian Period	586–539	Destruction of Jerusalem and exile
Persian Period	539–332	Return from exile: Ezra & Nehemiah
Hellenistic (Greek) Period	332–141	Between the Old and New Testaments
Roman Period	37 BC–324 AD	Life of Christ and the early church

Timelines of nations: From Abraham to Solomon page 77. Hebrew kings page 63. Egyptian Kings page 42. Assyrian kings page 26. Babylonian kings page 69. Persian kings page 54. Roman emperors page 100.

in white at the top left corner of the case (though sometimes at the bottom).

It is never possible to guarantee that all the items referred to will be on display, or that all the rooms will be open. When you arrive, go to the **Information Desk** in the Great Court and check on specific rooms that you may wish to see. Whilst the details in this book are accurate at the time of publication, because the Museum is constantly being upgraded we cannot guarantee that the items are in the locations recorded here.

If you have a copy of this guide prior to visiting the Museum, we encourage you to read it through before your visit. **In this guide we follow an approximate themed route:** Assyria, Egypt, Persia, Babylonia, the ancient Mesopotamian culture of Abraham, then Syria and the Philistines and finally Rome. This is not the chronological order, but saves over much back-tracking. The chronological order is: Mesopotamia, Egypt, Assyria,

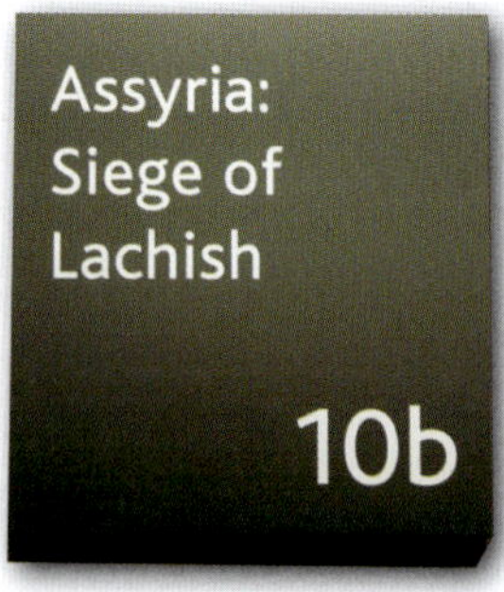

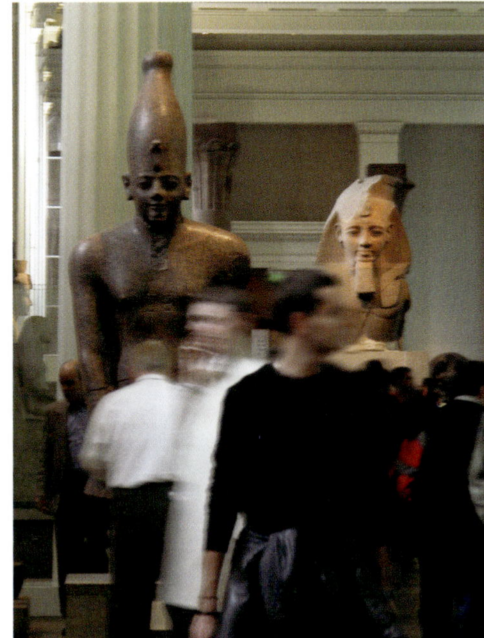

Right: Archaeology enables those in the present to walk among those of the past, like these visitors to the Museum passing Tuthmosis III, with Ramesses II in the background. One of these Pharaohs was probably in charge at the time of the Exodus

Babylonia, Persia and Rome. The Greek empire of the Macedonian, Alexander, comes in the period between the Testaments and is not our focus here.

Timeline and technical words

You will sometimes see references to periods such as 'Early Bronze Age'. The Timeline on page 12 will help you to identify these periods. However, they are only rough guides for dating; for example, it is known that iron was in use by 4,000 BC, even though the 'Iron Age' does not begin until 1200 BC.

A new chronology of the ancient world has been proposed in recent years. However, this has not found general acceptance and this guide follows the traditional timetable. For a reasoned response to the new chronology see, *The Third Intermediate Period in Egypt* by K.A. Kitchen, 2004, ISBN 0–85668–298–5.

Due to continuous study and discoveries, scholars may alter names (and spelling) for kings and peoples from the ancient world; for the sake of clarity this guide generally uses those in current use on the Museum's identification labels.

A number of technical words will be encountered in our tour: they are explained in the 'Glossary of archaeological words' on page 118.

Archaeology is rubbish!

Archaeology is the science of reading history from the leftovers of previous civilizations. It involves uncovering the remains of buildings and of household bits and pieces. From these we learn who the people were and when and how they lived. Archaeology

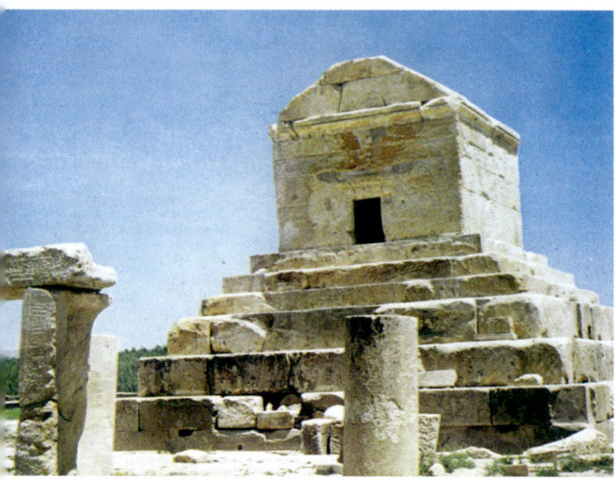

Left: The tomb of Cyrus II at Pasargadae. When Alexander the Great visited it in 322 BC, he discovered the tomb had been raided by grave robbers and the robes, cape, jewellery and scimitar of Cyrus were gone, and his bones lay all over the floor

has been called 'the study of durable rubbish.' We are looking through a window into the past and watching a way of life that would otherwise be wholly unknown to us.

A burnt and broken wall may speak of a long lost civilization that came to a violent end; a piece of shattered pottery with a hurried note scrawled on it informs us of a disastrous military campaign; a beautiful vase, clearly foreign to the location in which it was found, may tell us of international trade; a hastily buried cache of coins and household valuables points to the disintegration of a community. The past is right there in front of us.

The word archaeology comes from the Greek *archaios* which means 'ancient' or 'old'. Not until the early nineteenth century did the word 'archaeology' come to be used of items that could be dug out of the ground. Today the same word can cover anything discovered from the past, including manuscripts.

Grave events

The earliest 'archaeologists' were grave robbers who plundered ancient royal tombs for their treasures. Archaeology is a fairly young science. Little serious archaeological work was done before the nineteenth century, but after the defeat of Napoleon, British and French archaeologists worked together in Egypt and elsewhere. For the first time, the Bible was being looked at in the context of what we could learn about the nations surrounding Israel. Archaeological societies sprang into being, developing into what is today an exact and exciting science. Soon the names of some of the rulers of the ancient Middle East could be identified with those mentioned in the Bible, and in these early records names of kings of Israel and Judah, as well as place names mentioned in the Bible, occasionally appeared.

Today even seals and seal impressions (bullae) of kings of Israel and Judah, and their servants, have been discovered.

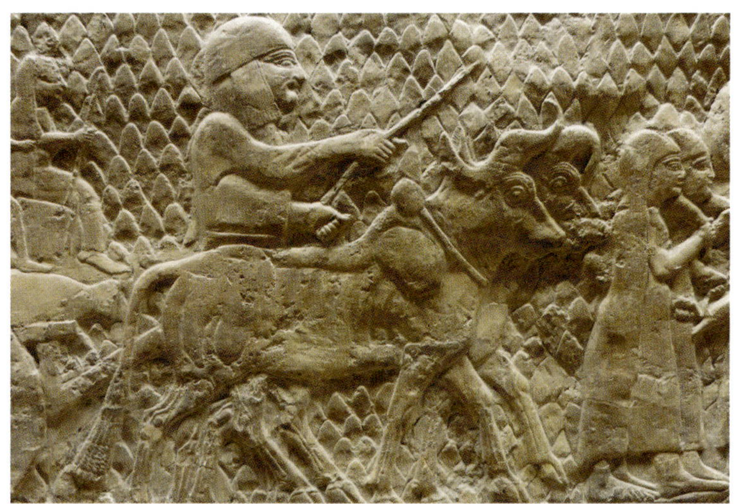

Above: Relief from the Siege of Lachish—an event from the time of king Hezekiah of Judah in 701 BC (see pages 34–37). As the defenders go into exile the detail of their starving animals is clearly shown

What does a Tell tell us?

Ancient civilizations built their towns on the rubble—often with the rubble—of the previous occupants. Much of what the earlier people left behind—their building materials, pottery, jewellery, messages, food remains, household utensils, weapons and even their own bones—were covered over by the newcomers. It is all this 'durable rubbish' that helps the archaeologist. As generation after generation built upon the trash of their ancestors—or of the enemy they defeated—the town grew higher and higher. The great mountain of earth that betrays the presence of an old city is called a *tell*, an Arabic and Hebrew word for 'ruin-mound'. This word is found in the names of Bible cities like Tel-melah and Tel-harsha (Nehemiah 7:61) and Tel-abib (Ezekiel 3:15).

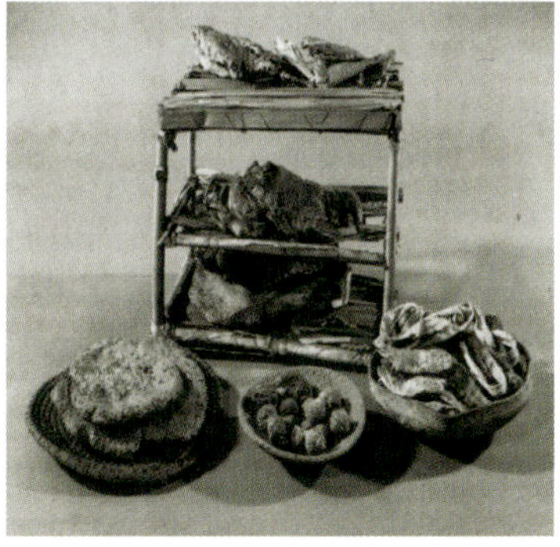

Above: Fast food from Thebes: including duck, bread, fruit and fish. These were included in Egyptian tombs as food for the Ka—the surviving spirit of the departed. Thebes was the ancient city of Upper Egypt on the banks of the Nile. By 1600 BC it became the capital of all Egypt but was destroyed by the Assyrian king Ashurbanipal, see Naham 3:8–10

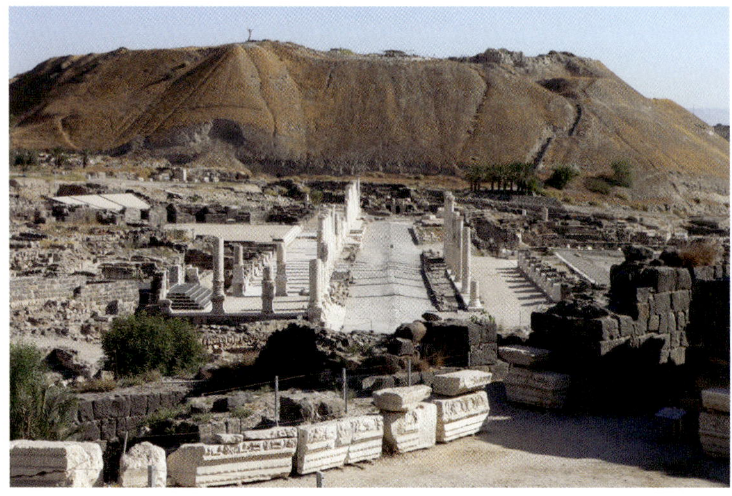

Above: The tell of Beth Shan, where the Philistines paraded the bodies and armour of King Saul and his sons (1 Samuel 31), now stands 80 metres high and reveals a long history of occupation from the fifth millennium BC to the eleventh century

Dating exhibits

In the Bible, events are often dated precisely, but the dating is never given with reference to the calendar as we know it. Sometimes a natural phenomena is used as the marker, as in Amos 1:1 'The words of Amos … two years before the earthquake when Uzziah was king of Judah …' or more often the reign of another king as in 2 Kings 13:1,10, and of course the census at the time of the birth of Jesus Christ (Luke 2:1). But this only helps us if we can locate those events or reigns at a point in history. In order to establish a chronology (that word comes from the Greek word for time: *chronos*), the Bible's dates are compared with events in the surrounding nations; even so, exact dating is not always possible, and this is why the date

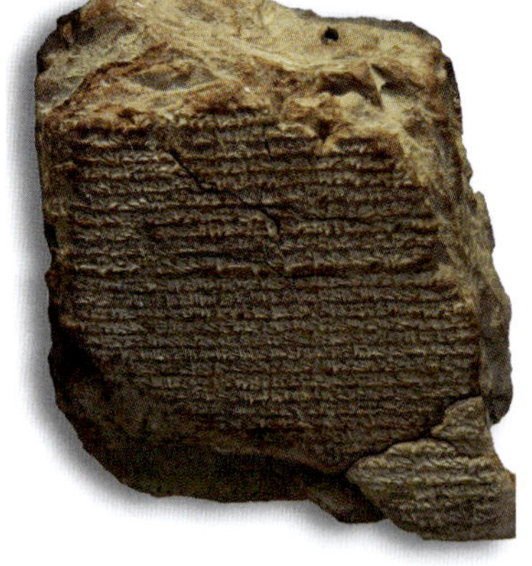

Above: The Babylonian observation of Halley's Comet (WA 41462), which is to be found in room 52, illustrates one way by which scholars are able to fix early dating. See page 59

for many exhibits is given as *circa* (or just *c.*), meaning 'about'.

As with any science, archaeologists must be cautious and ready to change when new evidence is uncovered. We must beware of drawing firm conclusions from little support. Archaeologists, like all scientists, are not infallible and they do make mistakes, change their mind, and disagree with each other's conclusions. However they can often offer precise dates through diligent work, especially when the ancient records refer, for example, to an eclipse of the sun or the appearance of a comet (see the Babylonian Chronicle on p 67 for an example of this).

COMMENCING YOUR TOUR

Remember the Museum room plan is on the inside back cover of this Guide.

We begin our tour in the **Great Court**

The Queen Elizabeth II Great Court was opened in the year 2000 and visitors gain the wonderful experience of feeling that they are in the open air whilst being warm and dry. Around the Great Court are sculptures that represent the various galleries. In the centre is the historic Reading Room and on either side are two impressive marble staircases that lead you to the upper galeries.

The circular Reading Room is appropriately at the very heart of the Museum. With reference to the nineteenth and twentieth centuries it has been referred to as 'The intellectual hub of the Empire.' It was first opened in 1857 and scores of

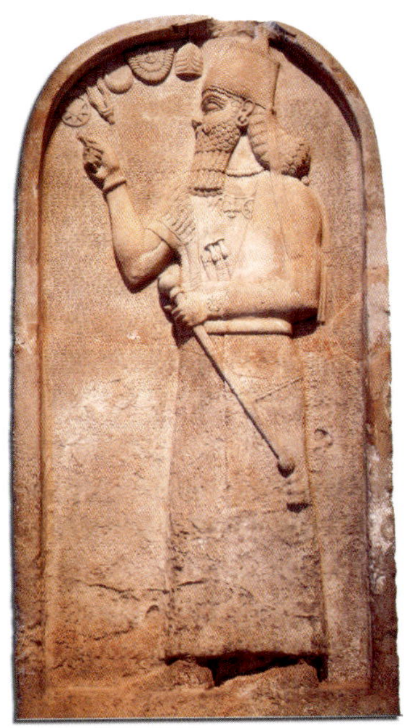

Above: The stele of Ashurnasirpal II (ANE 118805) in the Great Court. He ruled over the Assyrian empire during the reigns of Asa and Jehoshaphat in Judah. Above his hand and on his wrists are the conventional symbols of his gods

prominent people have studied here. They are listed either side of the entrance inside and include Thomas Carlyle, Charles Dickens, Edward Elgar, Charles Darwin, Karl Marx (Lenin visited here to pay homage to Marx), Arthur Conan-Doyle (the inventor of Sherlock Holmes), and John Keys—the personal secretary of Charles Haddon Spurgeon. At the time of publishing, the Reading Room is not open.

Follow round to the right as you face the Library beyond the staircase and cross over to **Room 1 Enlightenment.** Enter and turn left to the replica *Rosetta Stone*.

This room, once known as The King's Library and built between 1823 and 1827 to house the library of King George III, has been set out to reflect the so-called Age of Enlightenment during the eighteenth and nineteenth centuries, and represents how the Museum first grew with objects from all over the world. The beautiful timber floor is over two hundred years old.

As an introduction to much that we will see later, we begin with the Rosetta Stone. We will see the original in Room 4 (page 45) but this exact replica enables you to examine it in more detail.

The Rosetta Stone

The Rosetta Stone was discovered by a French officer in 1799 in the western Delta of Egypt and was surrendered to the British at the end of the Napoleonic war and brought to the British Museum in 1802. The stone is carved on black basalt and is valuable because it contains the same message in two forms of ancient Egyptian writing and one in Greek. The Egyptian writing at the top of the stone is hieroglyphic writing, whilst the second section is demotic Egyptian; the third section is in Greek capital letters (known as 'uncial'). The Greek was translated relatively easily and proved to be part of a citation by Egyptian priests in Memphis to celebrate the first anniversary of the coronation of Ptolemy V in 196 BC.

In 1824 A French scholar, Jean-François Champollion, recognised that the two Egyptian scripts were the equivalent text to the Greek and, once deciphered, this helped scholars to understand ancient Egyptian writing. The hieroglyphic script would have been known to Israel during their time in Egypt, and Moses, who was educated in the Royal Court of Pharaoh (see Acts 7:22), would have been accustomed to reading a script like this.

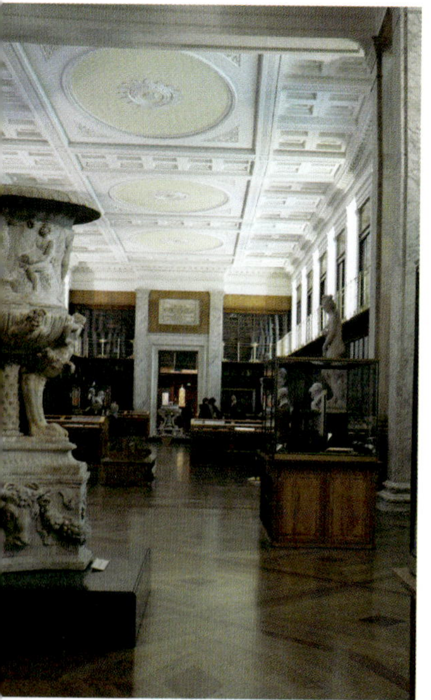

Left: Room 1 Enlightenment is laid out as it was when first completed in 1827 to house the library of 60,000 volumes of King George III which his son donated to the nation

Above: The Rosetta Stone (EA 24) has been in the museum since 1802 and was important in helping scholars to decipher the ancient Egyptian hieroglyphic script. The bottom left corner has been cleaned to show its original condition.

See Box: A Short History of Writing (page 20). Important proclamations in the ancient world were often recorded in three languages—the most famous of all being the sign above Jesus on the cross 'written in Aramaic, Latin and Greek' (John 19:20).

Behind and to the right of the Rosetta stone there are bricks stamped with the name of Nebuchadnezzar II. A fine example is *no. 90082*. This is the king responsible for the final destruction of Jerusalem in the time of Judah's last King Zedekiah in 586 BC. Daniel had been taken into exile by Nebuchadnezzar in 605 BC.

To the right and below Nebuchadnezzar's bricks, in *case 72 (on the bottom plinth)* you will find the **Samaritan Inscription** (*BM 127387*). The Samaritans included the people originally imported in 722 BC by Sargon, the king of Assyria, from across his empire to repopulate the land of Israel in the north. They integrated their pagan beliefs

A short history of writing

Writing is one of the important marks of civilization, and the earliest known development of writing comes from Sumer (now southern Iraq) shortly before 3000 BC. Simple pictures (pictograms) were drawn in vertical columns on clay tablets with a pen made from a sharpened reed.

In Egypt, writing appeared slightly later. This hieroglyphic script of about 700 pictorial signs was written from left to right, right to left, or downwards! A cursive (joined up) form, called 'hieratic' (meaning 'of the priests') was developed in the Old Kingdom, and 'demotic' script (a form of shorthand meaning 'of the people') was in use from about 700 BC.

Cuneiform 'wedge' script developed from the pictograms in Sumer. With about 300 signs, its use was confined to trained scribes, as was Egyptian.

From about 2,000 BC, cuneiform was the common script across the Fertile Crescent but the alphabet began to replace it after 1,000 BC. With only 22 consonantal signs, its comparative simplicity meant more people could write and read it. Hebrew and Aramaic were written with the alphabet. As Aramaic became the official language under the Persian Empire in the 6th century BC, the alphabet was current from southern Egypt to the Indus River.

The conquests of Alexander the Great from 330 BC, brought Greek to replace Aramaic, and so spread the Greek alphabet over the same area.

Nevertheless, the Aramaic script survived and gave rise to both the modern Arabic and Hebrew alphabets.

The Egyptians invented papyrus (a form of paper made from the papyrus reed) and that, or leather (vellum was a high quality leather), became the normal writing material wherever the alphabet was current. The 'paper and ink' referred to in 2 John 12 was almost certainly papyrus and the ink was made from soot mixed with gum.

See also Room 56 case 3 on page 86.

with Judaism and accepted only the first five books of Moses (the Pentateuch); consequently they were always considered as 'heretics' by the Jews—hence the point of the parable of the Good Samaritan (Luke 10 and compare John 4:9). This inscription is part of the Pentateuch in their own script and comes from the 13th century AD. See Box: Khorsabad, the home of Sargon (page 32).

Directly behind you in *case 15 Ancient Scripts—the search for Babylon.* A fascinating retelling of the discovery of Nineveh by Claudius James Rich in the early nineteenth century. He discovered hundreds of items covered in cuneiform writing, but was unable to read them.

In *case 16, behind 15,* follow the story of breaking the code of Egyptian hieroglyphs—read this case from left to right. The French scholar Jean François Champollion deciphered hieroglyphs in 1824 using the Rosetta Stone.

Continue down this room past the door through which you entered. You will experience what the Museum contained when items now in the Natural History Museum, the Science Museum and the British Library were exhibited here. Notice the two display cases (nos. 5 and 6) on the *Birth of Archaeology.*

Above: Egyptian hieroglyphic writing from the sarcophagus of an Egyptian priestess in the time of Jeremiah. Her name appears in the cartouche (EA 32 Room 4)

Below: A clear example of the wedge shaped cuneiform script from a genealogy in the Assyrian palace of Adad-Nirari 810–783 BC. (WA 1118925 Room 8)

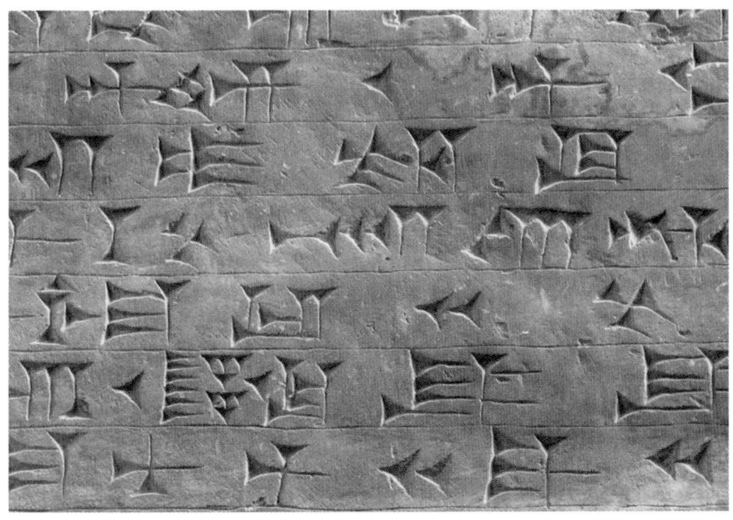

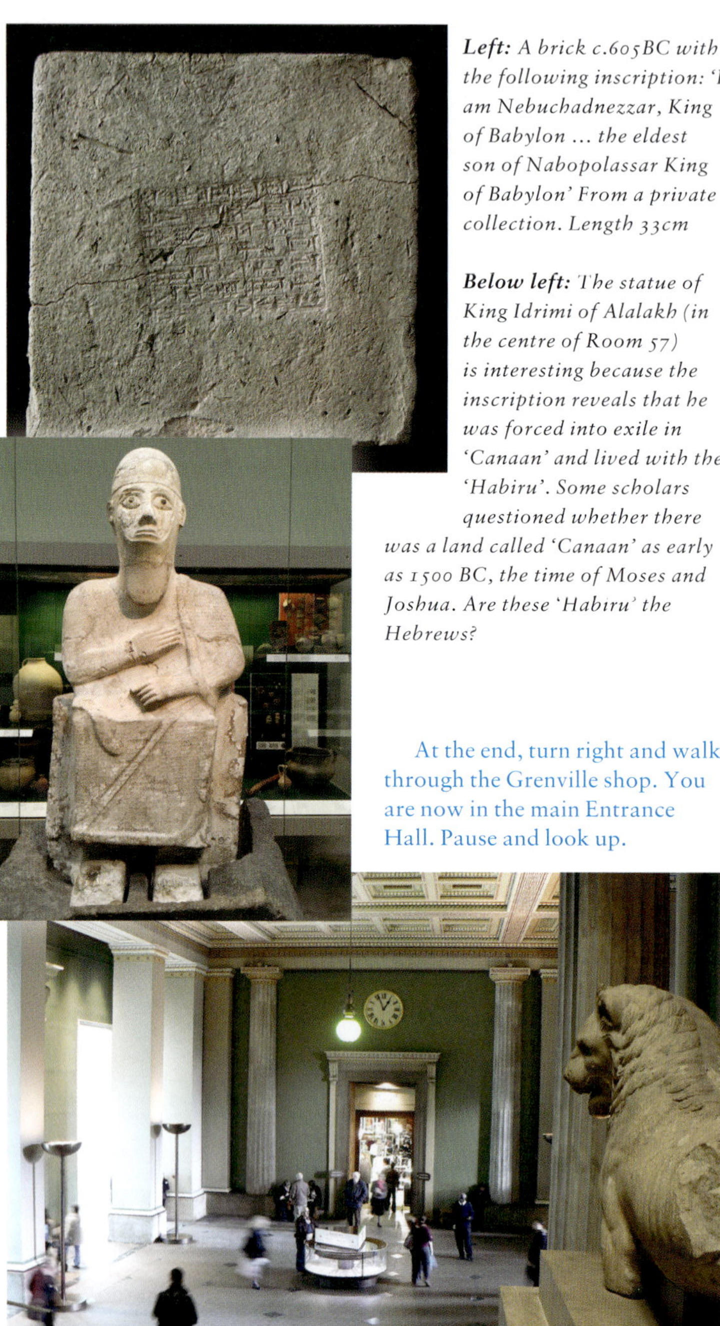

Left: A brick c.605BC with the following inscription: 'I am Nebuchadnezzar, King of Babylon ... the eldest son of Nabopolassar King of Babylon' From a private collection. Length 33cm

Below left: The statue of King Idrimi of Alalakh (in the centre of Room 57) is interesting because the inscription reveals that he was forced into exile in 'Canaan' and lived with the 'Habiru'. Some scholars questioned whether there was a land called 'Canaan' as early as 1500 BC, the time of Moses and Joshua. Are these 'Habiru' the Hebrews?

At the end, turn right and walk through the Grenville shop. You are now in the main Entrance Hall. Pause and look up.

Above: Looking into the main entrance hall from the Victorian staircase

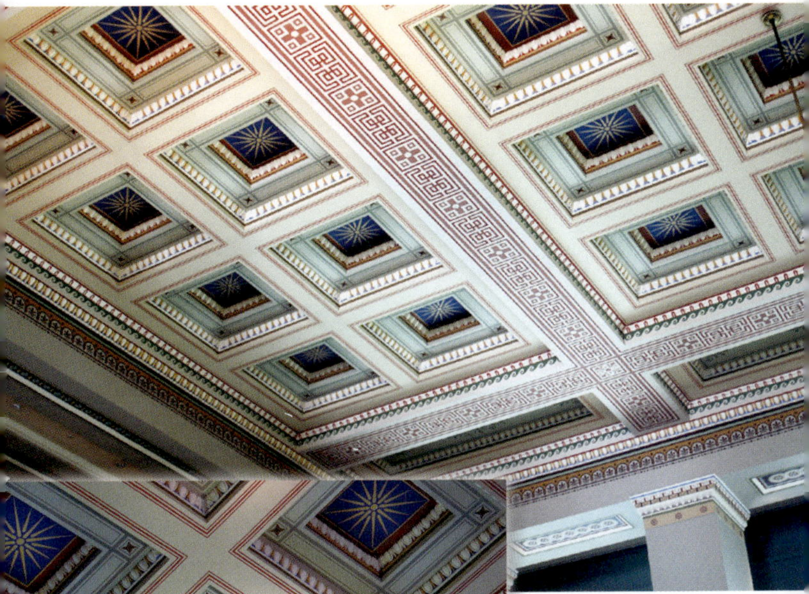

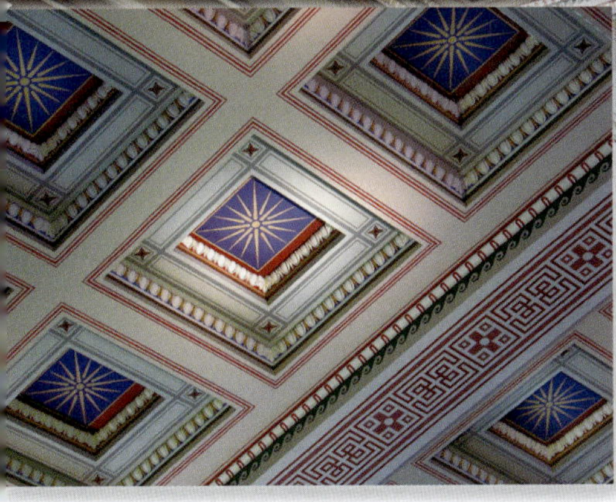

Above and inset: The exquisitely colourful ceiling of the Victorian Entrance Hall illustrating the buildings of ancient Athens

The Victorian Entrance Hall

This was opened in 1847 and the Polychrome scheme on the ceiling used motifs taken from buildings in ancient Athens. The Hall was damaged during World War II but the restoration that was completed in the year 2000 reinstated it to the original design of 65 different colours. This colourful ceiling is how many of the now colourless exhibits in the Museum from ancient palaces and temples (including the Elgin Marbles) would have appeared originally.

Walk through the corridor to the left of the staircase, passing the cloakroom on your left. This will bring you to **Room 6 Early Greece**. Turn right into **6a Assyrian Sculpture** to the *Black Obelisk* on your right.

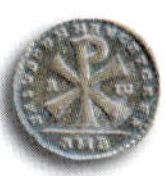

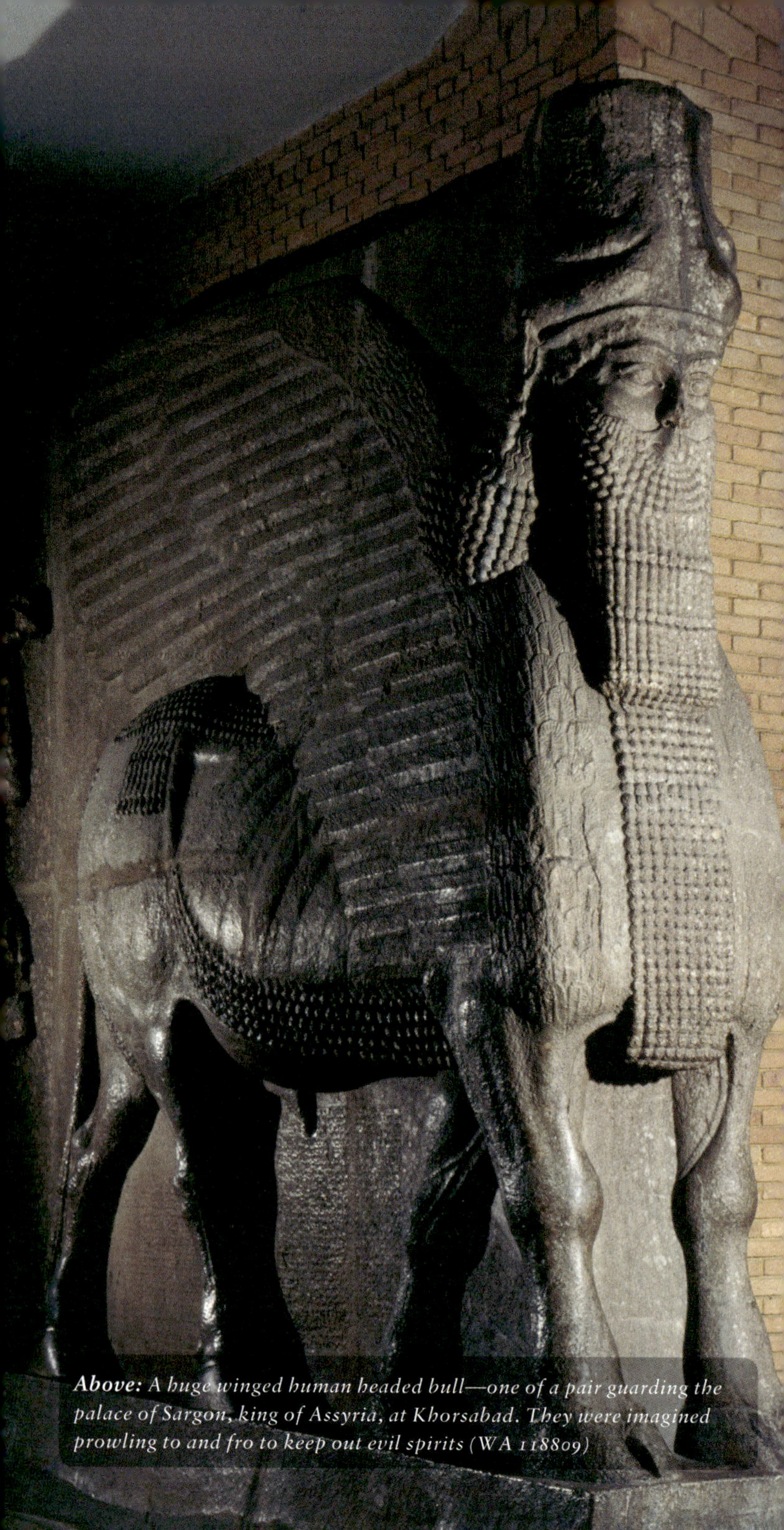

Above: *A huge winged human headed bull—one of a pair guarding the palace of Sargon, king of Assyria, at Khorsabad. They were imagined prowling to and fro to keep out evil spirits (WA 118809)*

❷ Fire from the North

Brilliant mathematicians, astronomers, engineers and warriors, yet the men from the land of Ashur struck fear and terror into many hearts. Lord Byron wrote, 'The Assyrian came down like the wolf on the fold' and to many these people were just a bunch of vicious thugs. Cruelty and fear were certainly weapons in the Assyrian military arsenal

Room 6a Assyrian Sculpture

By entering Room 6 we now step into the time of the Assyrian kings.

The Assyrians are coming!

The land of the Assyrians was in upper Mesopotamia and it was at the height of its power during the 8th and 7th centuries BC—from Uzziah to Hezekiah kings of Judah. The Bible places the Assyrians as the descendants of Ashur, the second son of Shem and thus a grandson of Noah (Genesis 10:22). One of their chief cities was Nineveh where Ishtar, the goddess of sex and war, was their patron deity. Assyria was one of the most feared nations of all in the ancient world. Some of the best known names from the Assyrian Empire are found in the Bible, including Sargon and his son Sennacherib.

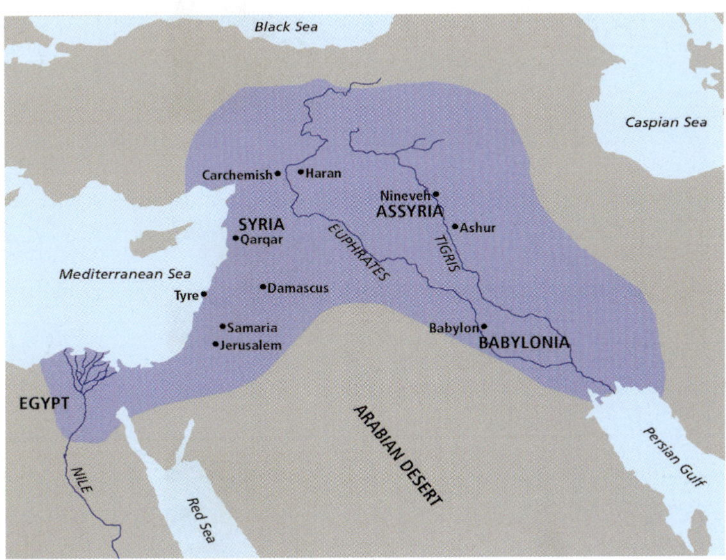

The Asyrian empire in the time Hezekiah

Assyrian kings

Assyrian kings ruled much of what we know as northern Iraq and Syria from 1300–1050 BC. They lost power in the face of Aramean tribes until about 925 BC, and as they reasserted their rule, they came into conflict with the kings of Israel and Judah. Note that only the first Old Testament reference to each king is given.

	BC	
Tukulti-Ninurta II	890–884	The reigns of Asa and Baasha, kings of Judah and Israel.
Ashurnasirpal II	883–859	The time of Ahab King of Israel and Elijah and Elisha the prophets.
Shalmaneser III	859–824	His records mention subduing Ahab and Jehu (See the Black Obelisk on page 27).
Shamsi-Adad V	823–811	The reigns of Joash and Jehu, kings of Judah and Israel.
Adad-nirari III	810–782	Probably the deliverer in 2 Kings 13:5.
Shalmaneser IV	782–773	During the reigns of Amaziah and Jeroboam II.
Ashur-dan III	772–754	Probably king when Jonah went to Nineveh.
Ashur-nirari V	754–744	During the reigns of Azariah and Menahem.
Tiglath-pileser III *	744–727	2 Kings 15:29 (also the Pul of v 19). His records name Menahem, Pekah and Hoshea of Israel, and Ahaz of Judah.
Shalmaneser V*	727–722	2 Kings 17:3–6.
Sargon II*	722–705	Isaiah 20:1. The destruction of Samaria in 722.
Sennacherib*	704–681	2 Kings 18:13, The siege of Jerusalem in 701BC.
Esarhaddon*	680–669	2 Kings 19:37
Ashurbanipal*	668–627	The Aramaic name Osnapper is used in Ezra 4:10, though some translations use Ashurbanipal. See pages 31.

End of Assyria with the fall of Nineveh to Babylon at Carchemish in 612.

* These kings are mentioned by name in the Bible

Timelines: from Abraham to Solomon page 77. Hebrew kings page 63. Egyptian kings page 42. Babylonian kings page 69. Persian kings page 54. Roman emperors page 100.

In Room 6 turn to your right

The Black Obelisk

Discovered in 1845 by Henry Layard, the black limestone obelisk commemorates the triumphs of the Assyrian king Shalmaneser III. Part of this victory obelisk describes his defeat of Ben-Hadad and Hazael of Damascus (see 2 Kings 8:7–15) and depicts rulers in national costume bringing tribute to the king. The second row down shows a kneeling figure in Israelite dress with the inscription above which reads, 'Tribute of Yaua, son of Humri: I received silver,

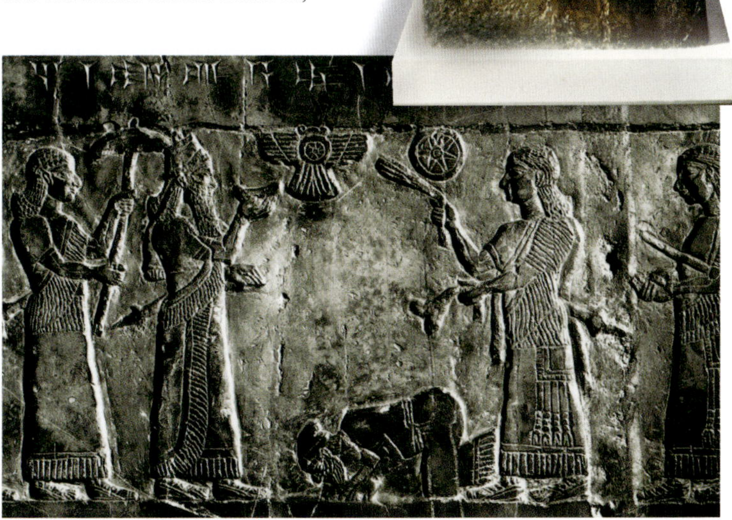

Above: Detail of the Black Obelisk showing the Israelites bringing tribute. The kneeling figure may well be that of Jehu himself

gold, a golden bowl, a golden vase with a pointed bottom, golden tumblers, golden buckets, tin, a staff for a king, spears.' This is Jehu the son of Omri. Jehu was not the direct son of Omri, but was a usurper and the fourth in line from Omri. In ancient near east languages, including Hebrew, there is no distinct word for grandfather/grandson.

From the ninth to the seventh centuries Assyrian records often called Israel, *humat-Humri*—'land of Omri', or *bit-Humri*—'house of Omri'. Behind the kneeling Jehu is a line of his servants laden with the items of tribute. To date, this is the only known depiction of an Israelite king.

Jehu was known to be a furious charioteer, and a ruthless soldier who destroyed the line of Ahab, including the infamous Jezebel (2 Kings 9–10). Having killed both the kings of Israel and Judah he needed a strong ally, and Shalmaneser provided that. Shalmaneser's account on the obelisk does not mention a defeat of Israel, but he received tribute nevertheless. However, the story did not end there. In order to make a friend of Shalmaneser, Jehu abandoned Hazael of Damascus (in Syria). For this treachery Jehu and Israel paid dearly in later years as 2 Kings 10:32 reveals.

Immediately behind the Black Obelisk are the stele of three kings.

We three kings of Orient are...
The one on the left is *Shalmaneser III (ANE 118884)*. This is the king of Assyria who, though not mentioned by name in the Old Testament, mentions both Ahab and Jehu in his records. The writing on the reverse of this stele describes his military campaign in the west in 853 BC. He confronted and defeated an alliance of twelve kings and he lists the strength of each army. He refers to 'Adad-idri of Damascus' (Ben-Hadad of Syria) and 'Ahab the Israelite' and claims that Ahab's army had 2,000 chariots and 10,000 infantry. This battle is not referred to in the Bible but perhaps can be placed during the three year 'reconciliation' (and

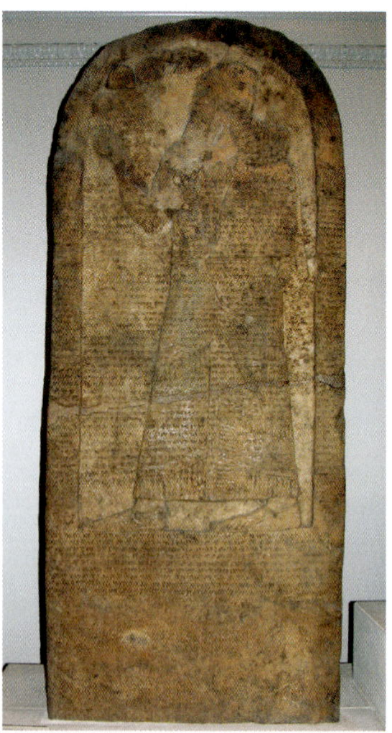

Above: Shalmaneser III, the king of Assyria who refers to both Ahab and Jehu in his own records (ANE 118884)

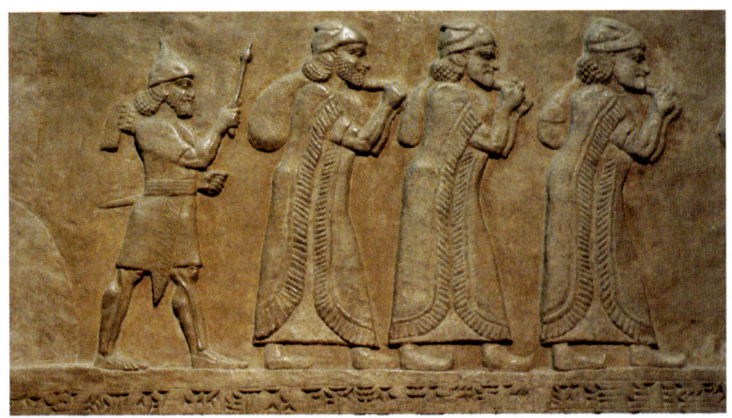

Above: Israelite prisoners being taken into exile from the city of Ashtaroth after the defeat of the northern kingdom in 740BC (ANE 118908)

hence alliance) between Ahab and Ben-Hadad (1 Kings 20:13–34; 22:1–3).

Beside Shalmaneser III is his father, **Ashurnasirpal II**. The third king is Shalmaneser's son.

(Note: do not confuse Shalmaneser III with the Shalmaneser referred to in 2 Kings 17:3 and 18:9 during the time of Ahaz and Hezekiah, kings of Judah—that one is Shalmaneser V).

To the left of the three kings is a wall relief of Jewish prisoners being taken into exile in the time of **Tiglath-Pileser III** (745–727 BC) from the city of Astartu. This is the Ashtaroth of Deuteronomy 1:4 and 1 Chronicles 6:71; their dress distinguishes them as Israelites. These were part of the ten tribes of Israel taken into exile at this time. Tiglath-Pileser is also known as Pul (2 Kings15:19) and is seen here in his chariot. The reference in 2 Kings 15:29–30 of him deporting 'the people to Assyria' is supported by his own claim to have replaced Pekah with Hoshea on the throne of Israel; Pul probably arranged the assassination of Pekah. To avoid the same fate, Ahaz, King of Judah, became his vassal by sending tribute as 2 Kings 16:7–10 records.

To your right, the **Temple of Ninurta at Nimrud,** see the panel **God and monster** (ANE 124571–2). Ninurta was the Assyrian god of war and farming. The Bible refers to 'Nimrod…a mighty warrior on the earth…a mighty hunter before the Lord' (Genesis 10:8, 9); he founded the city of Nineveh, which became the chief city of Assyria (vs.10–11). Nimrod possibly passed into legend as Ninerta.

The relief of the **protective spirit wearing a fish cloak** (ANE 124573) illustrates the significance of the protective fish cloak to the ancient Assyrians. Jonah's maritime experience would doubtless have impressed the inhabitants of Nineveh!

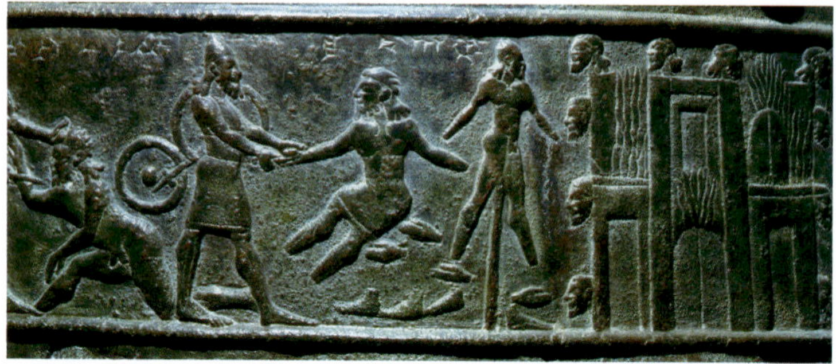

Above: *The gruesome detail of the bottom panel of the Balawat gates of Shalmaneser III (ANE 121651). Notice those impaled on stakes which was a forerunner of crucifixion—compare Ezra 6:11. This is possibly how the bodies of Saul and his sons were displayed at Beth Shan (1 Samuel 31:10)*

Now pass between the two winged lions opposite (*ANE 118801–2*) **in Room 6b** with the big gates in front of you

The lions were to protect the throne-room from evil spirits. In addition to the fact that they have wings and human heads they also have five legs; from whatever perspective they were ready for action and it was thought it made them all the better to cast out evil spirits.

'But Jonah ran away'

The Balawat Gates—like father, like son

These replica gates illustrate the massive gates that guarded the palace of the Assyrian king Shalmanezer III in the 9th century BC. They are an example of a type of gate used in many Assyrian official buildings. Shalmanezer's father, Ashurnasirpal II was unbelievably cruel, and once boasted:

'I built a pillar over against the city gate, and I flayed all the chief men who had revolted, and I covered the pillar with their skins. Some I walled up within the pillar, some I impaled upon the pillar on stakes, and others I bound round the pillar; and I cut off the limbs of the officers who had rebelled. From some I cut off their hands and from others I cut off their noses, their ears, and their fingers, of many I put out the eyes. Their young men and maidens I burned in the fire. The rest of them I consumed with thirst in the desert of the Euphrates.'

His son was no less cruel, and to prove the point, examine the bottom panel of the great bronze gates on your left, or on the reconstruction. You will see the grisly portrayal of enemies being dismembered or viciously killed. Though Jonah lived 100 years later, it is little wonder that he was reluctant to go to a city with kings like this in control

(Jonah 1:3). He headed for Tarshish —today, Benidorm!

Walk into **Room 7 Assyria: Nimrud**

The walls are decorated with reliefs from the palace of **Ashurnasirpal II** (883–859 BC).

Immediately on your left and right notice the Assyrian *eagle-headed protective spirit* (WA 124584 and 118804). This was used as the model for Tash in 'The Last Battle' by C S Lewis. The ***Standard Inscription*** of Ashurnasirpal gives the extent of his conquests. He lived at the time of Elijah, Elisha and Ahab and went as far as Tyre and Sidon; this gave a warning to Israel of the threat to come from future kings of Assyria.

Take the first exit to your left into **Room 10a Assyria: Lion hunt** and follow the lion hunt round. These panels show king **Ashurbanipal** (686–627 BC), the last great king of Assyria, hunting lions. The lions were released from captivity not merely for the sport of the king, but to demonstrate his power and authority over all creation. See Nahum 2:11 where, significantly, the destruction of the lion and lioness are symbols of Nineveh. Take particular note of the detailed relief of the lioness in her death agony; the observation and skill of the craftsman is evident.

Exit this room at the far end into **Room 10c Assyria: Khorsabad** and continue between the two huge winged bulls to the two figures at the top of the stairs on your left.

Famous for one line

You are standing in front of the great king *Sargon II (ANE 118822).* Sargon is facing one of his high officials or more probably his son the crown prince **Sennacherib.** For years it was presumed that a king by the name of Sargon never existed

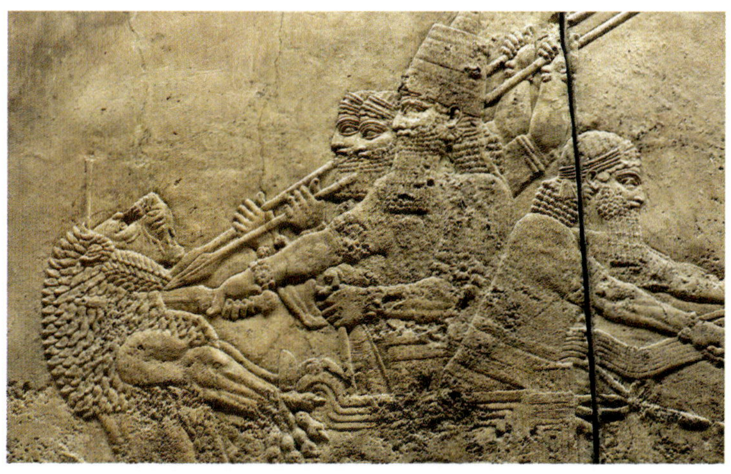

Above: *Part of the lion hunt by Ashurbanipal of Assyria. The hunt was intended to demonstrate the absolute power of the king*

Khorsabad, the home of Sargon

In 1843 Paul-Emile Botta, a French vice-consul and archaeologist in Mosul (northern Iraq), discovered at Khorsabad on the banks of the River Tigris, 8.5 miles (12 kilometres) to the northeast of Nineveh, a great palace guarded by huge **human-headed winged bulls** each weighing around ten tons and standing 15 feet high (4.8 metres). The walls were lined with great slabs of stone carved with pictures and cuneiform writing. Botta had discovered the palace of King Sargon who is now one of the best known Assyrian kings and who was one of the most powerful rulers in the ancient world. Of the many documents left behind by Sargon, several contain a reference to his defeat of Israel: 'In the first year of my reign I besieged and conquered Samaria … I led away captive 27,280 people who lived there.' Sargon's own documents confirm that he replaced them with people from other nations he had defeated (see 2 Kings 17:24), and these brought their own religions and practices with them (vs 29–33). From now on the people from Samaria became a mixed race with a mixed religion—this is why 'the Jews had no dealings with the Samaritans' (John 4:9).

because the only reference to him came in Isaiah 20:1. In the year 721 BC Sargon became king of Assyria; he continued the siege of Samaria begun by his predecessor Shalmaneser V (2 Kings 17:5–6 and 18:9–11) and when the city was destroyed he took all the credit. Sargon was the ruler of a vast empire and with a great ancestry, but he is mentioned in just one line —this is because the focus of the Bible is upon Israel.

To your left the two massive **human-headed winged bulls** (WA 118808–9) from Khorsabad were the guardians of the palace of King Sargon. See Box: Khorsabad, the home of Sargon. Look at the base of the one on the right. Recently discovered squares scratched on it show that guards had been playing the *Royal Game of Ur* that we will discover later in Room 56 (pages 78, 79). This game predates the time of Abraham.

Ashurbanipal tells us that his grandfather, Sennacherib, was assassinated between 'two colossi'—therefore at Nineveh it was probably two great bulls like these that witnessed the murder of Hezekiah's enemy. 2 Kings 19:37 also records the murder of Sennacherib by his sons whilst he was worshipping his god Nisroch.

Tribute from Hezekiah
Cross to the alcove opposite which is **Room 10c Assyria: Khorsabad.** The *Inscription from under the stomach of a human headed winged bull* (WA 118815), which is in a poor state of preservation, includes the most detailed surviving account of the tribute sent by Hezekiah, king of Judah, after the Assyrian campaign in Palestine in 701 BC —see 2 Kings 18:13–15. There is an interesting discrepancy between the 'three hundred talents of silver and the thirty talents of

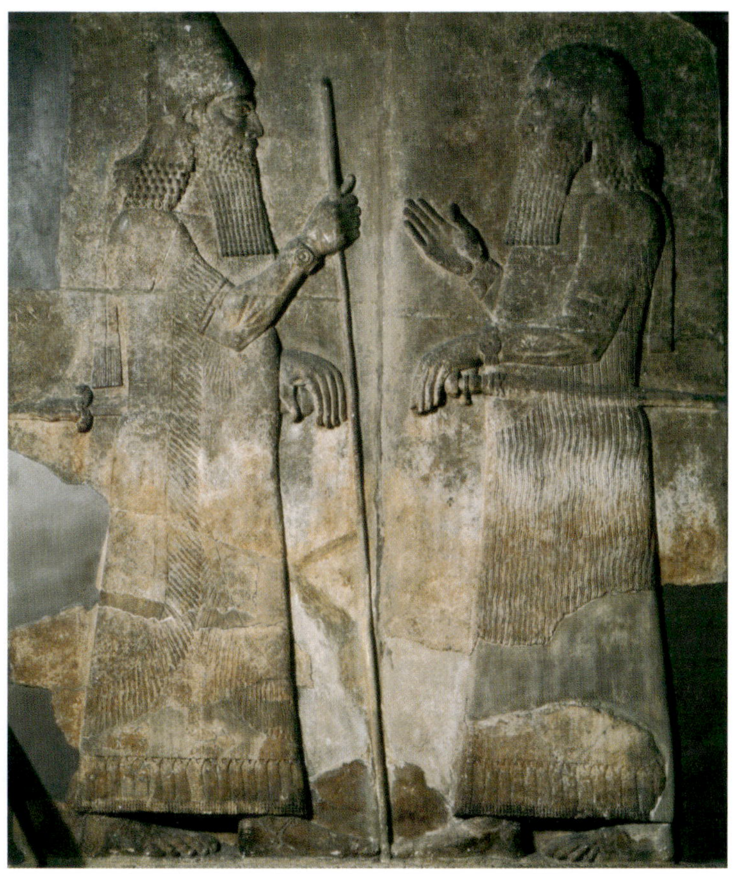

Above: Sargon of Assyria (left) with what is thought to be his son,
Sennacherib (ANE 118822)

gold' mentioned in v.14, and the Assyrian record here which states that it was 800 talents of silver and 30 talents of gold. Archaeologists now know that whilst the method of weighing gold was the same for both Judah and Assyria, for silver it was different and items other than silver could be included in Assyrian 'silver'.

Above you is the colossal head of a winged bull (WA118893). This is one of the few surviving sculptures from the palace that **Esarhaddon**, the son of Sennacherib, left unfinished at his death. His accession to the throne of Assyria is referred to in 2 Kings 19:37.

Go back to the rear of the two bulls and turn left into **Room 10b Assyria: siege of Lachish**

The siege of Lachish

When Austin Henry Layard discovered this stone relief in 1847 it generated great excitement in Victorian England because it was the first archaeological confirmation of an event in the Bible. The prophet Micah warned of the destruction of Lachish (1:13).

The wall reliefs in this room of a terrifying siege have been described as the finest example from the ancient world of a portrayal of siege warfare. In 701 BC Sennacherib, the son of Sargon, laid siege to Jerusalem. This took place during the reign of King Hezekiah and is vividly retold in 2 Kings 18–19, 2 Chronicles 32, and Isaiah 36–37. In this room you have Sennacherib's record of part of his campaign.

Isaiah 36:1–2 informs us: 'Sennacherib, King of Assyria, attacked all the fortified cities of Judah and captured them. Then the king of Assyria sent his field commander with a large army from Lachish to King Hezekiah at Jerusalem'.

Sennacherib destroyed scores of towns across Judah, but he was unable to enter Jerusalem. When he returned to his capital at Nineveh, it was the destruction of Lachish, and not Jerusalem, that adorned the walls of his victory room. See Box: The Taylor Prism (page 70).

Artillery

The battle for the strategic city of Lachish begins in the second panel on the wall facing you as you enter. The top of the panel shows grapes and figs on the trees indicating that the attack took place in late summer. Among the soldiers, different nationalities are represented, including some Israelites captured and forced into battle and Iranians with

Below: The Assyrian stone slingers in action at Lachish in 701 BC

Inset: Some of the stones discovered at the ruined gateway in the battle for Lachish (WA 132127–40)

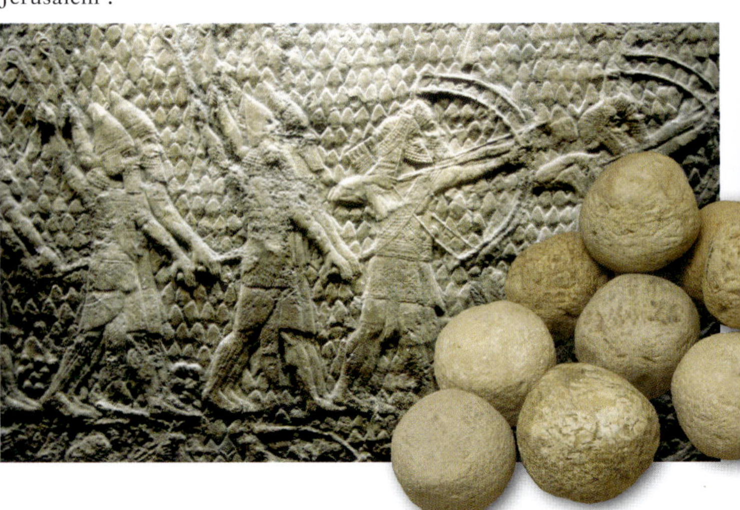

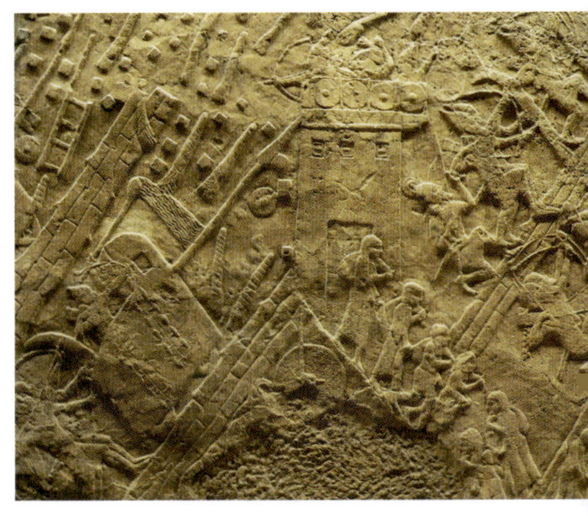

Right: The battering ram at the siege of Lachish

Below: A detail of the siege of Lachish with captives being impaled—a cruel early form of crucifixion

long skirts. Notice the ranks of archers firing over the walls into the city; some kneel, protected by the tall leather shields of the javelin throwers. Behind them are the bearded artillerymen with long pointed helmets and wielding their slings as they keep up a barrage of small but lethal missiles.

Cross over behind you to the corner case containing some of the actual stones discovered at the main gate in Lachish from this battle in 701 BC (WA 132127–40). The sling stones were one of the most lethal weapons in ancient warfare and hunting. Slings and stones were found in the tomb of the Egyptian pharaoh Tutankhamen who died in 1325 BC and the Romans expected every legionary to be able to handle a sling. Each stone is around the size of a billiard ball and in the hands of a well trained man they could reach speeds in excess of 120 mph and a distance of a quarter of a mile.

According to Judges 20:16 (so far the oldest known reference to the sling) the tribe of Benjamin could boast 700 left handed slingers who were so accurate that they could aim at a hair and not miss. In fact, some were equally agile with left or right hand (1 Chronicles 12:2). David used the same weapon against a nine foot giant. When he ran down to the stream he was looking for 'five smooth stones' of this size (1 Samuel 17:34–36,40).

The octagonal prism in this case (WA 10300) is Sennacherib's description of his campaigns,

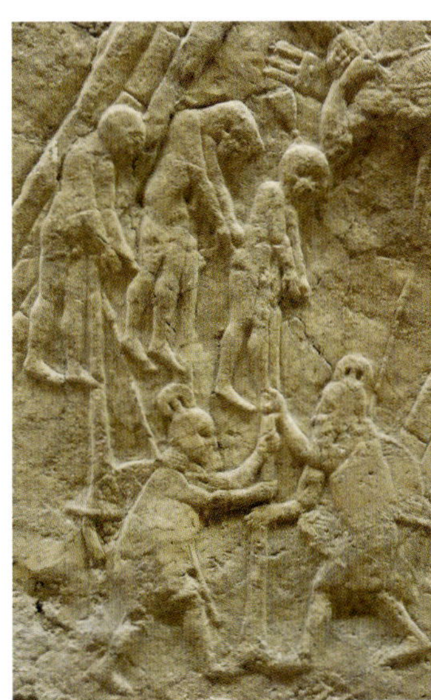

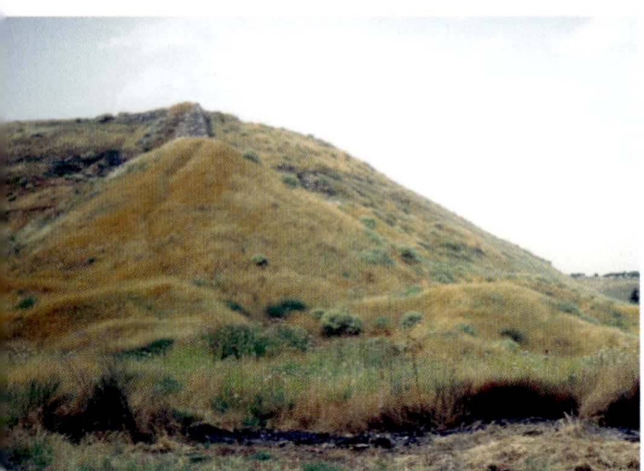

Left: The siege ramp built by Sennacherib's army at Lachish is still visible today. It is estimated that between 13,000 and 19,000 tons of rubble was used and Judean prisoners from earlier Assyrian victories in this campaign were employed

including Lachish and the siege of Jerusalem in 701 BC and his rebuilding of Nineveh in 694 BC. This is not the Taylor Prism (for which see page 70).

Return to the wall reliefs opposite and move right

Storm troopers and battering rams

Soldiers are scaling the walls, firing arrows for a protective shield as they advance. The air is thick with missiles. The siege-engines trundle up the earth and stone ramps to the walls of the city. Each engine encloses an archer, a man to guide it, and a 'fireman' who, with great ladles of water, douses the constantly falling fire-torches of the defenders as they try to set fire to the protective leather covering of the battering ram .

For their part, the defenders are desperately hurling their fire-bombs and rocks upon the attackers; some soldiers are falling over the wall, victims of advancing archers. At the bottom of the panel is the gruesome scene of those who tried to escape the city and have been impaled on long stakes in the sight of the defenders. Groups of men and women, with children clinging to their mothers, are led away into exile taking their possessions with them on camels and in heavily laden ox carts; the ox clearly shows signs of starvation. Notice carefully the helmets of some of these Judeans; we will find them as slave prisoners in room 9 (see page 37). The leaders of the city are spread-eagled and flayed alive, whilst others are summarily executed.

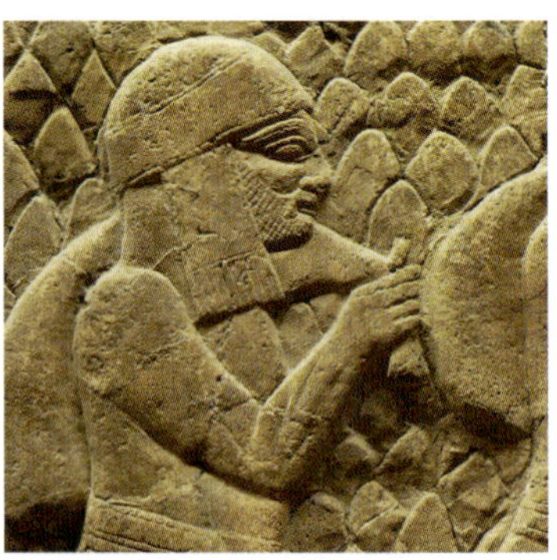

Above: The distinctive headwear of Judean prisoners from Lachish are seen again among the slave prisoners in Nineveh in Room 9 (ANE 124822)

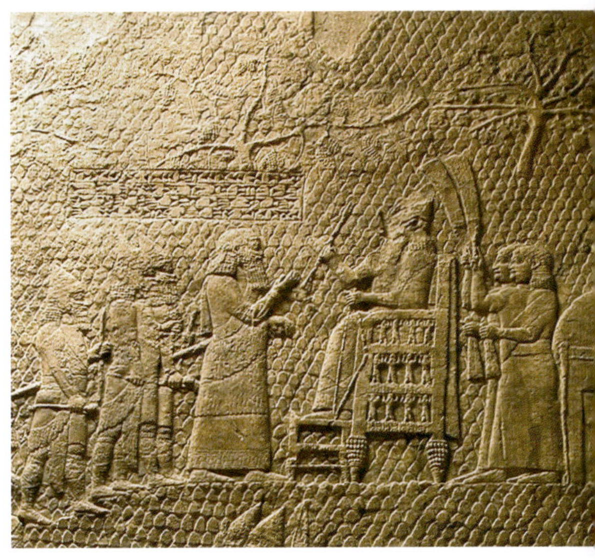

The great king loses face!

Sennacherib himself took part in this siege and he is seen receiving the defeated prisoners as he sits upon his high throne. The inscription reads, 'Sennacherib King of the world, King of Assyria, on a throne he sat and the booty of Lachish passed before him.'

Notice how the king's face has been hacked out. In 612 BC the Babylonians, whose capital had been devastated by Assyria in 689 BC, took their revenge and destroyed Nineveh; it was a common practice to deface the image of an enemy believing that this would delete him from history!

As you follow the relief round you will notice the picture of the base camp with priests offering sacrifices to their gods and the servants busy in their tents. See Isaiah 37:36–37. This is the end of the Lachish sequence. The remaining panels depict Assyrian cavalry, slingers and archers, and prisoners being led away under the watchful and taunting eye of the Assyrian guards. Some prisoners (though they are not Judean) are playing their lyres, which is reminiscent of Psalm 137.

Return out of this room and, passing between the two winged bulls, turn right into Room 8 Assyria: Nimrud and first left into **Room 9 Assyria: Nineveh**

'Fire will devour you'

This room depicts Nineveh in the time of Sargon and Sennacherib. Half way down on the right are detailed plans showing how those ten-ton bulls would have been carved and then lifted upright (WA 124823). Look for the slaves with those Judean helmets that we saw depicted on the Lachish reliefs in Room 10. Here they are hauling the ropes (ANE 124822). Clearly they must have been transported back to work as slaves for Sennacherib to build what he intended to be his 'palace without rival'.

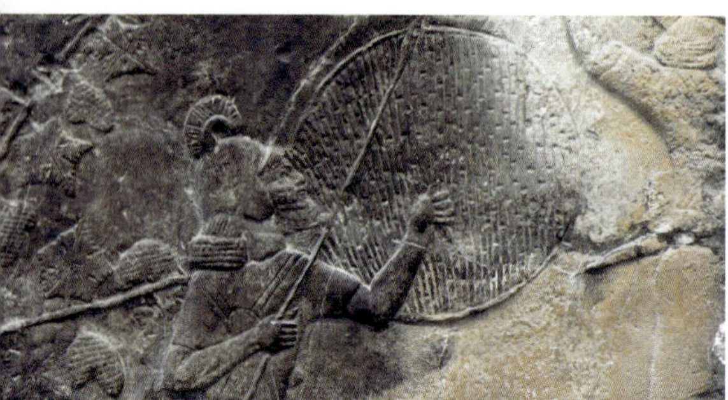

Left: The scorching effect of the fire that finally ravaged Nineveh is clearly seen on these wall reliefs from the time of its destruction by Babylon in 612 BC (WA 124785)

Some of the stone reliefs from Nineveh on the side panels at the far end of this room show the scorching effects of fire that illustrate well the words of the prophet who warned of the end of Nineveh—'the fire will devour you' (Nahum 3:15). This happened when the city was destroyed by a coalition of Medes and Babylonians in August 612 BC.

So completely was the whole city buried and lost to human memory that two centuries after its destruction, the Greek historian Xenophon sat on top of the sand covered ruin mound and had no idea what city it had been. Some scholars even questioned whether such a great city as that described in the Bible had ever existed. In 1847 Austen Henry Layard discovered the palace of Sennacherib and the reliefs of the siege of Lachish. These fire blackened walls recovered from the palace at Nineveh revealed just how accurate Nahum's prophecy had been.

Return down the room and on your right two-thirds of the way notice the grisly picture of a soldier being rewarded for the number of enemy heads he has gained *(WA124953–5)*. Macabre though this is, it was unchallenged proof of a defeated enemy. Only when David cut off Goliath's head did the Philistine army run. According to 1 Samuel 17:57 David was carrying the giant's head when he came into the presence of Saul. Later the Philistines did the same to Saul and Jonathan (31:8–9).

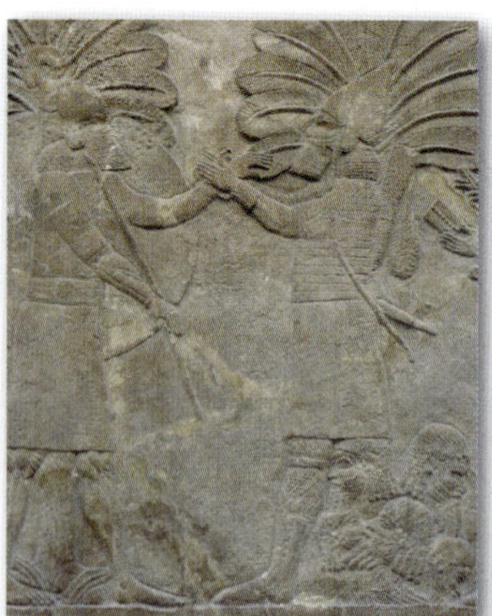

Above: The Assyrian soldier rewarded for the number of enemy he has killed reflects the significance of decapitation in ancient warfare (WA124953–5)

Blood and guts

As you exit from Room 9 into **Room 8 Assyria: Nimrud,** look immediately to your right. Here is a relief of **Tiglath-pileser III** with his foot on the neck of a defeated enemy (WA 118933). He is also known as Pul in the Bible and was the king of Assyria (2 Kings 15:19). It was common for a victorious king to put his foot literally on the neck of his defeated enemy. This act is reflected in Joshua 10:24 where Joshua summoned his commanders to 'Come here and put your feet on the necks of these kings…' In this wall relief the bow and spear pointing to the prisoner is a sign of death.

On the wall to your right is a carving of a vulture carrying intestines (WA 118907). In older translations of the Bible, 'bowels' is a word used to denote not only the physical organs of the abdomen, but also the seat of mercy and affection. This slab shows how all who resist the Assyrians would be treated: without mercy.

On the central columns of Room 8 are two reliefs. The one on the right is *Tiglath-pileser III* (WA 118900) and on the left is one of his *arms-bearers*. When Ahaz, king of Judah, was threatened by a coalition of Israel and Syria he sent tribute to Tiglath-pileser III to rid him of his troublesome neighbours (see page 29). Ahaz then corrupted the worship of the LORD by copying an impressive altar that he saw in Damascus of Syria (2 Kings 16:1–20).

Assyrian records show that King Hoshea was Tiglath-pileser's puppet king in Israel. Shalmaneser V considered Hoshea to be a traitor because he stopped paying tribute and sought Egypt's support, so he attacked Samaria

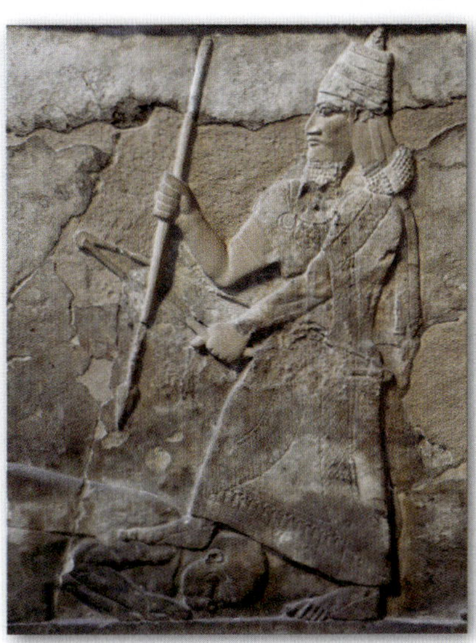

Above: Tiglath Pileser III signifies the death of his defeated enemy by the ominous direction of his spear and bow (WA 118933)

and deported many Israelites into Assyria. (See 2 Kings 15:29; 17:1–6). This policy of wholesale exile by the Assyrians contributed to the breakdown of cultural barriers and paved the way for the future spread of Greek culture and later, Christianity.

Note: because you are close to the Elgin marbles and its associated rooms, you may wish to turn to Paul and the Parthenon on page 112 and visit these rooms now. It will save you a significant walk later. This is recommended

Then return to the tour from Room 8

Continue ahead between the two (smaller) human headed bulls into Room 7 Assyria: Nimrud, and at the end turn left into Room 6 and turn left into **Room 4 Egyptian Sculpture.**

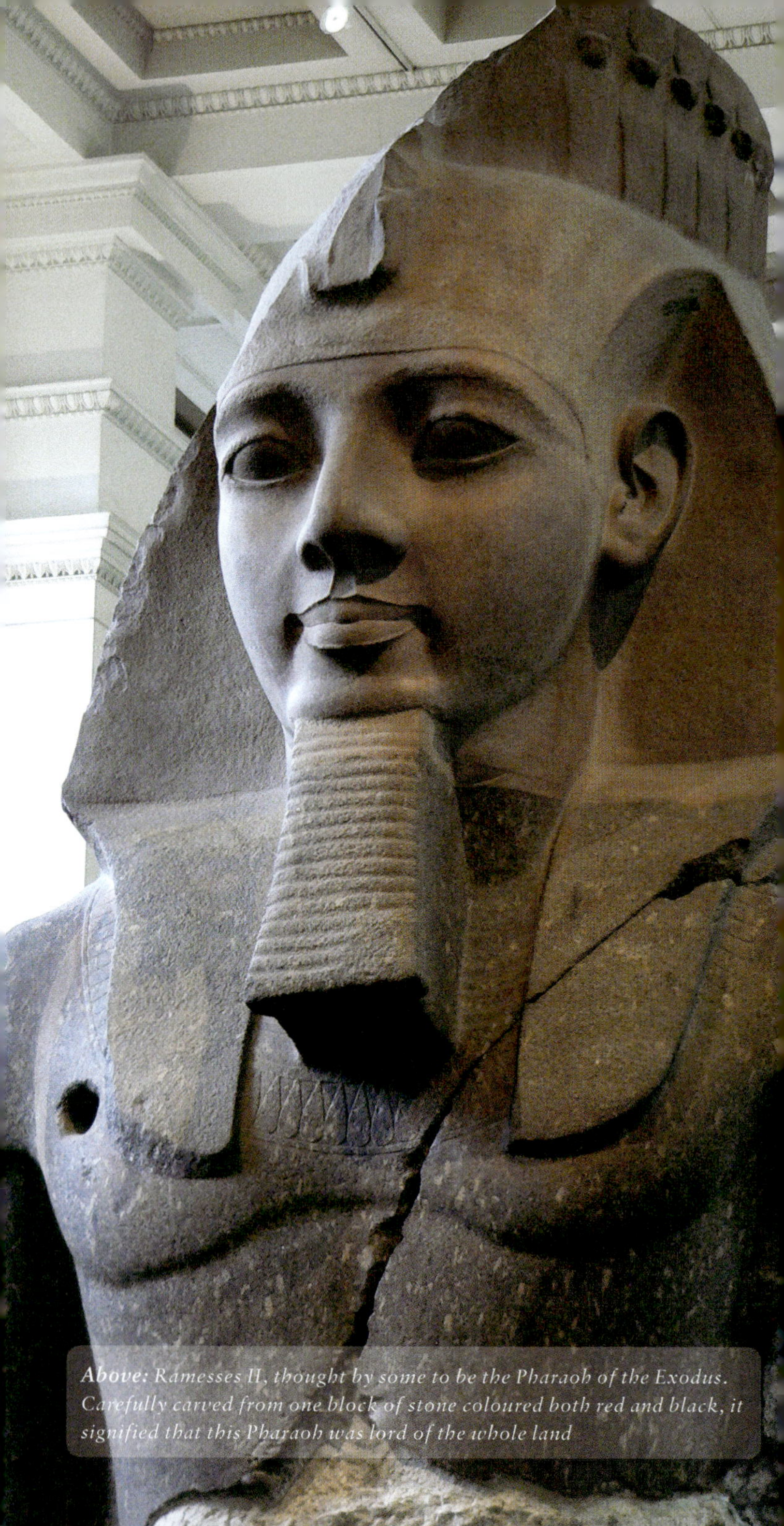

Above: Ramesses II, thought by some to be the Pharaoh of the Exodus.
Carefully carved from one block of stone coloured both red and black, it
signified that this Pharaoh was lord of the whole land

❸ Red land—black land

An exotic land full of mummies, myths and monuments, beloved by authors and filmmakers because of pyramids, romance, adventure and fabulous discoveries. Marvel at the skill of the craftsmen and learn something of this ancient culture

Room 4 Egyptian Sculpture

The Egyptians

One of the earliest civilizations known to man, the ancient Egyptians called their land by two names: *Kemet* (black land), referring to the black mud left by the receding flood waters of the Nile in which crops could be grown, and *Deshret* (red land), because in certain light the desert appears to glow red as a warning to any traveller.

Egypt owed to the Nile its security, prosperity, religion and even its calendar—the three seasons of the Egyptian year were governed by the flow of the river. Manetho, an Egyptian priest and historian in the third century BC, wrote a history of Egypt called *Aegyptiaca* and he is credited with dividing Egyptian history into dynasties.

Thebes in the southern part of Egypt was a magnificent capital and many items in the Museum come from that area. It was once fabulously wealthy—until the Assyrians under Ashurbanipal looted and destroyed it in 663 BC. Warning the Assyrian capital of her own coming destruction, the prophet Nahum has only to point back to the devastation of Thebes as an illustration of what awaits Nineveh: 'Are you better than Thebes situated on the Nile?… Yet she was taken captive' (Nahum 3:8–10). The chief deity of Thebes was Amun who eventually was combined with the sun god Ra, to become Amun-Ra, king of the gods. Amun-Ra was usurped by the Aten during the Amarna heresy (see below under

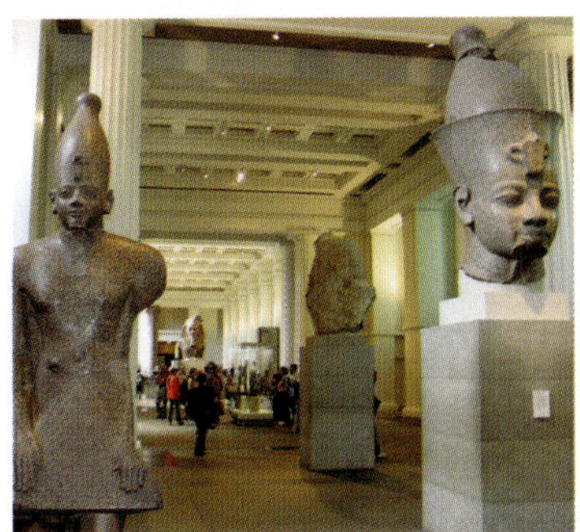

Above: The room of Egyptian Sculpture (Room 4) is a significant attraction for the millions of visitors to the Museum. The exhibits here include the Rosetta Stone and the busts of many Egyptian Pharaohs connected with biblical narratives

List of Egyptian kings

A precise chronology for the dynasties of Egypt is not possible. We have listed only those Pharaohs associated with the Bible. For the chronology of Joseph see a timeline from Abraham to Solomon on page 77.

	BC	
Khety II	2115–2070	Abraham into Egypt about 2091BC (Genesis 12:10–20).
Amenemhat II	1922–1878	Joseph probably entered his service in 1885 (Genesis 41:41).
Sesostris II	1880–1874	Jacob settled in Egypt (Genesis 47:9).
Sesostris III	1874–1855	Joseph probably Prime Minister in his reign and Jacob died.
Amenemhet IV	1808–1799	Joseph died during his reign in 1806.
Ahmose	1550–1526	Ordered the death of the Hebrew boys (Exodus 1:15–16).
Amenhophis I	1526–1504	Or this was the Pharaoh responsible for the above.
Tuthmosis II	1492–1497	Moses fled from Egypt (Exodus 2:15).
Tuthmosis III	1479–1425	The Pharaoh of the oppression and/or the Exodus (early date).
Amenophis (Amenhotep)II	1427–1400	Or the Pharaoh of the Exodus if we take an early date for the Exodus. Part co-regency with Tuthmosis III.
Tuthmosis IV	1400–1390	Joshua enters the Promised Land of Canaan.
Amenhotep III	1390–1352	See The Amarna Letters (page 94).
Amenhotep IV (Akhenaten)	1352–1336	As above. See page 43.
Tutankhamun	1336–1327	Items from his tomb illustrate many biblical objects.
Horemheb	1319 –1292	The eventual successor to Tutankhamun
Ramesses II	1279–1213	The Pharaoh of the Exodus if we take a late date for the Exodus..
Siamun	978–959	Possibly the Pharaoh when Solomon sealed an alliance by marrying his daughter (1 Kings 3:1)
Shoshenq I*	945–924	Shishak who sacked the temple in Jerusalem in 925 (1 Kings 14:25).
Osorkon IV*	734–715	The grandson of Shishak and referred to in 2 Kings 17:4 as So.
Taharqa*	690–664	Tirhakah who threatened Sennacherib in 2 Kings 19:9.
Tantamani	664–656	Assyrian king Ashurbanipal sacked Thebes (Nahum 3:8–10).
Necho II*	610–595	Defeated Josiah and imprisoned Jehoahaz (2 Kings 23:29–35).
Apries (Hophra*)	589–570	The Hophra referred to in Jeremiah 44:30.
Augustus *	27 BC– AD 14	Augustus was the first Roman Emperor to take the title of Pharaoh in Egypt. Joseph took Mary and the infant Christ to Egypt (Matthew 2:13).
Arab conquest	AD 640	Muslim invaders reduced the Christian church.

* These kings are mentioned by name in the Bible

Timelines: from Abraham to Solomon page 77. Hebrew kings page 63. Assyrian kings page 26. Babylonian kings page 69. Persian kings page 54. Roman emperors page 100.

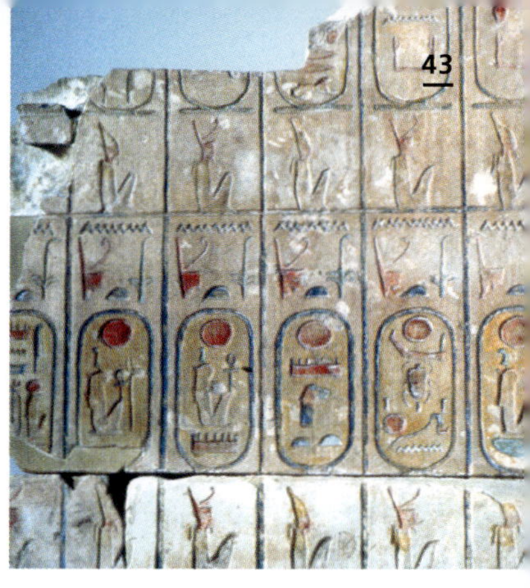

Right: This Egyptian king list from the palace of Ramesses II deliberately ignored history that the Egyptians preferred to forget (EA117)

Fragments of a list of kings) and during this time was considered to be the father and mother of all creation and was depicted as the sun disk.

As you leave Room 6 with the Ballawat Gates behind you, turn left into **Room 4 Egyptian Sculpture**

Heresies and wing nuts

Immediately on your left as you turn into **Room 4**, pause at the statue of *Amenhotep III* (*EA 5*). He was the grandfather of the famous Tutankhamun, and the most wealthy of all the Egyptian Pharaohs. Many of the Amarna letters (see page 94) were addressed to him by tribal kings in Canaan at the time when Joshua was leading the conquest of the Promised Land.

On the wall to your right is the *Fragments of a list of kings* (*EA 117*) from the temple of Ramesses II at Abydos. This block of Egyptian hieroglyphics is interesting in that it omits four Egyptian kings. This was a deliberate omission because these kings, including Tutankhamun, were involved in what is known as the 'Amarna heresy'. Amenhoteph IV (husband of the Egyptian beauty Nefertiti), changed the national religion from polytheism to the sole worship of the Aten, depicted as the sun disk. Amenhoteph changed his name to Akhenaten (worshipper of Aten).

Although Tutankhamun reinstated the old religion, ancient historians simply ignored unpalatable events. This was a common practice in the ancient world because to record something was to perpetuate it. Elsewhere in the Museum, we can find a *Votive Inscription* (see page 117) on which the emperor Caracalla erased all reference to his wife Plautilla and his brother Geta. He did the same on coins of his realm. The same happened to both Nero and Domitian when condemned by a decree of the Roman Senate. The Romans knew it as *damnatio memoriae*— the damnation of memory.

For this reason we would not expect the Egyptians to record the devastating plagues under the hand of Moses or the escape of so many slaves with the loss of imperial charioteers. Similarly the Assyrians would not record the adoption of Israel's God after the preaching of the prophet Jonah (Jonah 3:5) or the destruction of Sennacherib's army in the time of Hezekiah (2 Kings 19:35). By stark contrast, the Old Testament records the defeats and failings even of its greatest heroes, such as King David.

Right: Sesostris III (EA 684686) is sometimes playfully nicknamed 'wing nuts' because of his large ears. This may imply that he was ready to listen to his people

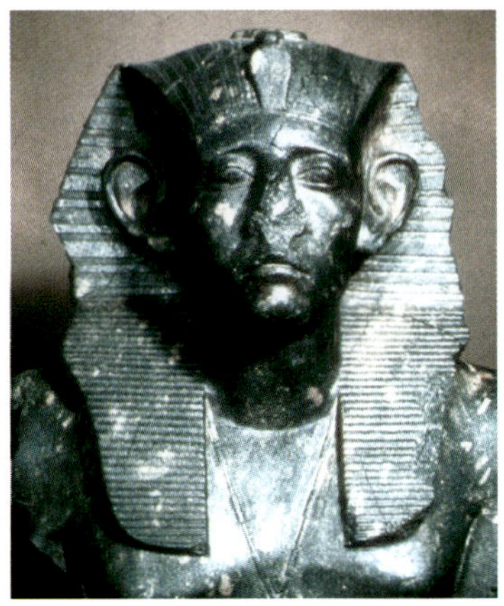

Continue along on the right and up three steps to the figurine in a case *(EA 1239)*. Notice that Egyptian men were clean shaven and in Genesis 41:14 Joseph, when released from prison, shaved himself before he came before Pharaoh. The figure is walking with his left leg foremost; this was the norm in ancient statues because it was the leg on the side of the heart—putting your heart into it.

Return to the other side of this room to the three statues of *Sesostris III (EA 684686).* He may have been the Pharaoh in whose time Joseph was Prime Minister and Jacob died. These three are in black granite, but a head of Sesostris in red granite is behind you *(EA 608)*—black land, red land.

More Pharaohs of Egypt

Further down on the left is a *red granite standing figure of a king* Tuthmosis III *(EA 61)* alternatively some believe that it is the statue of Amenophis II who, under the early date, would make him Pharaoh of the plagues and Exodus (Exodus 14). See Box: The date of the Exodus.

Beyond Tuthmosis III in a glass case between the two pillars the *Limestone dyad of man and wife* (EA 36). This is an

---

The date of the Exodus

Biblical scholars are divided between two alternative dates for the Exodus, these are 1446 BC ('early date') and 1220 BC ('late date').

The main evidence for the early date is based on 1 Kings 6:1. Solomon began the construction of the Temple in the fourth year of his reign which was 480 years after the Exodus. David's death and Solomon's succession to the throne is set around 970 BC. If this date is exact the Pharaoh of the Exodus was probably Tuthmosis III (1479–1425) or Amenhotep II (1427–1400 BC).

The main evidence for the later date is the reference to the store cities of Pithom and Ramesses in Exodus 1:11; archaeological evidence would appear to locate the Exodus in the time of Ramesses II who reigned from 1279–1213 BC and who mentions using slave labour called the *Hapiru* to build his grain cities—perhaps the Egyptian word for the Hebrews. However, it could be that the Israelites in Exodus were building cities that were later rebuilt in the time of Ramesses. The chronology in this guide assumes the early date.

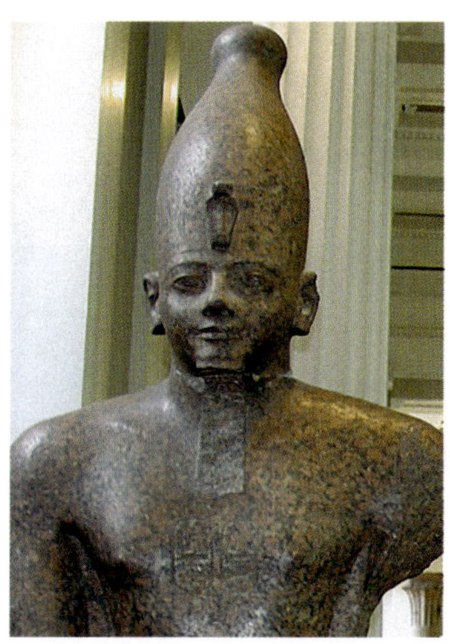

exquisitely detailed example of Egyptian costume and head dress typical of the time of Joseph and Moses. Brought to the Museum in 1837 the identity of the figures remained unknown until an Anglo-Dutch team discovered the missing hands in the tomb of Pharaoh Horemheb at Saqqara in 1976; a cast of the hands made in 2009 fitted perfectly. Before his accession, Horemheb was in charge of the army of Tutankhamun and is seated here with his wife Amenia.

Cross over to the inevitable crowd gathered round the **Rosetta Stone** in the centre of the room

The story of the Rosetta Stone and its significance you will find on page 18. In the Enlightenment Gallery we saw more closely a perfect replica of this.

Continue down Room 4 and on the left a **Statue of Panehsy** (EA 1377) the treasurer to Ramesses II. Only the Pharaoh had ultimate control over the treasures in Egypt, and Moses may have been in line for the post of treasurer (Hebrews 11:26).

The large bust in the centre of the room is that of **Ramesses II** (EA 19). See page 40. He is considered by some to be the Pharaoh of the Exodus (see Box: The date of the Exodus) Notice the skilful workmanship that made use of a single block of coloured granite. The two colours—black and red—signified

that he was Pharaoh of the whole land. Ramaesses lived to the age of 90 and was on the throne for 66 years. He was a great builder (there are more statues and temples of him than of any other pharaoh), family man (he had over 100 wives and concubines and more than 100 children), and warrior (he fought the Hittites for half a century and entered into the world's oldest known peace treaty to date). His 4' 8"mummy is in the Cairo Museum.

Behind Ramesses II, *granite ram of Amun with King Taharqa* (EA 1779. The large granite ram represents the god Amun. The king is the 'Tirhakah king of Cush' in 2 Kings 19:9. Cush was south of Egypt in what we know as Nubia or northern Sudan. Taharqa was the 'broken reed' that Hezekiah relied on as an ally when he was threatened by Sennacherib of Assyria (Isaiah 36:1–6). Sennacherib's own records refer to that failed attempt by the Egyptians to come to the aid of Hezekiah.

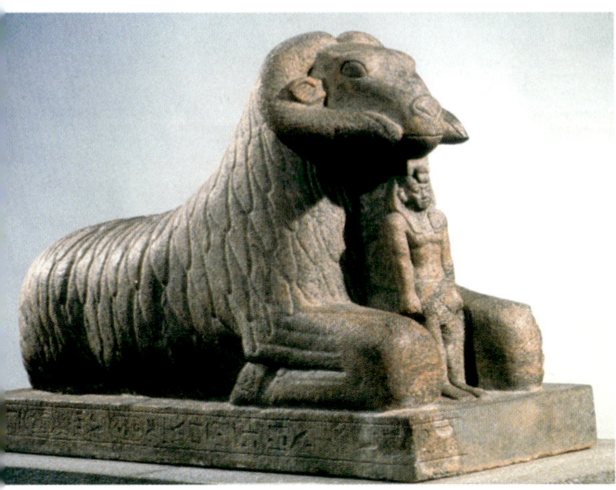

Left: The god Amun in the form of a ram with Pharaoh Taharqa (EA 1779). This Pharaoh was the 'broken reed' of Hezekiah's trust. The inscription on the plinth describes how Taharqa 'fully satisfies the heart of his father Amun'

Further along is a beautifully carved black basalt *sarcophagus of Ankhnesnerferihre* (EA 32). An excellent example of Egyptian hieroglyphic writing. This high priestess was alive in the time of Jeremiah (in the sixth century BC) who warned of judgement on the Pharaoh: 'I am going to hand Pharaoh Hophra King of Egypt over to his enemies' (Jeremiah 44:30). See page 21 for a picture of this. Her name appears in the cartouche.

The Romans in Egypt

In the far right hand corner of Room 4 are two stele of the Roman emperors Tiberius (EA 617) and Domitian *(EA 709)*, both taking the title of Pharaoh of Egypt. Under Tiberius, Jesus Christ died, and probably under Domitian, the apostle John was exiled to Patmos (Revelation 1:9). See list of Roman Emperors on page 100.

Exit by the door beside you, ascend the **West Stairs** (a lift is available at this point) and turn left to enter The Michael Cohen

Gallery **Room 61 Egyptian Tomb-chapel of Nebamum**

The items in this room come from the tomb chapel of Nebamum, a rich accountant who died c 1350—almost exactly at the time Joshua died. They illustrate everyday life in Egypt at the time of Moses.

Turn right to *cases 4B and 4C* **Fashion.**

No. 12 is a gold ring of Thuthmosis III *(EA 71492)* who is one of the possible pharaohs at the time of the Exodus. Notice also here the fine jewellery and a pair of sandals woven from palm leaf. Under **Beauty** notice the bronze mirror (no 19 *EA 38332*). Exodus 38:8 informs us that the bronze basin at the tabernacle was made from 'the mirrors of the ministering women'; these probably came from Egypt (Exodus 12:36) and were therefore similar to the one here. Beauty treatments (for both men and women) about the time of Moses are also illustrated here and include the type of items that would have been used by

Potiphar's wife in the time of Joseph. Notice no 20 a bronze razor (*EA5593*), probably of the kind used to shave Joseph when he was taken from prison to the royal court (Genesis 41:14).

Continue across the entrance to *case 6B*. No1 **Living conditions**. The wooden headrest (*EA 29565*) illustrates Jacob at Luz: 'Taking one of the stones there, he put it under his head and lay down to sleep' (Genesis 28:11). It may appear uncomfortable, but it served the purpose of keeping the head (and therefore ears and hair) above the ground-crawling insects and allowed the circulation air for the upper part of the body in a hot climate. Look out for many more head rests in the Egyptian galleries, some in ivory. Also here is a child's sandal and a board game. No. 4 (*EA32610*) is a model of an Egyptian house.

The case on **Work and Survival** depicts the kind of implements the Israelites would have been familiar with in Egypt. As you turn right at the end of the gallery, pause to watch a reconstruction video (2 minutes) of the inside of Nebamum's tomb chapel. It well

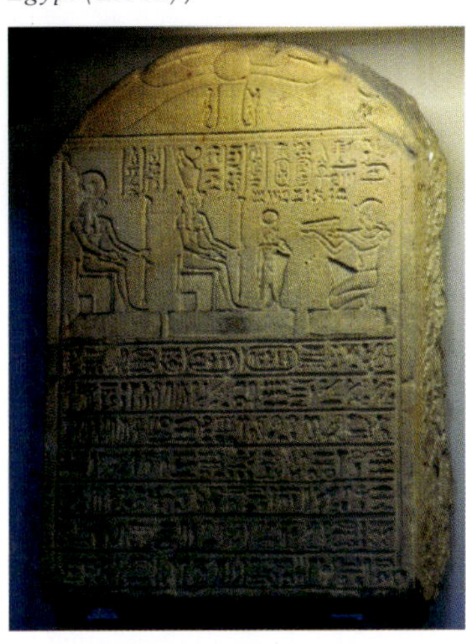

Below: A stele of the Roman emperor Tiberius as Pharaoh of Egypt kneeling before three gods of Egypt (EA 617)

illustrates the beautiful colouring of buildings in the ancient world that we noted on page 23.

Immediately round the corner on your right in *case 3* **Building the tomb-chapel** note especially the painter's minerals used for the colours, and his palette (nos 5 & 6). No 7 is a list of absentee workmen!

The whole wall on your left from *cases 2G to 2A* holds pictures of Nebamum's ideal future life: the garden, hunting, banqueting etc. 2D contains a display of food offered before the statue of Nebamum and his wife: figs, dates and dom palm.

Before you leave this room, cross to *case 5* **The wealthy home** and **gods in the home.** This

Above: A bronze mirror from Egypt (EA 38332). It was mirrors such as this that Israel used for the large basin at the Tabernacle. This item is currently not on display

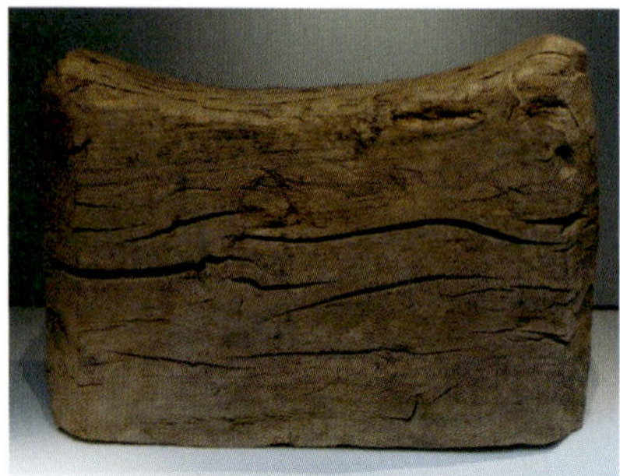

Left: A wooden headrest from Egypt, though Jacob had to be content with stone! (EA 29565)

Below: The painter's palette and mineral blocks remind us how colourful many ancient buildings and tombs were

illustrates the decoration of the wealthy home and also a model of a town house in Egypt (no.1). There are more head rests here.

Continue into Room 62 **Egyptian death and afterlife, Mummies.** In these rooms you are advised to follow the directions here closely, there is so much of interest that you can easily spend the remainder of your time in these next two rooms!

Immediately on your left in *case 28* **Mummies of sacred bulls.** *(EA 6773)*. These are of later Roman date, but the practice was unchanged from the time of Israel in Egypt. The sacred Apis bull (herald of the god Ptah), Buchis bull (sacred to Ra and Osiris), and Mnevis bull (sacred to Ra at Heliopolis) were worshipped, and when they died were embalmed and buried. Another young bull—without blemish—had to be found to take its place. The plague recorded in Exodus 9:1–7 would have affected the current sacred bulls. It is the worship of the sacred bulls that lies behind the episode of the golden calf in Exodus 32, and Israel

were still worshipping a golden calf in the time of Jeroboam I (1 Kings 12:28 & 2 Chronicles 13:8). Centuries later the prophet Ezekiel reminded Israel that many of them had never left Egyptian worship behind them: 'Nor did they forsake the idols of Egypt' (Ezekiel 20:8).

The book of Genesis closes with the words 'Joseph died… They embalmed him, and he was placed in a coffin in Egypt' (Genesis 50:26). Joseph, as a man of high rank, would have been embalmed and mummified exactly as you see examples in

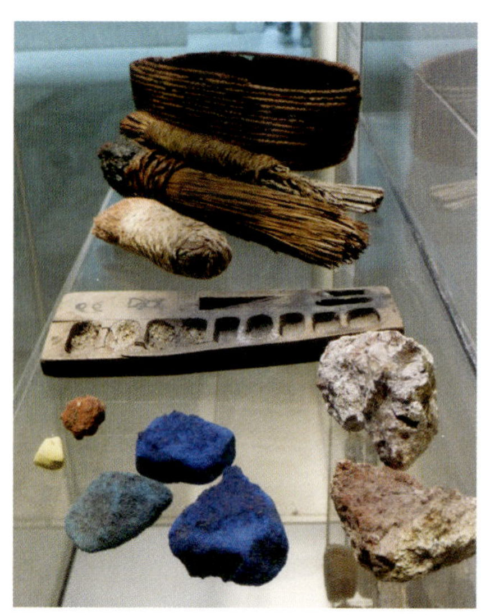

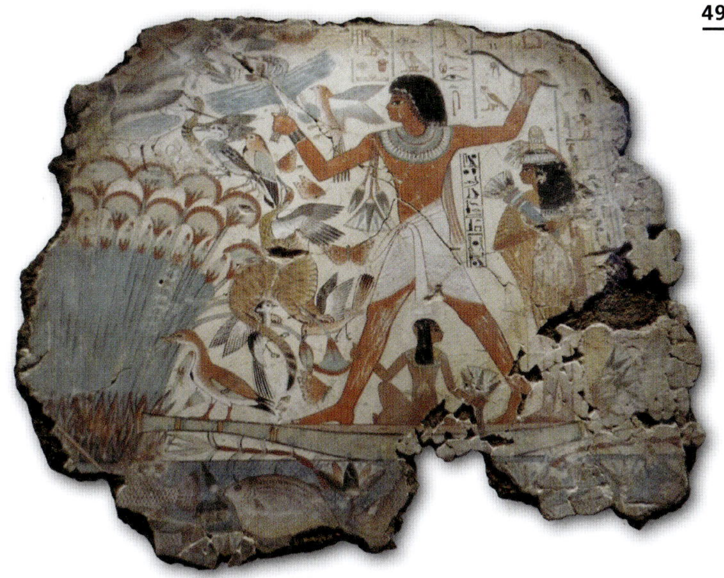

Above: Nebamum's ideal future life—a hunting scene

these rooms. His body would have been placed in a great wooden coffin, or perhaps stone, and we may wonder whether his coffin included the elaborate drawings and plans to direct the spirit of the deceased to the underworld or whether he had left instructions that such was unnecessary!

On the right hand wall in *case 24* notice the example of the **Book of the Dead**, no 8 (*EA 9901/3*). See Box: The Book of the Dead page 51.

Enter **Room 63. Egyptian death and afterlife, Mummies** and turn immediately left. In *case 11* there is a collection of **food offering** from the tombs in the Valley of the Kings: pomegranates, loaves, cakes, dates and duck. Much of our knowledge of Egyptian life comes from the small models that were included in the tombs of the great people in Egypt. These models were all buried in the coffins of those wealthy enough to be 'mummified'. The belief was that they would come to life and serve their master or mistress in the next world.

Continue along this wall and at the doorway turn right to *case 8*

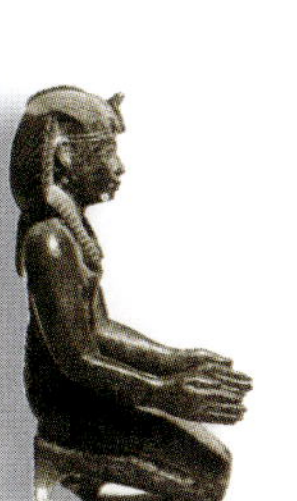

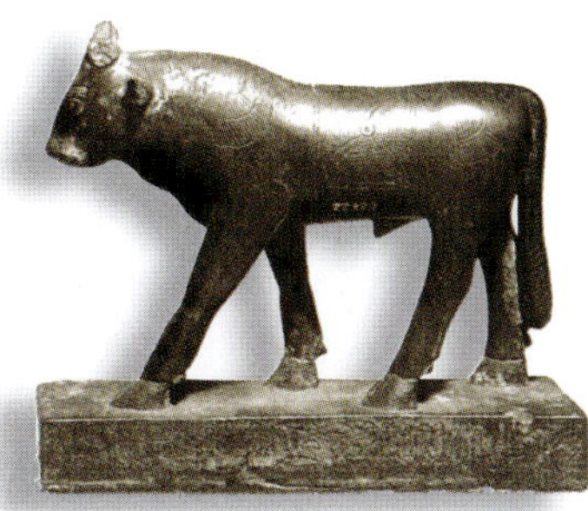

Left: A bronze statuette of an unnamed Egyptian ruler worshipping an Apis bull, c.600 BC (EA 22920). This is not currently on display in the Museum

The nearest mummy to the time of Joseph you will find here, the **mummy of Ankef** (EA 46631). It is dated c 1950 BC.

In *case 5 on your left* there are examples of baking, brewing and butchery, and other household items that would have been familiar to Israel in Egypt.

Case 4 contains the coffins of Gua. This explains the Egyptian approach to death with reference to the major gods Osiris and Ra. Here is the large cedar coffin of Gua around 1850 BC (EA 30839), the time of Joseph (Genesis 39–50). The large eyes, always on the east side of coffins, enabled the deceased to look towards the rising sun; inside is a painted door to allow the spirit Ba, to go in and out on its journey. See Box: The Book of the Dead on page 51. Notice in this case the painted wooden statuette of a female servant (EA 30716) which illustrates the history of the baker in the story of Joseph (Genesis 40:16).

Cross to the right hand wall *case 3* **Mummification**. The example shown is of a woman who lived at the time of Pharaoh Tirhaka (see page 45).

Enter **Room 64 Early Egypt.** On the right in *case 1* is *a reed basket* (EA 58695). Though much older than the time of Moses it recalls the story of Exodus 2. According to Exodus 2:3 that basket, unlike the one you are looking at, was waterproofed with 'tar and pitch'.

At the far end on the right by the door look at the display on

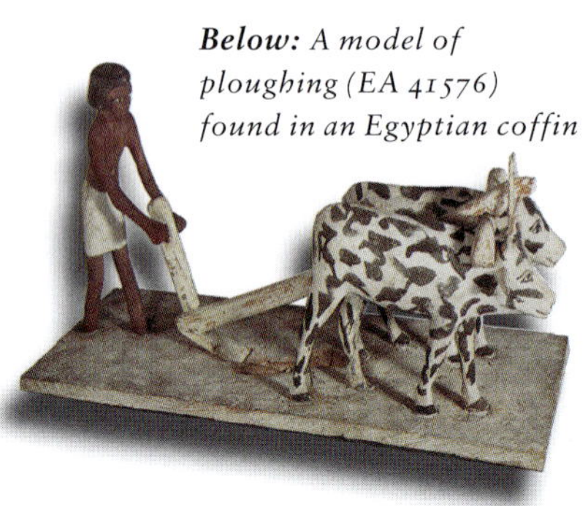

Below: A model of ploughing (EA 41576) found in an Egyptian coffin

The Pyramid of Khufu. When first seen by European travellers they were mistakenly thought to be the store houses Joseph built (Genesis 41:48). Here is a fragment of the limestone-casing block from the largest pyramid, built for Khufu (EA 490).

Enter **Room 65 Sudan, Egypt and Nubia**

Although much in this room is well before Moses, Egyptian culture would have changed little over the years.

Cross to the opposite door, and in *case 1* is a **Cuneiform tablet from El-Amarna** (WAA 29791). See the Amarna letters page 94. This is a letter from Tushratta king of Mittani to Pharaoh Amenhotep III and it contains a request for a

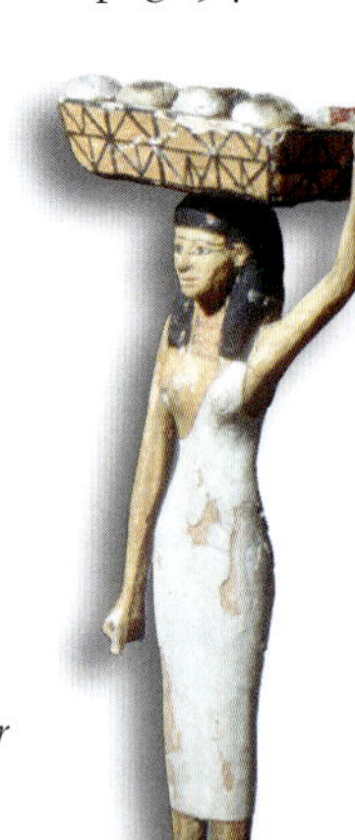

Right: A female servant carrying a tray of cakes on her head (EA 30716) (Height 34 cm)

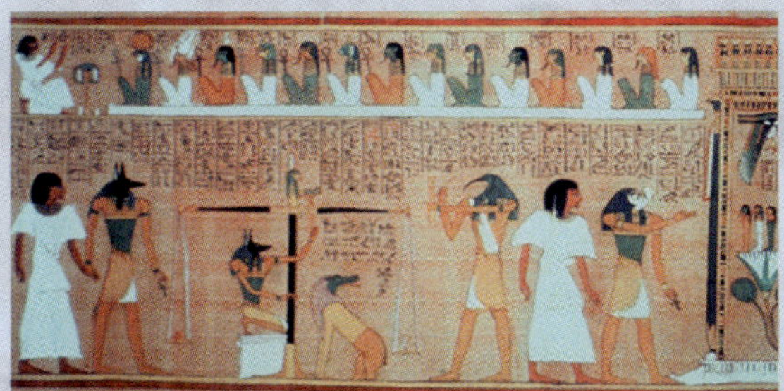

Left: Spell 125 from The Book of the Dead where the heart is weighed against the feather of truth (EA 9901/3)

The Book of the Dead

There were several versions of the Book of the Dead (sometimes known as the Book of the Two Ways). Gaining access to the happy land 'located somewhere in the Far West', depended on leading a virtuous life on earth. The deceased had to pass through a series of ordeals: the ferry-man must be persuaded to take the dead across the River of Death, then came the twelve gates guarded by fearful serpents. Amulets and a copy of the Book of the Dead—with relevant spells and a map to work out how to pass the many dangers—were buried with the dead person. At the Lake of Fire, forty-two Assessors read out a list of sins and wrong doings and the deceased had to swear that he was innocent of them all. If that test was passed, he was admitted to the judgement hall of Osiris, where the heart was weighed against the feather of truth. Sometimes an inscribed scarab beetle has been found placed over the heart of a mummy with the words: 'My heart do not testify against me at the judgement!' If the life had been full of sin, the scales would tip against the deceased and they would be fed to Ammut—the crocodile-headed monster. If the life had been virtuous, the deceased could join the ancestors in the kingdom of the West.

gift as 'gold is as dust in the land of my brother.' This helps us to understand what riches Moses gave up when he left Egypt, considering 'disgrace for the sake of Christ as of greater value than the treasures of Egypt' (Hebrews 11:26).

Exit this room and pause at the top of the East Stairs which is **Room 53 Ancient South Arabia**, before entering Room 53. Turn to the next chapter.

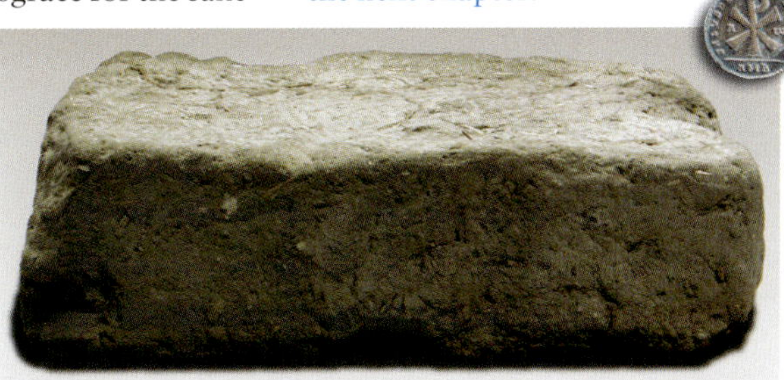

Above: A Nile mud brick from the time of Ramesses II. This is currently not on display in the Museum (EA 6020). Length 38cm

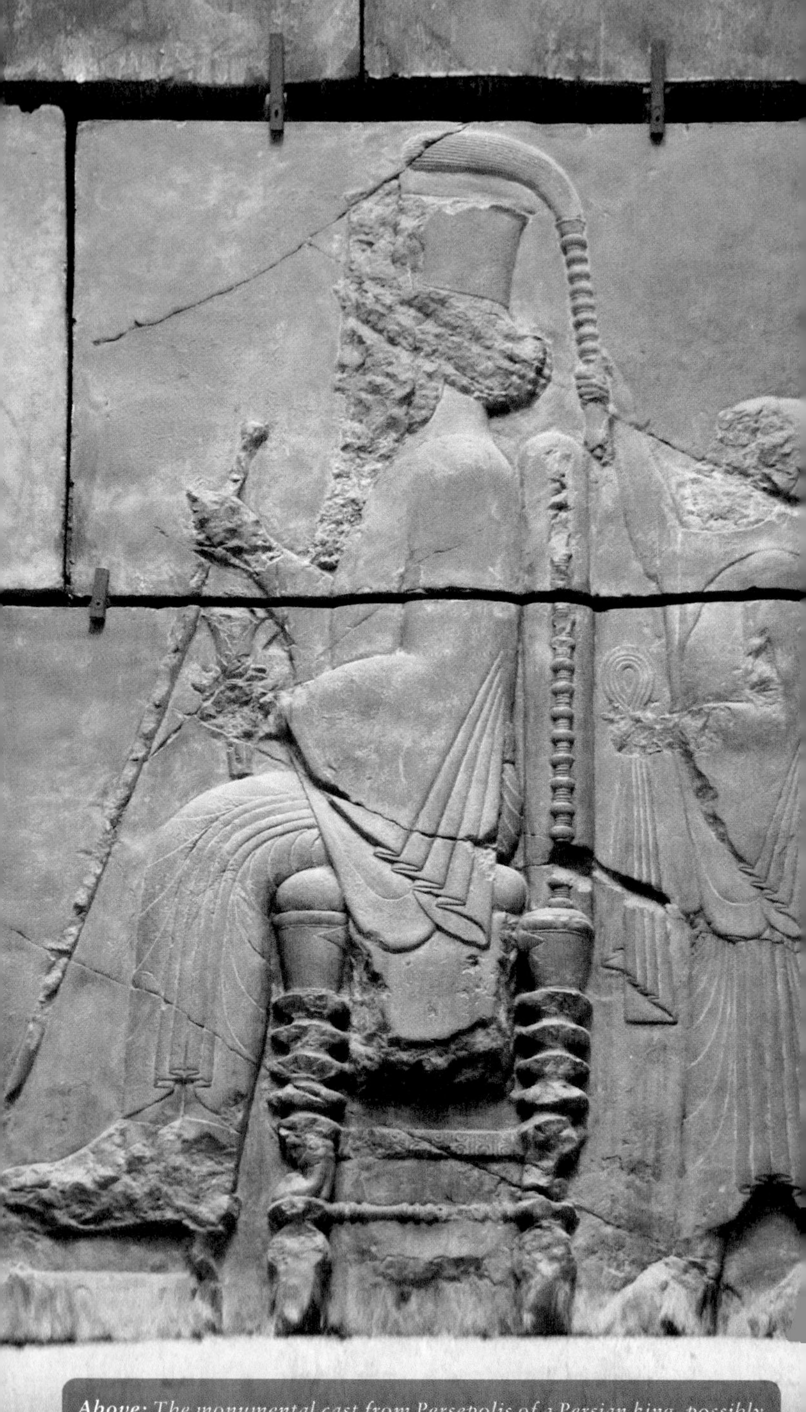

Above: *The monumental cast from Persepolis of a Persian king, possibly Xerxes the king referred to in the book of Esther (NE 225). Notice the sceptre in his hand*

4 Persia—land of the Great Kings

A new and more powerful empire arose, and bandits provide us with an insight into the fabulous wealth of this mighty empire that eclipsed those of Assyria and Babylon. A great road from Sardis in Turkey to Susa in Iran enabled the first pony express to keep the empire informed of the King's edicts. This was truly the first world Empire

Before you enter Room 52, pause at the top of the East Stairs in **Room 53 Ancient South Arabia**

Facing you on the wall above the stairs is an impressive nineteenth century (1892) *Plaster cast from* Persepolis *(ME 225).* This Persian king on his throne, thought to be Xerxes (referred to in the Bible as Ahaseurus—Esther 1:1), holds a sceptre in one hand and a lotus flower in the other. Esther was his chosen queen when Vashti (Herodotus calls her Amestris) fell from favour. The sceptre reminds us of Esther's courageous act when she approached the king on behalf of her people, the Jews. The king 'held out to her the gold sceptre that was in his hand. So Esther approached and touched the tip of the sceptre' (Esther 5:1–2).

Unlike Cyrus (page 56), Xerxes

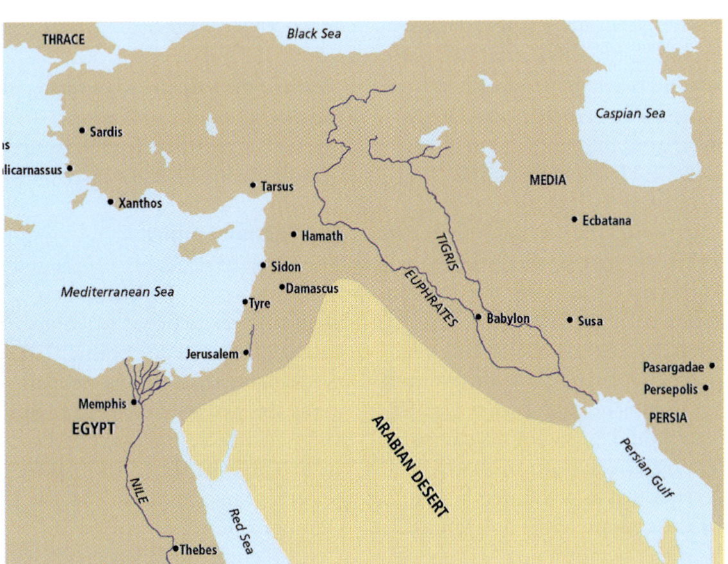

The extent of the Persian Empire

List of Persian kings

	BC	
Achaemenes	700–675	Founded Persian kingdom and the Achaemenid dynasty.
Cyrus I	640–600	Persia not yet a world power.
Cyrus II*	559–530	Established Persian dominance and captured Babylon. Jews return to Jerusalem and rebuild Temple. Ezra 1:1–4.
Cambyses II	530–522	Jews becoming re-established in their homeland.
Darius I*	522–486	Extended the empire into northern India and ranged into Europe. Temple completed. Persian Wars failed to subdue the Greeks. Haggai and Zechariah prophesying.
Xerxes I*	486–465	Ahaseurus* in the Bible. Lost Persian Wars and the decline of Empire began. Esther queen.
Artaxerxes I*	465–424	Ezra sent to Jerusalem by the King (Ezra 7:1). Nehemiah his cupbearer (Nehemiah 2:1).
Darius II	424–404	Beyond the Bible.
Darius III	336–330	Defeated by Alexander the Great and end of Persian Empire.

* These kings are mentioned by name in the Bible
Timelines: from Abraham to Solomon page 77. Hebrew kings page 63. Egyptian kings page 42. Assyrian kings page 26. Babylonian kings page 69. Roman emperors page 100.

was no friend to his defeated nations: he heavily taxed Egypt, destroyed Babylon and invaded Greece. He took a massive Persian army into Greece and confronted the 300 Spartan heroes at Thermopylae who killed 20,000 Persians before being slaughtered to the last man. Xerxes then destroyed Athens c. 480 BC. The gap between the third and seventh year of his reign in Esther 1:3 and 2:16 would allow for his campaign against Greece (481 to 478 BC). Xerxes was assassinated in 465 BC by the captain of his bodyguard. Vashti, the mother of Artaxerxes I, outlived Xerxes and is known to have been a cruel and vengeful woman; she had already mutilated the mother of one of Xerxes' lovers. We may fear for the future of Esther which is unknown.

The Persian Empire
The Persians probably originated from southern Russia and their main cities were Ecbatana, Susa Pasargadae and Persepolis, all in modern day Iran. They came late in the story of the Old Testament, and we come across them first in 2 Chronicles 36:20, 'the kingdom of Persia came to power.' In October 539 BC the armies of Cyrus II entered Babylon and heralded the great Medio-Persian Empire.

In Daniel 5:30 'Darius the Mede took over the kingdom'; this is either an alternative royal title for Cyrus, or more likely a reference to a subordinate—possibly Gubaru who was known to have governed Babylon on behalf of Cyrus.

Persia remained the new world power, controlling three million square miles from Ethiopia to India, until Alexander the Great of Macedonia, defeated the Great King Darius III in 331 BC.

Cyrus, Darius, Xerxes (Ahaseurus) and Artaxerxes, were the Persian kings of the latter part of the life of Daniel, the history of Esther and the return to Jerusalem as recorded in Ezra, Nehemiah and the prophets Haggai, Zechariah and Malachi.

The Greek historian, Herodotus, wrote his *Histories* in the same century when Esther was queen in Susa. Translations of Herodotus' book can be purchased from the Museum bookshop.

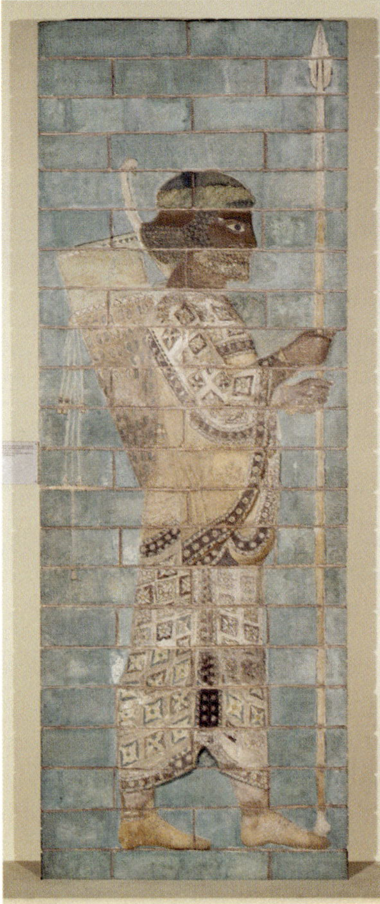

Above: One of many beautiful panels of glazed brick from Susa in the time of Esther (WA 132525)

Bricks and bandits

As you enter **room 52 Ancient Iran** in case 5 in the middle on the left (*Architecture of the Persian Empire)* is a colourful *panel of glazed brick* (WA 132525) showing a guard on duty at the east gate of the palace at Susa. It was here that Mordecai sat (Esther 2:21) and therefore he would have been familiar with these panels since this was one of hundreds like it. This once adorned the palace at Susa of Darius I, the Great King of Persia (522–486 BC). Darius built a magnificent palace at Susa and you can imagine the splendour of a building decorated with wall panels like these. He is referred to in Ezra 4:5; 5:6–7; 6:1; Haggai 1:1 and Zechariah 1:1. Perhaps the royal guards, Bigthana and Teresh in Esther 2:21, were dressed like this. His son was Xerxes (486–465 BC) and this would have been the

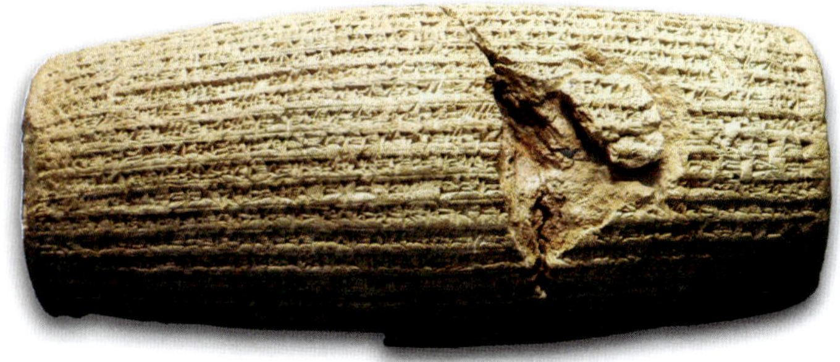

Above: The Cyrus Cylinder (ME1880,0617.1941) which records the policy of Cyrus, King of Persia, allowing exiles to return to their home and rebuild their cities and temples. Length 16cm

palace that Esther was familiar with when she became queen.

Also notice the **Royal Inscription of Xerxes** below (118840).

Around the walls of this room you will see casts of the stone carvings, made in 1892, from the Palace at Persepolis that Darius began and Xerxes completed. Here there are guards, officials and chariots. Though Persepolis was geographically at some distance from Susa, it is a good example of the architecture, costumes etc. that would have been familiar to Esther. Read Esther 1:3–7 to gain an impression of the lavish splendour of the Persian court.

You may not have time to watch the computer reconstruction of the palace beneath the side walls. It lasts for seven minutes. It well illustrates the beautiful architecture and likely original colouring of the palaces Esther was familiar with. This presentation is repeated on both sides of the room

Returning home

The glass case in the centre of this room, *case 4* contains **The Cyrus Cylinder** (ME 1880,0617.1941) Discovered in 1879 at Babylon, this is one of the most significant documents of the Persian Empire. It proclaims that King Cyrus of Persia (559–529 BC) allowed exiles taken captive during the time of the Babylonian empire to return to their own country and rebuild their temples, taking their gods with them.

According to 2 Chronicles 36:23 and Ezra 1:2–4 Cyrus king of Persia claimed that he had been charged by: 'The LORD, the God of heaven' to build a house for him at Jerusalem. Some 150 years before Cyrus came to power, Isaiah 44:28 referred to Cyrus as a 'shepherd' for Israel and prophesied the rebuilding of Jerusalem at his command. In the event, could Daniel have influenced this decree of Cyrus (see Daniel 6:28)?

Cyrus gave permission for the Jews in exile to return to their city and rebuild both the city and 'the temple of the LORD,

Below: A silver drinking bowl made for the palace of Artaxerxes I where Nehemiah was 'Cupbearer to the king' (ME 19940127)

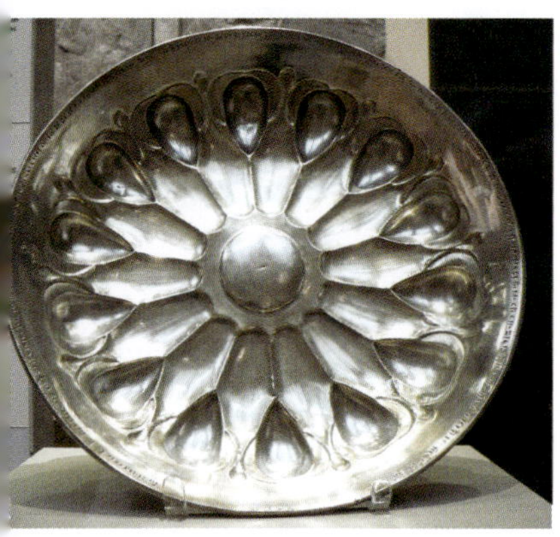

the God of Israel, the God who is in Jerusalem'. At one time it was questioned whether a pagan king would ever make such a concession to subject nations; however, this cylinder describes his peaceful victory over Babylon in 539 BC and how he took the king of Babylon (Nabonidus) prisoner and returned a number of the national gods to their temples and arranged for people who had been taken into exile to return home. The cylinder does not refer to the Jews, but it confirms the policy described in Ezra 6:3–5. In part it reads: 'I am Cyrus, king of the world, the great king, the mighty king, king of Babylon, king of Sumer and Akkad, king of the four corners of the universe…'

This Cyrus Cylinder has been referred to as an early 'charter of Human Rights', predating the Magna Charta by more than a millennium. Its significance is seen in the fact that a replica is kept in the United Nations Headquarters in New York and in 1971 it was translated into all official UN languages. It has become part of Iran's cultural identity.

In the left of *case 3 Ancient Iran* are silver *drinking bowls*. These were held in the palm of the hand. To the right, the three silver plates are also drinking bowls. The one on the left of the three *(ME 19940127)* has an inscription within the rim which in part reads: 'Artaxerxes … son of Darius the king, in whose house this silver drinking cup was made'. Nehemiah was cup-bearer to this king (Nehemiah 2:1) and it is therefore not impossible that Nehemiah handled this very bowl in the course of his duty, which was to taste the wine himself to show that it was not poisoned before presenting it to the king.

Above this silverware, notice in the panel **Historical Documents.** *No.1 (32234)* refers

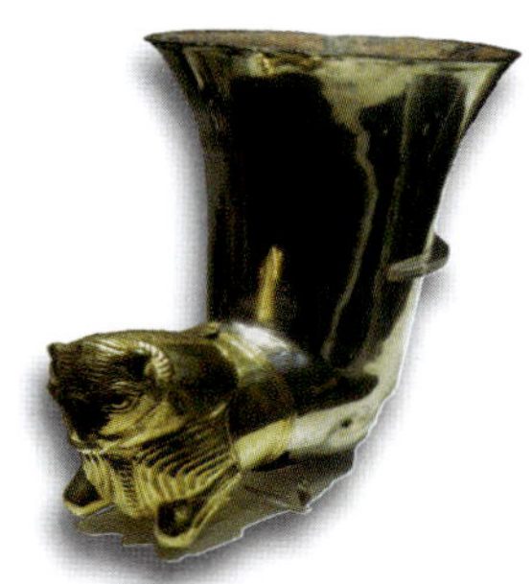

Above: A silver and gold drinking cup from Persia, probably similar to that used by Nehemiah as Cupbearer to the king (116411)

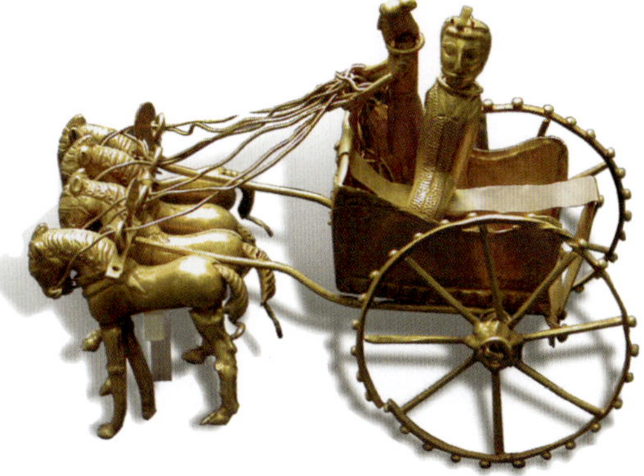

Right: An intricate gold chariot from Persia in the time of Esther (WA 123908). Length 9cm

to the murder of Xerxes by his son (some believe a bodyguard or courtier) on 14 August 465 BC. We have no record of the fate of Esther, though *no. 2 (85009)* interestingly informs us that little is known of Persian queens; this makes the book of Esther all the more significant. See also no.6 the **Cosmetic Bottles** which remind us of the preparation of Esther before she was presented to the king (Esther 2:12).

Continue right to the **Oxus Treasure,** which comes from the same period and illustrates the exquisite jewellery and other items of Esther's time; you will gain an idea of the wealth of Esther's court. Persia was fabulously wealthy and when Alexander destroyed Susa in December 331 BC it is claimed that he found 1,180 tons of gold, and a further 300 tons at Persepolis in January 330 BC. Notice, among many items, the exquisite **gold chariot models**. Continuing round this case 3, notice especially the **silver and gold drinking cup** *(116411)* which held the equivalent of two bottles of wine! A reminder of the banquet in the royal court recorded in Esther 1:7 'Wine was served in goblets of gold'.

Further on in *case 3* is the **Darius Seal;** this is a seal of the Great King Darius I *(89132)*. It is inscribed in three languages.

At the end of this case notice the **lion weight** *(E 32625)*. Weights in the form of a lion were common and the word 'mene' was the name given to a weight of about 500 gm. 'mene' is similar to the Aramaic word for 'numbered'. The Aramaic handwriting that appeared on the wall during

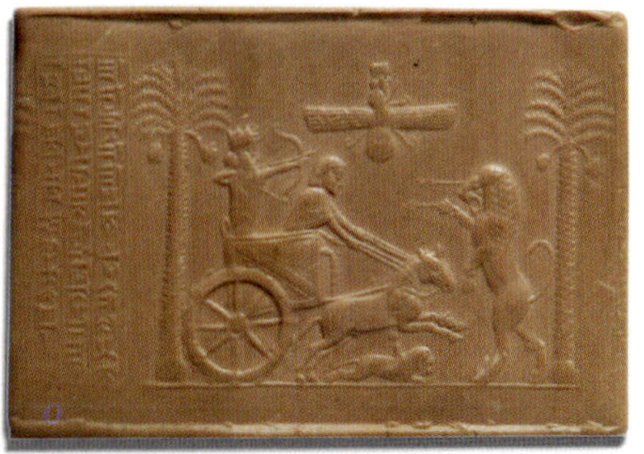

Left: A seal impression of Darius I (89132) during whose reign Haggai and Zechariah were prophesying. The title of Darius in the text to the left is written in three languages. Above the king is the winged disk emblem of the Ahura Mazda, the national god of ancient Persia. Length 5.5cm

Three merchants travelling to India were passing through Afghanistan in May 1880 with a large hoard of gold and silver that had been found on the north bank of the Oxus river. They were attacked and robbed by bandits, but their servant managed to escape and alerted the local British political officer, Captain F.C. Burton. Burton went in pursuit, caught up with the robbers and persuaded them to return a significant portion of the merchants' belongings. In a bag that had been cut open, a magnificent gold bracelet was discovered,

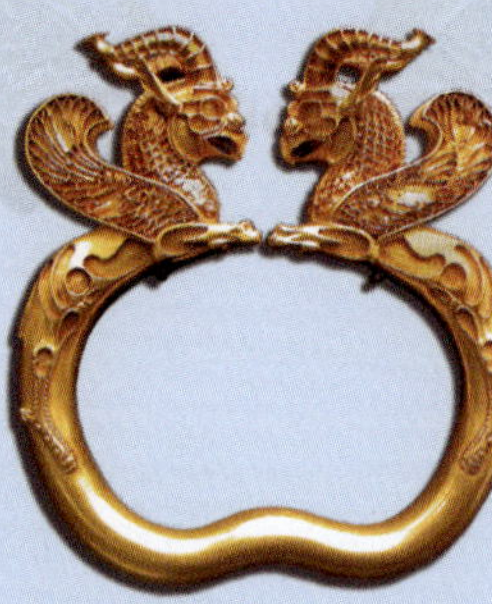

which Burton later bought. The merchants had been carrying over 170 objects from the Achaemenid period and 1,500 coins from the early fifth to the third centuries BC. This made up what you see here as the Oxus treasure. The merchants sold much of the treasure in Rawalpindi (Northeast Pakistan) to Major General Sir Alexander Cunningham who was Director General of the Archaeological Survey of India. Eventually this valuable collection was passed to the British Museum.

Pictured: A gold armlet from Persia in the time of Esther (124017). Width 10cm

the feast of Belshazzar read: 'Mene, mene, tekel and parsin' (Daniel 5:25). Daniel explained this as spelling the end of the king—he had been weighed and his days were numbered. 'That very night Belshazzar, king of the Babylonians, was slain.' The prophecy was fulfilled (Daniel 5:30–31).

Return down the room to *case 6* and notice the ***Babylonian Observation of Halley's Comet** no. 20 (41462)* which is dated precisely at 22–28 September 164 BC. See page 16 for a picture. Also above it, the record of ***the death of Alexander** the Great no. 17 (45962)*. These are included here as illustrations of one way scholars are able to fix early dating, namely by the record of planetary movements.

Return to **Room 53 Ancient South Arabia**

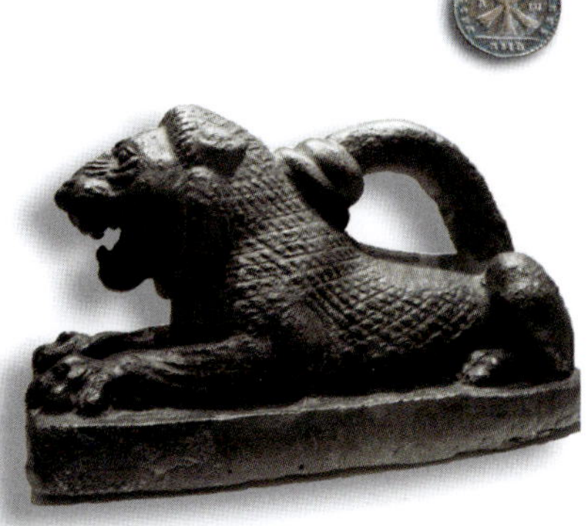

Right: *The Aramaic word for 'numbered' is mene and this 'mina' weight reflects Daniel 5:25 (E32625)*

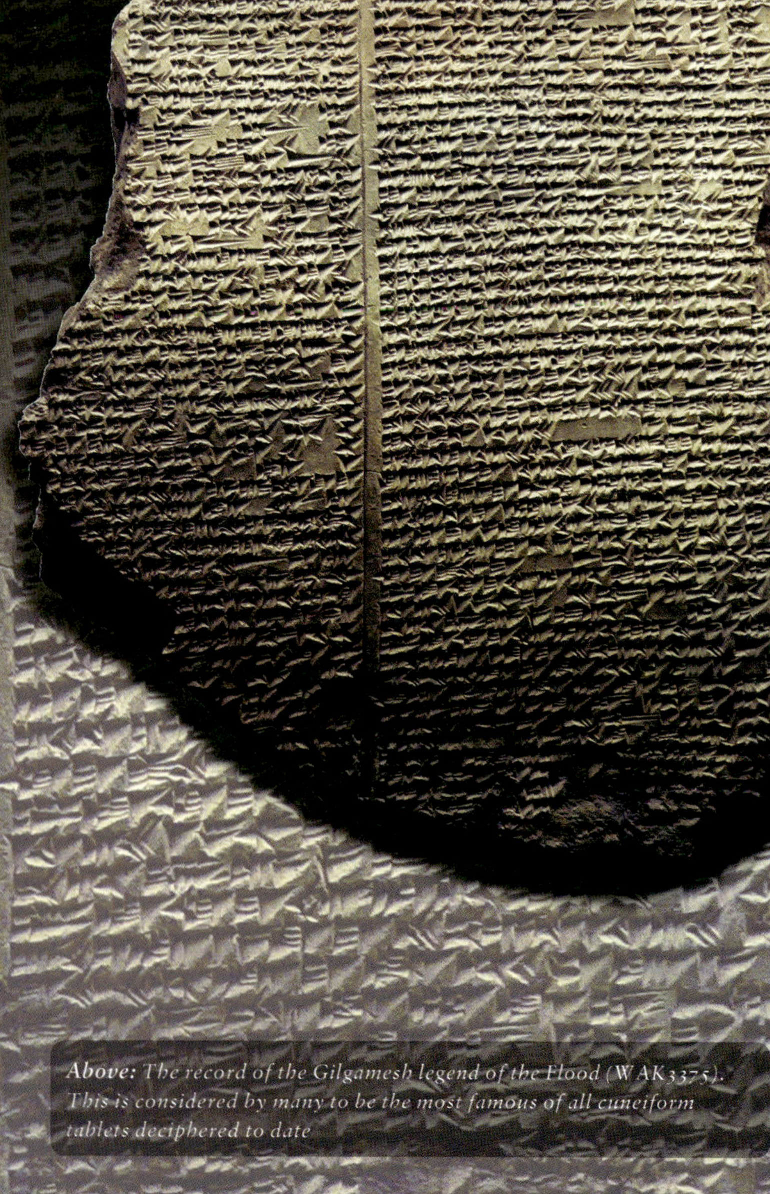

Above: *The record of the Gilgamesh legend of the Flood (WAK3375). This is considered by many to be the most famous of all cuneiform tablets deciphered to date*

🔴5 Who wants neighbours?

Israel found itself surrounded and constantly in battles and skirmishes with its immediate neighbours like the Philistines and Syrians. It was also the victim of the powerful empire-building war machine of the more distant Assyrians and Babylonians

We have provided here a background to the turbulent days of the judges and kings of Israel. The tour continues from **Room 53 Ancient South Arabia. Go into Room 54 Ancient Turkey**

Hittites—from the north west

Before the late 19th century the only known reference to the Hittites was in the Bible.

Abraham purchased a burial site for Sarah from Hittite merchants (Genesis 23). Their ancient capital of Hattusha (now Boghazköy in Turkey) was discovered in 1906. The Hittite empire was founded c1700 BC and the Egyptian Ramesses II fought them and made peace with them in 1258 BC. By 1200 BC their power was broken. However, the

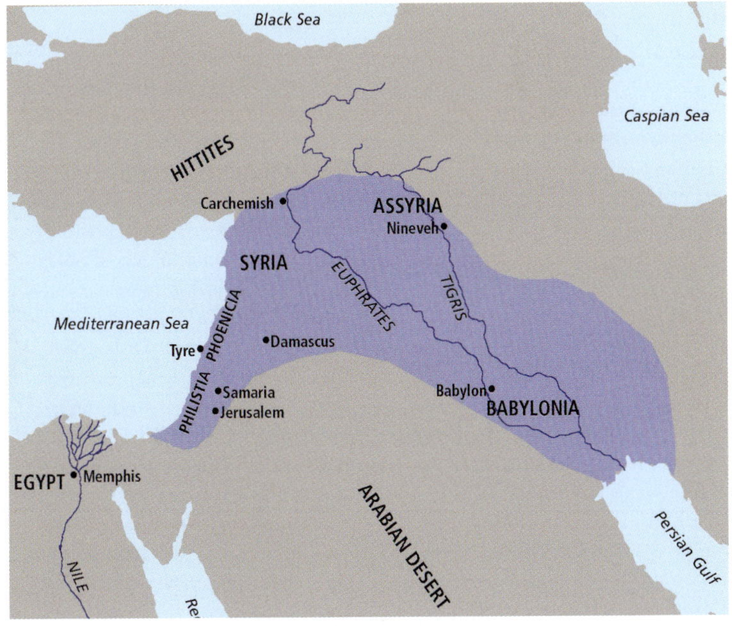

Israel's neighbours in the time of the kings of Israel and Judah

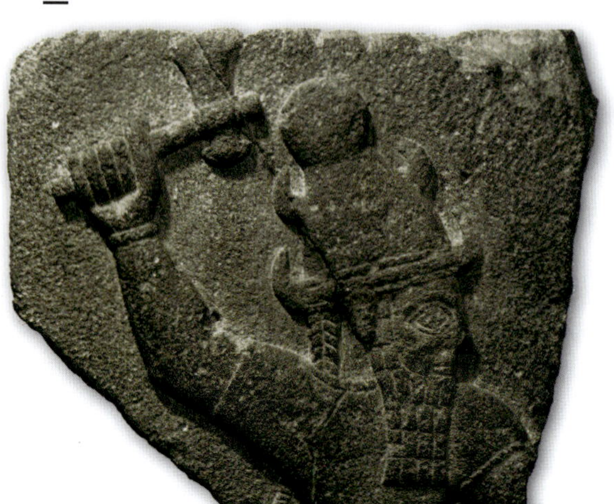

Left: Baal, the god of storm, was widely worshipped across the ancient Levant. He has a thunder club in one hand and a lightening fork in the other (WA 117909)

descendants of the Hittites still ruled some places in the time of David, and Bathsheba's Hittite husband Uriah was one of David's military officers (2 Samuel 11:3). In the time of Ahab (874–853 BC) a possible coalition between Hittites and Egypt could terrify the armies of Ben Hadad, King of Aram (2 Kings 7:6–7).

Babylonians—distant neighbours in the east

From a biblical viewpoint the most well-known of all Babylonian kings was the fearsome Nebuchadnezzar (also Nebuchadrezzar) who, at the Battle of Carchemish in 605 BC, destroyed a coalition of the Assyrian and Egyptian armies and made himself master of an empire reaching from the border of modern day Iran right down to Egypt. In the middle of this mayhem, Daniel and his young friends, and later Ezekiel, were taken into exile to Babylon. The Babylonians occupied territory to the east of the Aramaeans in modern day Iraq. They are referred to in Genesis 10:10 under the title 'the land of Shinar', whilst in Jeremiah 24:5 we find another common description: 'the land of the Chaldeans'.

The Assyrians—neighbours in the north-east

We followed their progress in chapter 2 (page 25).

Enter Room **54 Ancient Turkey**

Baal, the god of storm

Turn immediately left to *case 4* a small figurine of a god, probably Baal, on the back of a bull (*ME 140867*) and to his right is a relief of Baal (*ME 117909*). Baal was worshipped as Teshub by the Hittites. In Canaan this was the god Baal who is frequently mentioned in the Old Testament. Because he was the god of storm it was all the more significant that in the time of Elijah, Baal was defeated by fire from heaven on a clear day, in the contest on Carmel (1 Kings 18:20–40). The bull was his sacred animal and two bulls were sacrificed. Jesus

Hebrew kings: The kingdom divided—Israel and Judah

The dates for Hebrew kings can be established accurately by connecting them with kings and events of surrounding nations (especially Egypt, Assyria and Babylonia) whose dates are sometimes given by astronomical data. As a result, for example, we can fix the year of Ahab's death as 853 BC, and this enables us to work both backwards and forwards from there using biblical data. Only those kings mentioned in this guide are listed here. Co-regencies are not shown.

 *Those marked with an asterisk are also referred to by name in contemporary documents outside the Bible.

Judah (20 kings reigning in Jerusalem)		Israel (20 kings reigning in Samaria)	
(Rehoboam	930–913)	Jeroboam I	930–909
Asa	910–869	Baasha	908–886
		Omri*	885–874
Jehoshaphat	870–848	Ahab*	874–853
		Jehoram (Joram)	852–851
Joash*	835–796	Jehu*	841–814
		Sent tribute to Assyria	841
		Jehoahaz	814–798
Amaziah	796–767	Jeroboam II	782–753
		Menahem*	752–742
		Pekah*	737–732
Azariah* (Uzziah)	761–740		
Ahaz*	732–716	Hoshea*	732–723
		Fall of Samaria to Assyria	722
Hezekiah*	716–687	Sennacherib confronted Hezekiah in Jerusalem	701
Manasseh*	687–642		
Josiah	640–609		
Jehoahaz	609		
Jehoiachim*	609–597	Many Jews exiled to Babylon including Daniel and Ezekiel.	
Jehoiachin*	597	For three months before exiled to Babylon.	
Zedekiah	597–587	Fall of Jerusalem to Babylon (16 March 597). More Jews into exile. Final destruction in 587.	
	539	The fall of Babylon to Persia and Cyrus of Persia allows Jews to return and rebuild Jerusalem.	
	516	The Temple completed. Prophets Haggai and Zechariah.	
	458	Ezra in Jerusalem.	
	445	Nehemiah in Jerusalem. Malachi and close of OT.	

Timelines: from Abraham to Solomon page 77. Egyptian kings page 42. Assyrian kings page 26. Babylonian kings see page 69. Persian kings page 54. Roman emperors page 100.

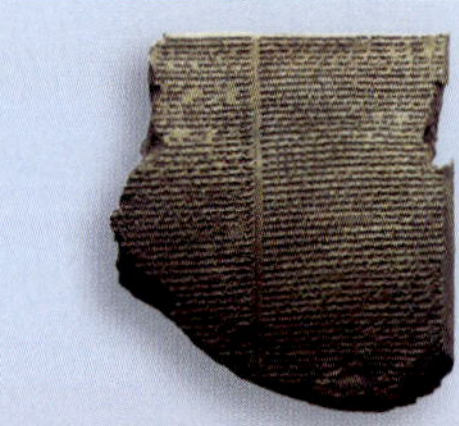

The Gilgamesh Epic
—a legend of a flood

Discovered by George Smith in 1872, this is the legend of Gilgamesh who seeks immortality. He meets the hero Utnapishtim who tells how he gained immortality by surviving the flood. There are interesting similarities, though wide divergences also, with the biblical record. Utnapishtim is instructed by the god Ea to build a great boat and bring his family and representatives of all living creatures into it. They ride out a terrible flood that destroys the rest of mankind. Utnapishtim finally sends out a dove, a swallow and a raven – the raven does not return. Together with his family and menagerie, Utnapishtim leaves the boat on Mount Nasir in what is now Kurdistan, and offers sacrifices to the gods. As a reward for good behaviour he and his wife are given immortality. These accounts, and there are other flood stories from the ancient world, at least point to the fact that stories of creation and a great flood were common in the world of Abraham. This tablet is dated around 650 BC but is clearly a copy of a much older original. Compare the Atrahasis Epic on page 82.

Flood stories occur in the ancient traditions of people groups from every continent and in scores of countries including Iran, Egypt, Russia, China, India, Mexico, Peru and Hawaii.

was accused of being an agent of Baal-zebub (Mark 3:22–23) who was the god of flies and dung, the prince of demons and identified with Satan.

Enter **Room 55 Mesopotamia 1500–539 BC**

On the left in *case 8* are clay documents from the Assyrian library in Nineveh relating to the time of Sargon, Sennacherib and Ashurbanipal kings of Assyria (See pages 32–38). In the second row down on the right notice the ferocity of the fire that destroyed Nineveh in 612 BC (*ME K5967*). This is reflected in the warning of Nahum 3:15.

In the next row down, second in from the right, notice the explanation of the substitute king (*ME K2600 and ME K112*). If the wise men prophesied any harm to the king, a substitute was placed on the throne and removed by death when the danger was over! An illustration of Christ dying as our substitute to remove the penalty of sin (1 Peter 2:24).

The next row down is an *Epic of Creation* (*ME K3473*). The creation accounts from the Ancient Near East bear little resemblance to the biblical account, unlike the traditions of a global flood.

Move to your right and note the text board indicating the exciting possibilities of what may be discovered among the 30,000 volume library of Ashurbanipal.

In *case 9* notice the images of *Fish-cloaked sages* (*apkallu*). These illustrate the fact that Jonah's experience in a great fish would not have surprised the Assyrians in Nineveh (Jonah 3).

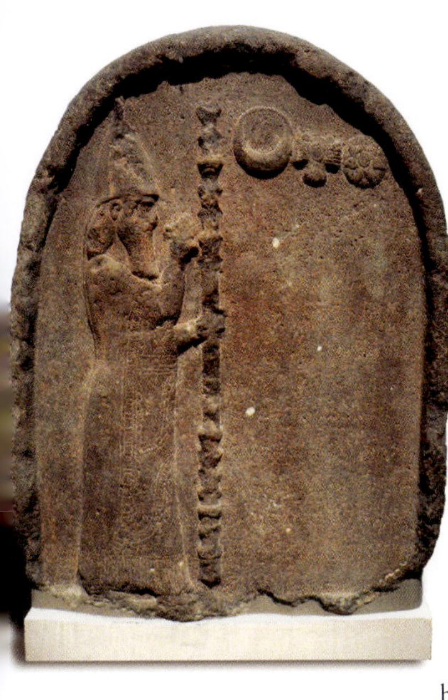

Left: Nabonidus, the father of the Belshazzar referred to in Daniel chapters 5,7,8, worshipping before symbols of the moon god Sin, the sun god Shamash, and the goddess of war and love Ishtar (ME90837)

Below: The Babylonian map of the world (ME92687)

Cross over to the case in the centre. **The Babylonian map of the world** (ME 92687). One of the earliest known geographic maps. Here, Babylon is seen as the centre of the world. Notice the reference in the text board to the fact that one mountain is identified as the place where the ark landed in the Babylonian account – Uratu is the Ararat of the Bible (Genesis 8:4).

In the reverse side of this case **King Ashurbanipal's Flood Tablet** (ME K 3375). This is the Gilgamesh Epic. See BOX: The Gilgamesh Epic – a legend of a flood.

Move to *case 7* on your right. See page 69 for the order of Babylonian kings. At the far left end of this case is **The Stele of Nabonidus** (ME 90837). Nabonidus was the last king of Babylon. He is worshipping three of his gods. His absence from Babylon campaigning in Arabia explains why Daniel was third ruler in the kingdom

(Daniel 5:29). The small clay **Chronicle of Nabopollasar (top shelf left)** (ME 22047) whose sudden death in 550 BC brought his son Nebuchadnezzar II to the throne. **Nebuchadnezzar king of justice** (ME 45690), a clay tablet extolling the greatness of Nebuchadnezzar. Three **Terracotta cylinders describing Nebuchadnezzar's building works**. Nebuchadnezzar was renowned for his magnificent buildings that would have dazzled Ezekiel, Daniel and their friends when they entered Babylon as exiles from Jerusalem.

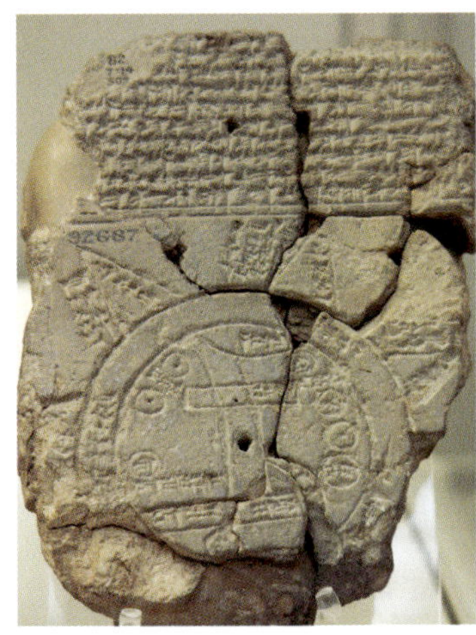

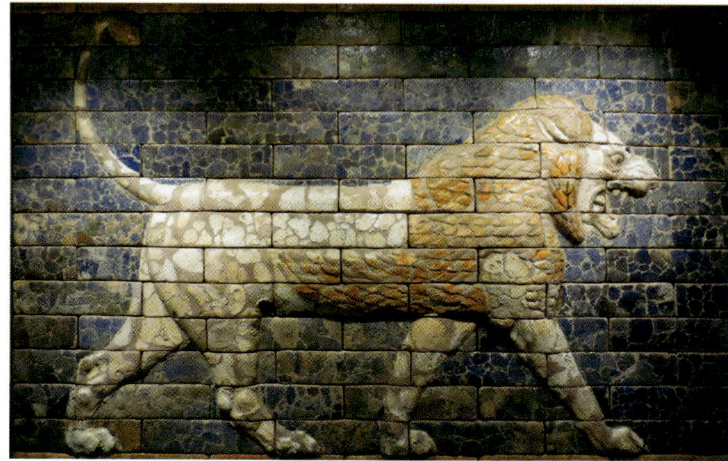

Above: A roaring lion from the Throne Room of Nebuchadnezzar. The brilliant colours of blue, yellow and white represent the divine and royal power of the king. 120 roaring and striding lions (together with dragons and bulls) lined the Processional Way and represented the king himself. See page 70

'The wretched, weary person weeps' (ME 40474) (top shelf 3rd on the right). Amel Marduk was a son of Nebuchadnezzar who was thrown into prison for some misdemeanour. Here is his lament of how unjustly he has been treated. He is the Evil-Merodach of 2 Kings 25:27 and likely he met up with King Jehoiachin in prison (2 Kings 24:15), because when he came to power in 562 BC he treated Jehoiachin above all the other royal exiles (2 Kings 25:27–30). The museum Staatliche Museen zu Berlin displays the ration book of supplies for *'Yaukin king of Judah'* and his family, discovered in the royal archives at Babylon.

Nabonidus was the last king of Babylon and was very unpopular. This is why the Persian entry into Babylon in 539 BC was without bloodshed, and business continued as normal. This poem **'He looks at those effigies and utters blasphemes…'** (ME 38299) ridicules Nabonidus in favour of Cyrus of Persia. **The fall of a dynasty** (ME 35382) records that Nabonidus was absent in Arabia for much of his reign. It was for this reason that his son Belshazzar was on the throne in Babylon when the Persians captured the city in the year 539 BC (Daniel 5).

Return to the left of the bottom row Babylon and the Bible. **Nebuchadnezzar captures Jerusalem** (ME 21946). This clay tablet lists the main events of the Babylonian kings. It is often known as a 'Babylonian Chronicle'. One side refers to the crucial Battle of Carchemish in 605 BC in which the Assyrians and Egyptians were soundly defeated by Nebuchadnezzar. On the side facing you, it records that in the seventh year of Nebuchadnezzar

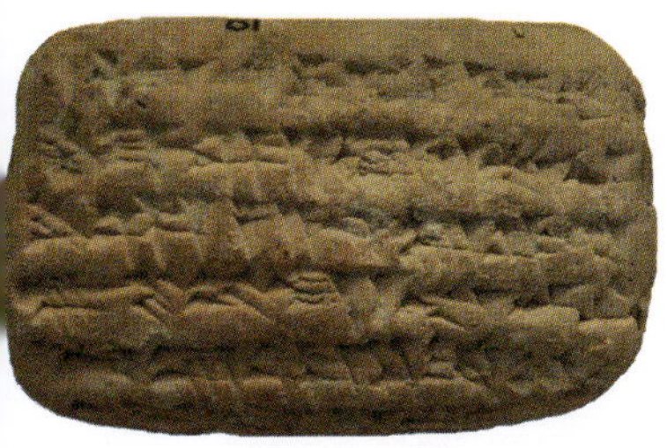

Left: The small clay tablet (ME 114789) of Nebo-Sarsekim referred to in Jeremiah 39:3 as one of the Babylonian officers present at the capture of Jerusalem in 597 BC

(598/597), in the month of Kislimu (November/December), he marched into 'Hatti-land' (Syria-Palestine) and camped against 'the city of Judah' (Jerusalem). The record continues to tell how on the second day of the month Addaru (Adar) he captured the city and its king, received tribute and appointed his own king. The event is recorded in 2 Kings 24:8–17. The Chronicle's careful dating means that we can fix the date for the first destruction of Jerusalem under Jehoiachin at 16 March 597 BC. Nebuchadnezzar II attacked Jerusalem three times: in 605, 597 and 587 BC.

The small (5.5 cm) clay tablet of ***Nebuchadnezzar's right hand man*** (ME 114789) records how an officer of Nebuchadnezzar lavished a gift of gold on a temple in Babylon. His name is Nabu-sharussu-ukin and it is dated to

the tenth year of Nebuchadnezzar in 595 BC. He is identified with Nebo-Sarsekim of Jeremiah 39:3 who, eight years later, was one of the Babylonian officers in charge of Jerusalem when the city finally fell to the Babylonians in the time of Zedekiah, king of Judah in 587 BC. The tablet was deciphered in 2007. The museum suggest that he 'probably' met Jeremiah the biblical prophet.

The suggestion at **One God** (ME 47406) that the Jews thought of the pagan gods as 'aspects' of their Yahweh is, of course, greatly mistaken. The two clay tablets ***Belshazzar and the Bible*** (ME 26740 and 91125) both give significant meaning to the reference in Daniel 5:1 to 'King Belshazzar'. See Box: The

Right: on the Babylonian Chronicle (WA 21946) the text (highlighted here) reads that the king: 'encamped against the city of Judah and on the second day of the month Adar, he seized the city and captured the king (this was Jehoiachin). He appointed there a king of his own choice (Zedekiah), received its heavy tribute and sent (them) to Babylon'. Height: 6 cm

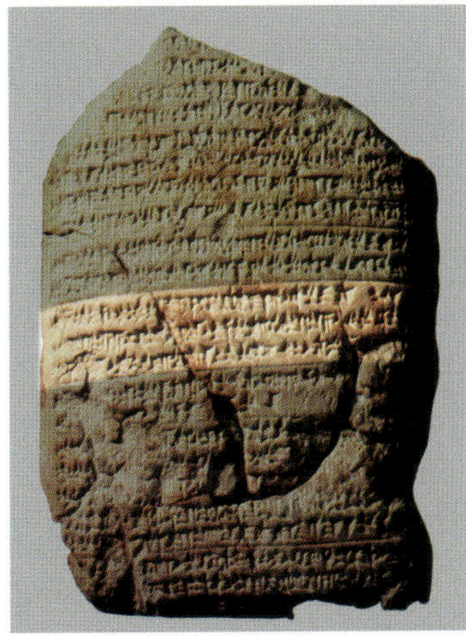

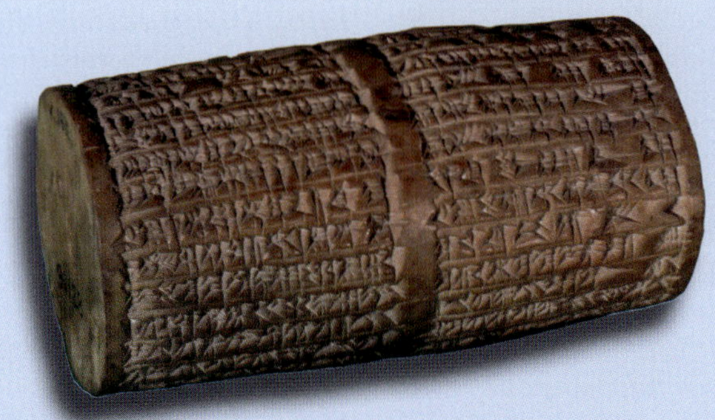

Above: The Cylinder of Nabonidus which refers to king Belshazzar and illustrates the detailed accuracy of the biblical record of the final days of the Babylonian Empire (WA91125). Length 10.4cm

The Cylinder of Nabonidus — Belshazzar, the king who never lived?

Nabonidus was the last king of Babylon, and Daniel lived through his reign. Nabonidus, who is not referred to by name in the Bible, restored two temples of the moon god Sin. Until 1854 the book of Daniel in the Old Testament contained the only known reference to Belshazzar, and some considered him to be a figment of the writer's imagination. In that year J E Taylor, the British Consul in Basra, was exploring the ruins of an ancient ziggurat at Tell el Muqayyar (ancient Ur of the Chaldees) in southern Iraq, when he discovered at the corners four identical clay time capsules of which this is one. They had been placed there by Nabonidus and on each he records the history of the ziggurat and adds a prayer for the long life and good health of himself and adds:

'…as for Belshazzar, the eldest son, the offspring of my heart, the fear of thy great divinity cause thou to exist in his heart, and let not sin possess him, let him be satisfied with fullness of life.'

Was Nabonidus aware of his sons extravagant banquets using the sacred vessels from the temple in Jerusalem?

In response to an omen, Nabonidus spent many years on campaign at the oasis of Teima in north-west Arabia, and Belshazzar remained at Babylon as co-regent and thus as de facto king. All this perfectly explains a number of issues that had puzzled scholars. Daniel 5:1 refers to Belshazzar as the King, and v 29 records that Daniel was proclaimed 'third highest ruler in the kingdom'. This dual reign of Nabonidus and Belshazzar also explains why, although the records of the Persian king Cyrus tell us that he took the king of Babylon (Nabonidus) prisoner, Daniel 5:30 records that the night on which the Persians broke into the city of Babylon, 'Belshazzar, king of the Babylonians, was slain'. (see also the Cyrus Cylinder in room 52 p 56).

Cylinder of Nabonidus on page 68.

Finally, the mina weights often in the form of a lion or a duck — as here, looking like Belgian chocolates! Note the Museum caption for this item. This illustrate the account in Daniel 5:27. See page 59 for a lion wieght.

Go to *case 6* **Building Babylon.** Here is *The East India House Inscription* (WA 129397) which records the devotion and achievements of Nebuchadnezzar. It includes a reference to the Processional Way and the Ishtar Gate, both known to Ezekiel, Daniel and the Jewish exiles in Babylon. The reference to the god Marduk in part reads: 'Create in my heart the worship of your divinity and grant whatever is pleasing to you because you have fashioned my life.' It is a clear example of cuneiform writing.

Moving to the right in this case is a picture of how the building of the Tower of Babel may have been, except that it has only seven levels. It was intended for the king to get close to his god Marduk; the museum suggestion of this being the inspiration of the biblical Babel (Genesis 11:1–9) assumes a very late date for the Pentateuch. Although the famed 'hanging gardens' of Babylon have never yet been uncovered, the clay tablet ME 46226 records many

List of Babylonian kings

	BC	
Nabopolassar	626–605	Babylon competing for domination.
Nebuchadnezzar II*	605–562	605 defeat of Egypt and Assyria at Carchemish.
(Nebuchadrezzar)		Babylonian supremacy.
		605 Jehoiachim of Judah became a vassal of Nebuchadnezzar (2 Kings 24:1) and Daniel was taken into exile (Daniel 1:1–2). 597 Jehoiachin and Ezekiel taken to Babylon. 586 Jerusalem captured, Temple destroyed and its treasures taken to Babylon.
Amel-Marduk*	562–560	Evil-Merodach of 2 Kings 25:27, Jews still in exile.
Nergal-Shar-usur*	560–556	Nergal-Sharezar of Jeremiah 39:3, Jews still in exile.
Labashi-Marduk	556	Jews still in exile.
Nabonidus	556–539	Belshazzar* son of Nabonidus, as co-regent. (Daniel 5:22). Babylon captured by Persia in 539 and the end of an empire. Note: Daniel served in the royal courts of the last five kings of Babylon and Cyrus of Persia.

* These kings are mentioned by name in the Bible

Timelines: from Abraham to Solomon page 77. Hebrew kings page 63. Egyptian kings page 42. Assyrian kings page 26. Persian kings page 54. Roman emperors page 100.

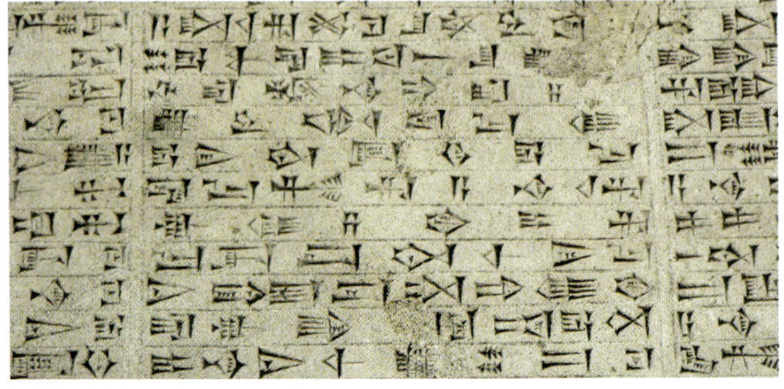

identifiable plants and herbs in it. To the right is one of an estimated 15 million baked bricks required for his extensive building works, thousands of which were stamped with the name of Nebuchadnezzar,.

In *case 5* (behind *case 6*) is the reverse side of the East India House inscription.

The impressive and colourful lion of glazed brick (see page 66) is typical of much of the magnificent architecture of Nebuchadnezzar's Babylon. Daniel and his friends would have been familiar with this. The excessive heat required for such glazing is well illustrated by the account of the fiery furnace in Daniel 3:19–21.

Case 3 top right is ***The Babylonian Chronicle and the Fall of Nineveh*** (ME 21901). This illustrates the deliberate warning in Nahum 3 that Nineveh would be destroyed by fire and water.

A bird in a cage

In the bottom left of *case 3* ***The Taylor Prism*** (ME 91032) was discovered in 1830 at Nineveh by Colonel Geoffrey Taylor, the British Resident in Baghdad, from whom it derived its name. It records the first eight military

Above: Part of the East India House Inscription which expresses the devotion and achievements of Nebuchadnezzar in clear cuneiform script. (WA 129397)

campaigns of Sennacherib, but it is the account of his third campaign, in the year 701 BC, that is of interest to us. By the time Hezekiah came to the throne of Judah in 716, Samaria in the north was already under the control of Assyria. Hezekiah's father, Ahaz, had made Judah a vassal state of Assyria, but Hezekiah decided to assert his independence and seek support from Egypt. When Sennacherib succeeded his father, Sargon, he turned his attention to Jerusalem. The details of what followed are recorded in 2 Kings 18–19, 2 Chronicles 32, and Isaiah 36–37.

Sennacherib left his own account on this six-sided clay prism. Having defeated the Phoenicians and received tribute from Moab and Edom, he intercepted an Egyptian force on its way to the relief of Jerusalem. Hezekiah had made a treaty with Taharqa of Egypt who proved to be a 'broken reed' (2 Kings 18:19-

The Taylor Prism

The king begins by introducing himself: 'Sennacherib, the great King, the powerful King, the King of Assyria, the unrivalled, the pious monarch, the worshipper of the great gods. The protector of the just; the lover of the righteous, the noble warrior, the valiant hero, the first of all the Kings, the great punisher of unbelievers who are breakers of the holy festivals. Ashur, the great lord, had given me an unrivalled monarchy. Over all princes he has raised triumphantly my arms.' Sennacherib then describes his defeat of the king of Babylon (Merodach-Baladan referred to in 2 Kings 20 and Isaiah 39) and the wholesale slaughter and pillaging that followed. Little wonder that 2 Kings 18:13–16 records Hezekiah's vain attempt to pay off Sennacherib by stripping the Temple of its gold. When Sennacherib finally arrived at the walls of Jerusalem he had already laid waste across Judah forty-six 'strong cities, fortresses, and small cities which were round them' and had 'captured 200,150

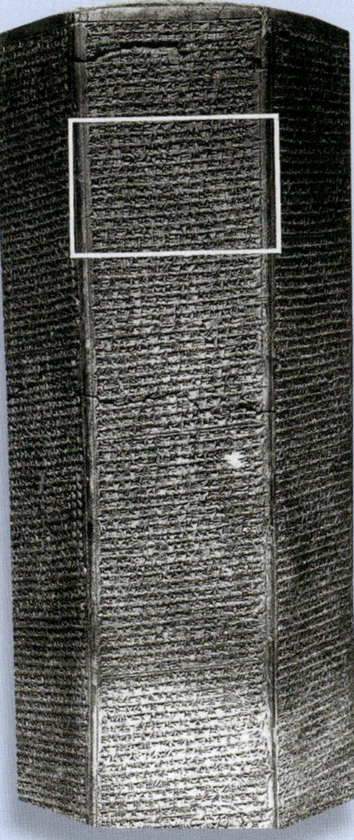

people, small and great, male and female'. His were no idle threats (vs 28–35). However, Isaiah stiffened the defenders' resistance (19:20–34), assuring them of God's intervention and even warning the king of Assyria that God would treat him as cruelly as he treated his captives (v 28). In his own record Sennacherib adds that, 'The terrifying splendour of my majesty overcame Hezekiah. The elite forces and his good soldiers he had brought in to strengthen his royal city Jerusalem, did not fight.' According to vs 35–37 they did not to need to! The king then lists the tribute that Hezekiah had sent to him. Inexplicably there is no mention of Lachish on this prism. Sennacherib withdrew and returned home where history records that he was assassinated some years later 'between two colossi' — perhaps very similar to the huge bulls we saw in Room 10 (page 24) or the ones in Room 9 being excavated.

Pictured: The Taylor Prism (ME 91032). The detail outlined in white describes how Sennacherib shut up Hezekiah in Jerusalem, 'like a caged bird'. Later the text describes the tribute Hezekiah sent to Sennacherib. Height: 38.5 cm

21). Sennacherib records that he shut up Hezekiah in his royal city 'like a bird in a cage'. In the event, it was Lachish and not Jerusalem that adorned the walls of his victory room in Nineveh. See pages 33–37. And also the Box: The Taylor Prism.

At the bottom right in *case 3* see **Erasing History?** (ME 90866). We meet this concept often in the Museum (see for example pages 43 and 117) where the erasing of a name or face on an inscription would delete them from history.

Cross over to *case 10*. **Assyria at war**, notice in the middle of the case the small size of the swords which illustrates the close combat expected in ancient warfare (compare the Romans also). Sennacherib was probably assassinated with a short sword like this – 2 Kings 19:37. The helmet, swords and armour illustrate the infantry Hezekiah confronted during the Assyrian invasion in 701 BC. Next to this is a panel illustrating Ashurbanipal's Assyrian campaign against Egypt in which Tirhakah was defeated. Tirhakah, when crown prince, has been defeated by Sennacherib in 701 BC and now, as Pharaoh, he was defeated by Assyria again in 671. Nahum refers to this defeat to warn Nineveh that in turn their end will be as inevitable!

On the top shelf of *case 13* **Glass and alabaster jars** discovered by Austin Henry Layard in the nineteenth century. ME 90952 has on it a cuneiform inscription: 'Palace of Sargon King of Assyria'. This is the Sargon II of Isaiah 20:1. It

reflects the fact that the art of glassmaking was known at least as early as the eighth century BC.

Below note the lion **Mina Lion weights** (ME 91220 and ME 91222); we met these in Persia on page 58.

In *case 14* **The deeds of Tiglath-Pileser I** (ME 91033). This Clay prism was given to four scholars in 1857 who had been independently trying to decipher cuneiform writing, one of whom was Sir Henry Rawlinson. The 'very remarkable coincidence' of their translations proved that cuneiform had at last been deciphered.

The case behind you in the centre contains a necklace composed of ancient cylinder seals dating from 2200 to 350 BC. The seals were collected by Austin Henry Layard, the British archaeologist who discovered Nineveh. He had them made into this necklace and presented it to his wife as a wedding present in 1869. See below for details of these seals.

Cross the room to *case 2*. Here is an interesting display of **Boundary Stones**. These were of great importance in the ancient world. See Proverbs 22:28, 'Do not remove an ancient boundary stone set up by your forefathers' also Deuteronomy 19:14; 27:17 and Hosea 5:10. To move a boundary stone ('landmark') was to steal a man's land and this deserved the judgement of God. In Babylonia a boundary stones was known as a *kudurru* and it acted as a legal document. It is possible that clay copies were placed on site, because these more

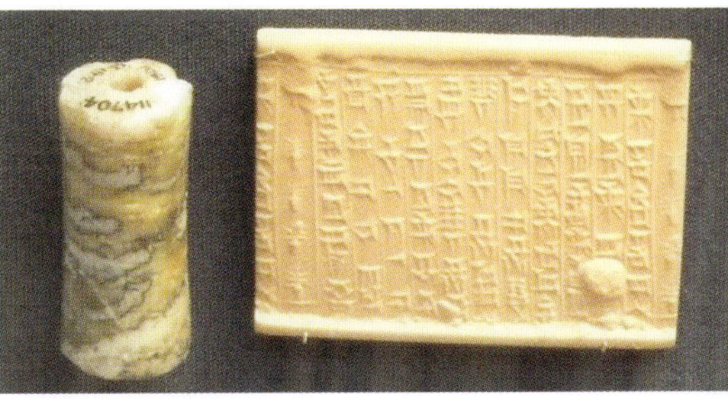

Right: A cylinder seal of a court treasurer of a Kassite king in the 14th century BC. Notice the hole in the cylinder through which a cord could be threaded

durable carvings on stone were all discovered in temples — the bank vaults of the day.

Ancient ID cards

In *case 1* to the left is a chalcedony seal of a treasurer to a Kassite king in the 14th century BC (*ME 114704*). The Kassites came from the mountains of Mesopotamia and infiltrated and effectively conquered Babylonia from around 1500 BC. They absorbed Babylonian culture and left no trace of their own; we know of them only through inscriptions – much as the Israelites when they entered Canaan at roughly the same time. The early Babylonians developed the cylinder seal and these are common throughout our tour of the Museum. They represent the Visa or ID card of the day. Rolled over soft clay the design became the owner's 'signature'. An interesting illustration of this is found in the sordid account of Judah consorting with what he thought was a prostitute but who was in reality his daughter-in-law, Tamar. When Judah was unable to pay her 'fee', she demanded as a pledge his staff and 'your seal and your cord' (Genesis 38:18). You will notice that each seal has a hole bored through the centre through which a cord could be threaded so that the seal could be hung safely around the owner's neck – or a pin inserted to fix to clothing. Jezebel used King Ahab's seal in order to secure the murder of Naboth (1 Kings 21:8).

Enter **Room 56 Mesopotamia 6000–1500 BC.**

Left: This boundary stone (ME 102485) records a gift of land; the carvings are emblems of the gods called upon to curse anyone who challenges the ownership of the property or who defaces the stone (c.1125–1100 BC). Height: 37 cm. Currently not on display

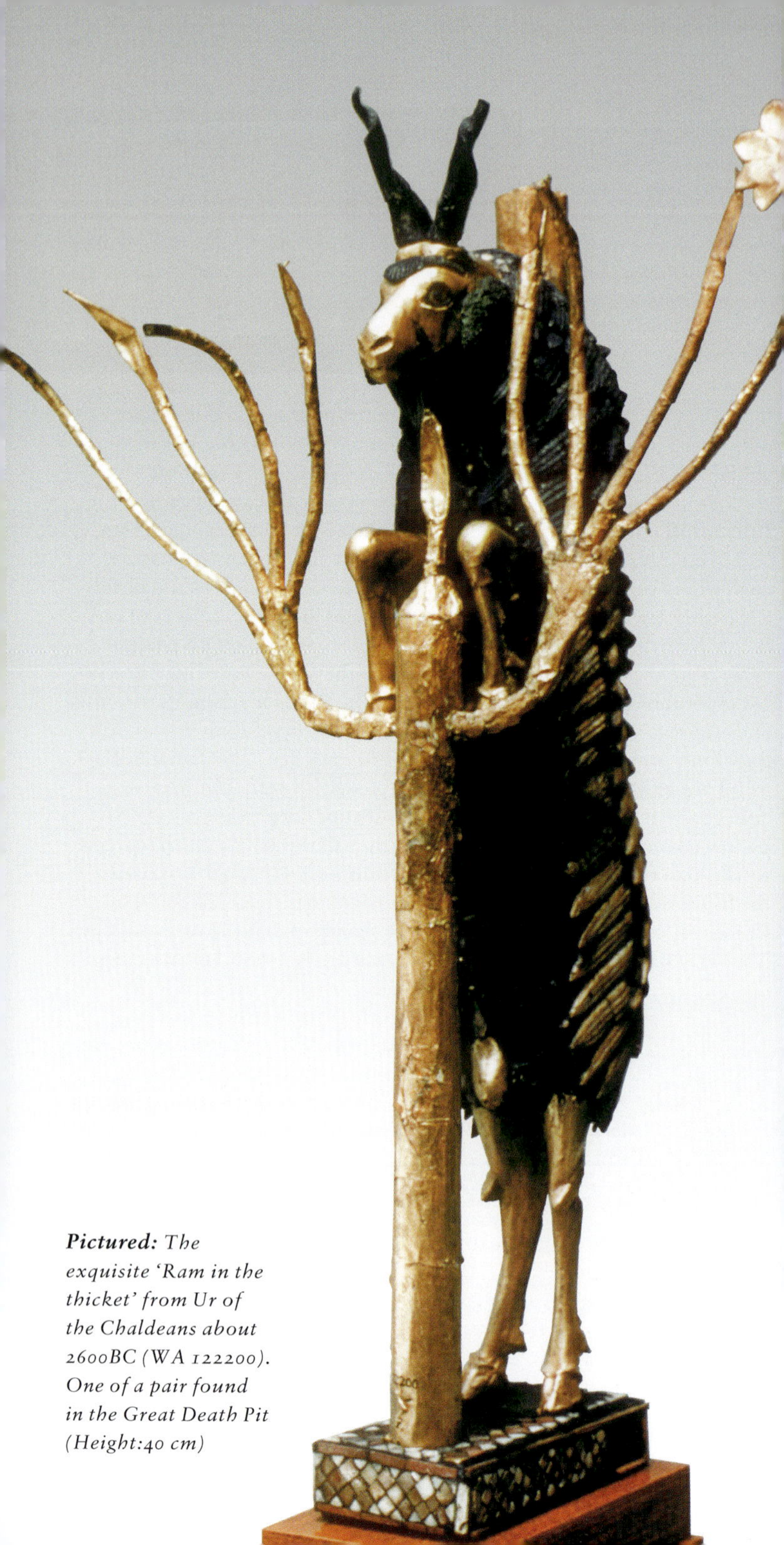

Pictured: *The exquisite 'Ram in the thicket' from Ur of the Chaldeans about 2600BC (WA 122200). One of a pair found in the Great Death Pit (Height:40 cm)*

6 Father Abraham

Four and a half thousand years ago southern Iraq was a sophisticated society and a vibrant centre of trade. Its impressive buildings, comfortable homes, exquisite jewellery and advanced technical knowledge make it a far cry from the primitive culture that many assume Abraham left in response to the call of God.

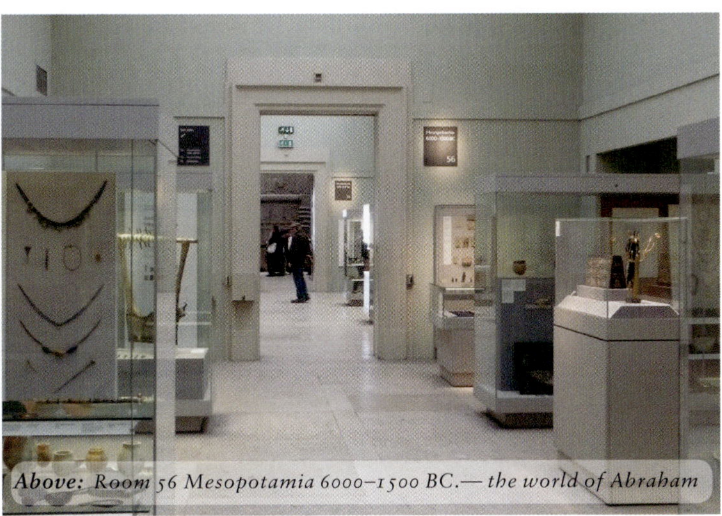

Above: Room 56 Mesopotamia 6000–1500 BC.— the world of Abraham

Room 56 Mesopotamia 6000–1500 BC

The world of Abraham—Early Mesopotamia

The word Mesopotamia means 'between the two rivers' and it refers to the land between the great rivers Tigris and Euphrates in what is now east Syria and down through Iraq to the Persian Gulf. This was the land of Israel's roots because from here, around 2000 BC, Abraham migrated firstly north to Haran and then south into the land of Canaan. In this room we will discover much that illustrates narratives in the book of Genesis and beyond; some of the names will be familiar to us.

Digging up Ur

The first serious archaeological excavations of Ur (now Tell el Muqayyar in southern Iraq) began in 1923 under the direction of Sir Leonard Woolley. It is generally

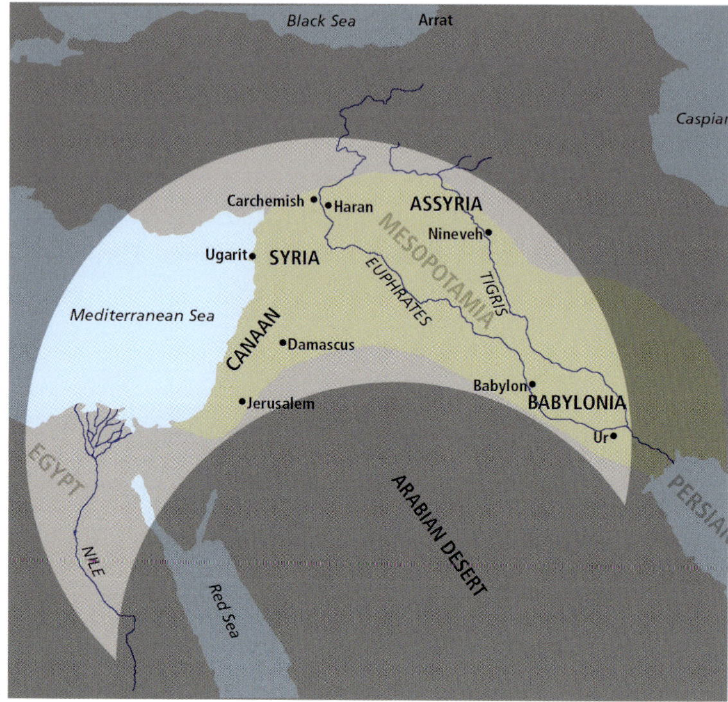

Above: *The Fertile Crescent from Egypt to Mesopotamia to the Persian Gulf—in the time of Abraham*

accepted that this is the site of the ancient 'Ur of the Chaldeans'—the birthplace of Abraham (Genesis 11:27–29). Although most of the artefacts in Room 56 are dated around 2500 BC—half a millennium prior to Abraham—they provide an accurate picture of the advanced civilization into which Abraham and Sarah were born.

A huge ziggurat (temple) dedicated to the moon-god Nanna (also called Sin) dominated the skyline and lifestyle of the people of Ur, and it is likely that Abraham once worshipped here (see Joshua 24:2). Such structures are reflected in the tower of Babel referred to in Genesis 11:1–9.

Contrary to popular belief, literacy was widespread at this time, and Sir Leonard Woolley discovered that one fifth of all homes in Ur contained clay tablets with writing. In addition, Abraham could have enjoyed the comfort of a two-storey brick house with a lobby, courtyard, kitchen and toilet, bedrooms and reception rooms; Sarah, similarly, would have been familiar with the beautifully intricate head-dresses and jewellery that you will see here. Trade, literature, mathematics and astronomy were highly developed.

A timeline from Abraham to Solomon

This timeline assumes the accuracy of the ages and periods stated in the Old Testament.

BC

2166	Abraham was born.
2091	Abraham left Haran at the age of 75 (Genesis 12:4).
2066	Isaac was born when Abraham was 100 (Genesis 21:5).
2006	Jacob was born when Isaac was 60 (Genesis 25:26).
1915	Joseph was born 17 years before entering Egypt which was 39 years before Jacob entered Egypt (Genesis 45:6 ie Joseph's age of 30 plus 7 years of plenty and 2 years of famine).
1898	Joseph was sold into Egyptian slavery at the age of 17 (Genesis 37:2).
1885	Joseph entered Pharaoh's service at the age of 30 (Genesis 41:46).
1876	Jacob settled in Egypt at the age of 130 (Genesis 47:9) and 430 years before the Exodus (Exodus 12:41).
1859	Jacob died at the age of 147 and 17 years after he settled in Egypt (Genesis 47:28).
1805	Joseph died at the age of 110 years (Genesis 50:26).
1526	Birth of Moses—he was around 80 at the time of the Exodus (Exodus 7:7 and Acts 7:30).
1446	The Exodus: the Hebrews left Egypt 480 years before Solomon's fourth year (1 Kings 6:1)—see page 44 for a note on dating the Exodus, but this guide assumes a fifteenth century date.
1406	Death of Moses at the age of 120, and the beginning of the conquest of Canaan (Deuteronomy 34:7).
	Joshua took command in his early 60s (on the basis that the 'young man' of Exodus 33:11 would not be much more than 20; see Numbers 14:26–30).
1399	Major battles for the Promised Land completed according to Caleb in Joshua 14:10.
1356	Joshua died at the age of 110 (Joshua 24:29), but much land unconquered.
1356–1050	Period of the Judges.
1050–1010	Saul's reign. Precise accuracy of these dates is not possible since Saul's exact age and length of reign in 1 Samuel 13:1 are not given.
1010–971	David's reign. He began at the age of 30 (2 Samuel 5:4) and therefore was born in 1040.
970–930	Solomon's reign (2 Chronicles 9:30).
966	This year is accepted by scholars as the fourth year of Solomon's reign. In this year he began to build the temple. This was 480 years after the Exodus (1 Kings 6:1). The Exodus itself was 430 years after Jacob settled in Egypt (Exodus 12:41).

Timelines: Hebrew kings page 63. Egyptian kings page 42. Assyrian kings 26. Babylonian kings page 69. Persian kings page 54. Roman emperors page 100.

On the move

For a century Ur was the capital city of the area, but around 2000 BC tribes from the north-west overran Babylonia; they are known to history as the Amorites. Genesis 11:31 reads: 'Tera took his son Abram… and they set out from Ur of the Chaldeans to go to Canaan.'

Strictly, the name Chaldea would not be given to the land for another thousand years. With the destruction of Ur, the Amorites strengthened Babylon, a city that would later give its name both to the area and to an empire so feared by the Hebrew kings. Marduk became the national god of Babylon and his massive temple adorned the city.

Enter **Room 56** and *in case 25 immediately to your left* notice the ***terracotta figurines and plaque.*** No 4 (ME 127497). These may be similar to the 'household gods' that Rachel stole from her father's home (Genesis 31:17–35), that Joshua complained of in

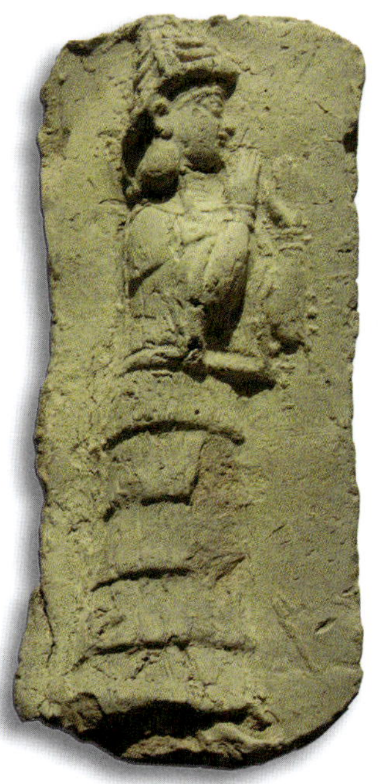

Below: A terracotta plaque of the intercessor goddess Lamma (ME 127497). From Ur c. 2000–1750 BC during the time of the patriarchs. Height: 40 cm

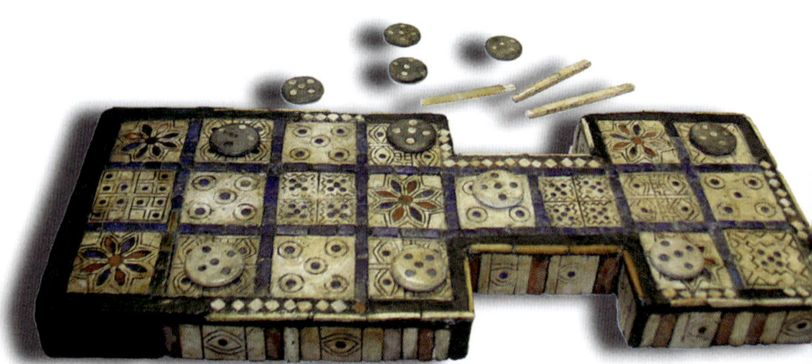

Above: *The Royal Game of Ur (ME 120834). Length: 28 cm*

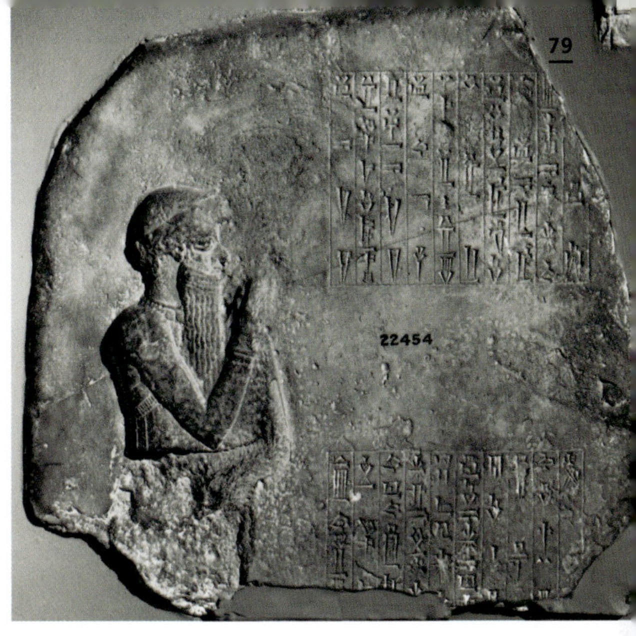

Right: A monument of Hammurabi in worship (ME 22454)— see page 80

Joshua 24:14–15, that Micah kept in his home (Judges 17–18), and that David's wife Michal owned (1 Samuel 19:13). These references reveal that for half a millennium some Israelites treasured household idols (see also later in Room 57 *case 10* page 93).

Behind you in the glass cabinet is **The Royal Game of Ur** *(ME 120834).* This is one of the oldest known games and it has been found as far away as South India; it predates Abraham by at least a millennium. Earlier (see page 32) we discovered that guards outside Sargon's great city of Khorsabad idled away their time by playing this very game—1200 years later! Other examples of this game that was scratched onto the base of the huge winged bulls, have been found in Nineveh; it was obviously a popular game and Abraham and Sarah may well have played it. You can buy a replica of the Royal Game of Ur in the Grenville shop.

In *case 24* **The Golden Age of Mesopotamian Trade**, notice the small tablets of clay which was the 'paper' of Abraham's day. Baked hard in the sun, the completed document would last almost indefinitely. Thousands of these official records reveal a bustling city of merchants and businessmen trading into Syria

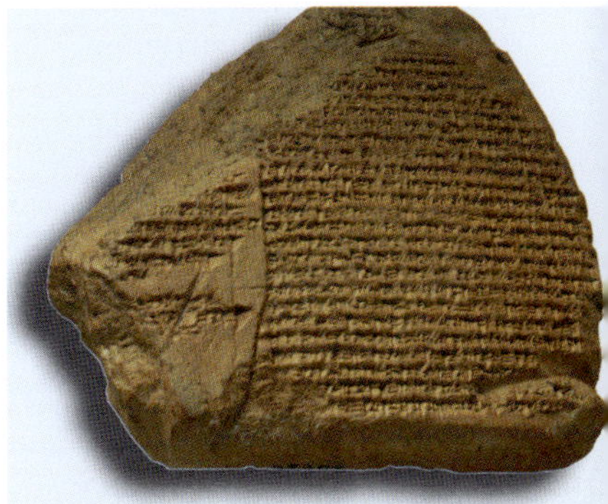

Above: A genealogy of the Kings of Babylon (ANE 80328) illustrates the significance of accurate genealogies in the ancient world—see page 80

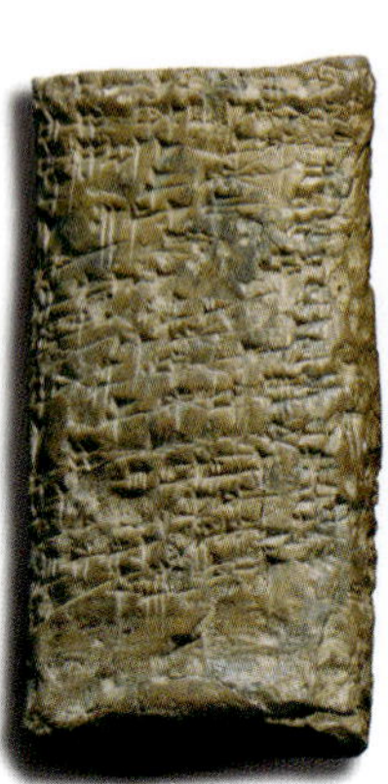

Clay letter

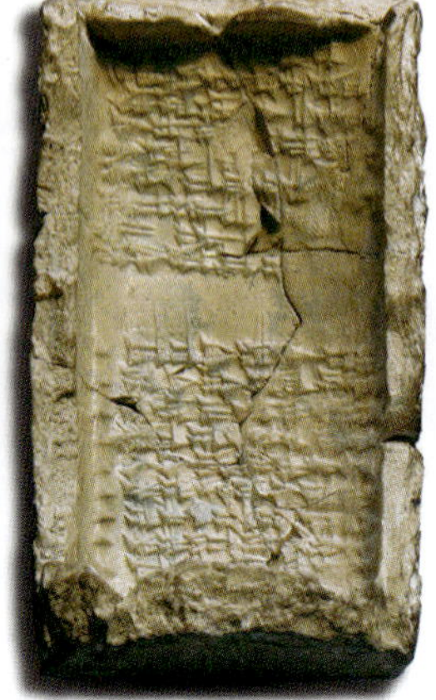

Inside of envelope

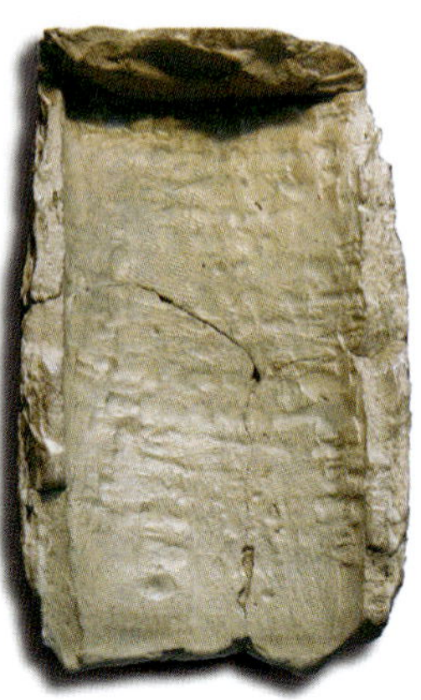

Top of envelope

Above: A Babylonian clay legal document and its envelope similar to WA 11357. This one, not yet on display in the museum, is dated early 18th century BC and is a contract with 11 witnesses for the purchase of an office in a temple. Notice how the writing on the back of the cuneiform text becomes impressed on the inside of the envelope. Height of envelope: 11cm

and down to the Persian Gulf. They record purchases (including complaints about wrong orders, see *ME 131236*), marriages, and all the events of the life of a busy city.

The Code of Hammurabi (sometimes spelt Hammurapi). He is not mentioned in the Bible, but was king of the Old Babylonian (Amorite) Dynasty from 1792–1750 BC, which places him somewhere between Abraham and Moses. See **Part of a votive monument** (ME 22454) His laws form one of the oldest known law lists in the world and some bear a resemblance to the Old Testament laws: for example his reference to dealing with the goring ox can be paralleled with Exodus 21:28–36. But the differences are equally significant and some of his punishments are excessive: anyone caught looting at a fire was to be thrown onto the fire, and the doctor who failed to cure his patients was punished! Hammurabi's prologue extols the virtues, achievements and piety of the king, but there is no sacrifice offered for those who fail to keep the laws. The original black stone text is in the Museé du Louvre in Paris.

Notice here also the genealogy of **Kings of Babylon** on a small clay tablet (ME 80328); family lists like these help archaeologists to fix dates. Genealogies (family trees) were very important in the ancient world. This is why we have the record of Abraham's ancestors in Genesis 11 and the long lists in Chronicles. The Levites in Nehemiah 7:61–65

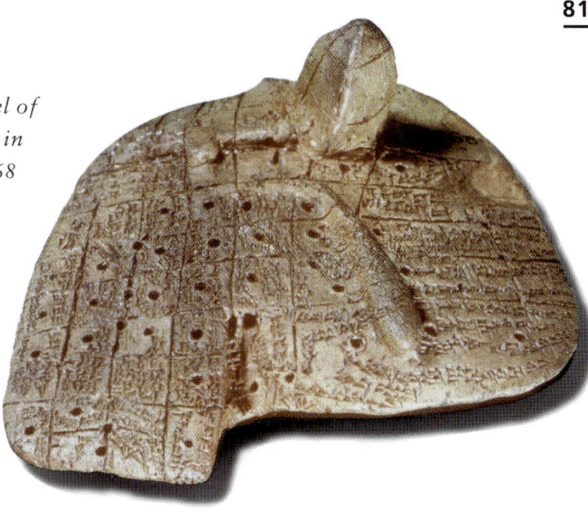

who could not find their family
records, were excluded from the
priestly service. The genealogies
of Jesus in Matthew 1 and Luke 3
are significant in establishing his
human ancestry.

Magic, myths and maths

In *case 22* the display of
***Babylonian science and
literature*** reveals the the society
into which Abraham and Sarah
were born. The priests of Ur were
busy with their elaborate duties
at the gigantic ziggurat of the
moon god, Sin. Under ***Omens***,
notice the clay model of a sheep's
liver *(ME 92668)*. Marks on the
livers of animals was used to aid
the priests in their divination
and this one may have been used
to teach trainees what to look
for in each section—hence the
holes. Ezekiel 21:21 records how
Nebuchadnezzar of Babylon 'will
seek an omen (and) examine the
liver' before deciding which city
to attack. Close by is a clay model
of a sheep's liver ***model of a cake***
(ME 17309) and ***stomach*** *(ME
96948)* for divination and a record
of ***magic spells*** *(ME 96704* and
ME 109215). The face of a demon

Humbaba *(ME116624)* is made
up of an animal intestines.

The ***Babylonian Story of the
Flood*** *(ME 78941)*, known as the
Atrahasis Epic is a Babylonian
legend of Creation and the Flood.
See Box: The Atrahasis epic
page 82.

Above this shelf notice the
large clay ***mathematical tablet***
(ME 15285). This and other
tablets reveal that the Babylonians
had a correct understanding of
astronomy, mathematics and
geometry—including the theorem
of Pythagoras nearly fifteen
hundred years before the Greek
philosopher wrote it down. They
knew the value of pi as 3 1/8
which is accurate to 0.06%! They
were also familiar with quadratic
equations to the 8th degree
and were skilled in algebra and
geometry. Hardly a primitive and
lawless people.

On the second shelf down we
have a ***Sumerian hymn*** *(ME
23584)* and an index giving us the
first lines *(ME 23701)*. Education
was as important then as now
and here is a ***School tablet with
proverb*** *(ME 104096)* on which
the teacher wrote out the exercise

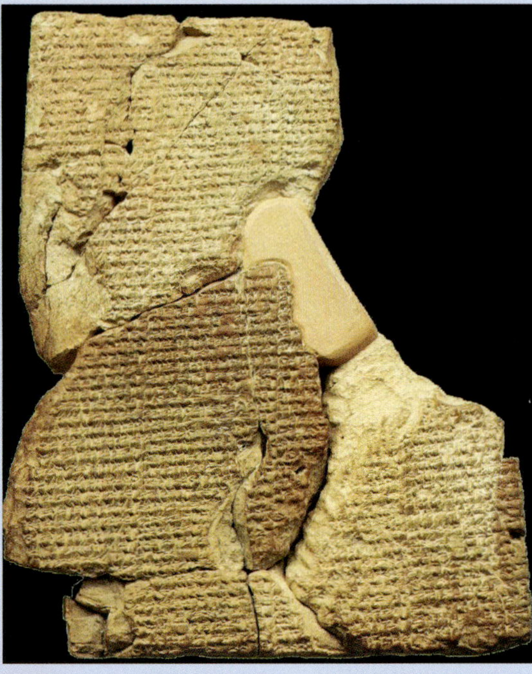

Right: A Babylonian legend of the Flood—the Atrahasis epic (ME 78941)

The Atrahasis epic a Babylonian legend of the Flood

This cuneiform tablet comes from after the time of Abraham, around 1635 BC, although the legend predates this. The account of creation has little in common with the version in Genesis. Anu is the god who rules in heaven, whilst Enlil rules the minor gods on the earth. When these minor deities down tools and refuse to work any more, man is created out of blood and clay. Unfortunately the noise from this rapidly increasing race gives Enlil a headache and so he deluges the earth with a flood. Here the story converges a little more with the biblical account of Noah. Atrahasis is the hero of the flood who, warned in advance, escapes in a boat with his family and the animals. When the flood recedes, Atrahasis offers sacrifice to the gods. Compare the later Gilgamesh Epic in Room 55 case 8. Page 64.

on one side and the pupil copied it on the other. Clay tablets like these are of immense help to archaeologists deciphering ancient languages.

An early account of a military campaign (*ME 139965*).

On the third shelf is an early prescription for drugs to cure a skin complaint (*ME 113970*).

Continue on your left into the alcove. It is worth pausing to read this display board **The Royal Cemetery of Ur**. Between 1922 and 1932 Sir Leonard Woolley uncovered a cemetery in Ur. The

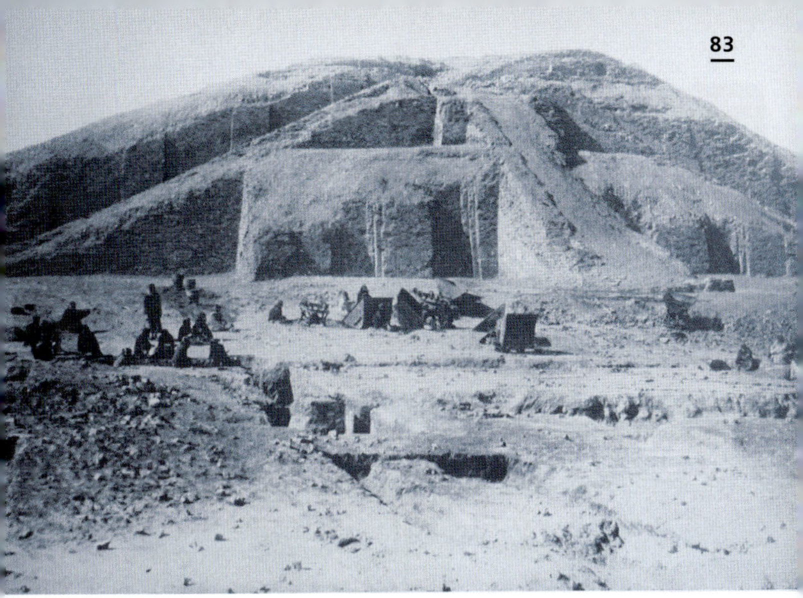

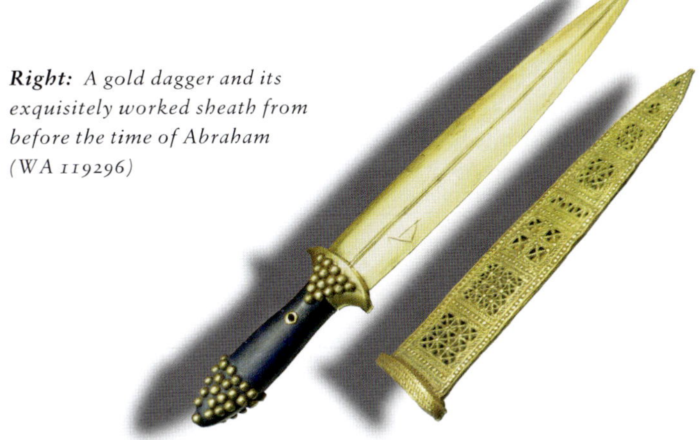

Above: *The remains of the ziggurat at the site of ancient Ur of the Chaldeans (now Tell al-Muqayyar), during excavations by Sir Leonard Woolley on behalf of the British Museum and the University Museum, Philadelphia. This is a building with which Abraham would have been familiar because he and his father almost certainly worshipped here before God revealed himself to Abraham—see Joshua 24:2*

sixteen tombs were dated around 2600 BC and were clearly the graves of royalty, revealing much of the splendour of the courts at that time. All the items displayed in cases here come from the royal graves at Ur. In a grisly display of hope in the future life, courtiers, attendants, grooms and guards would assemble the body of their master or mistress and then drink a poison in order to continue

Right: *A gold dagger and its exquisitely worked sheath from before the time of Abraham (WA 119296)*

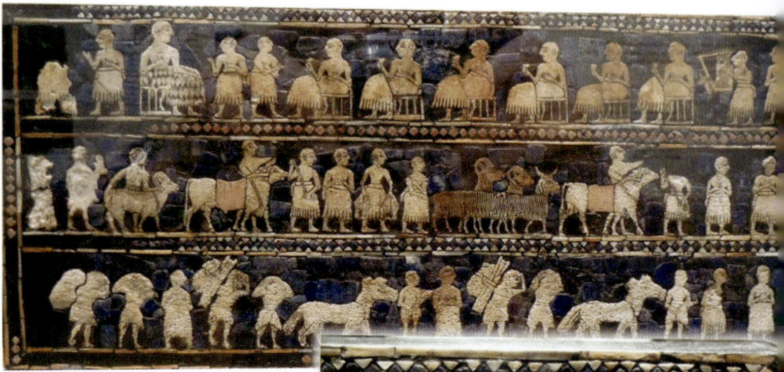

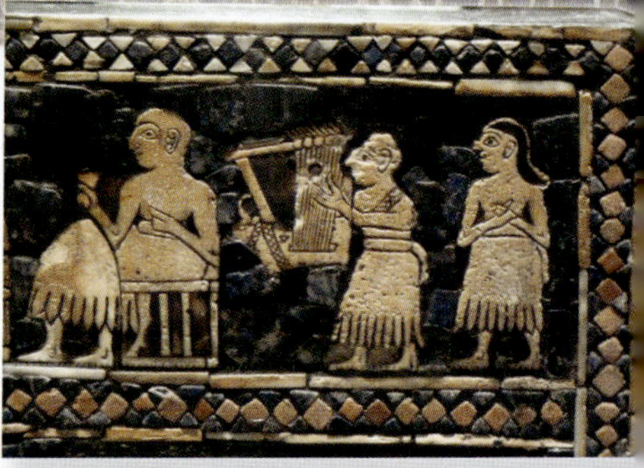

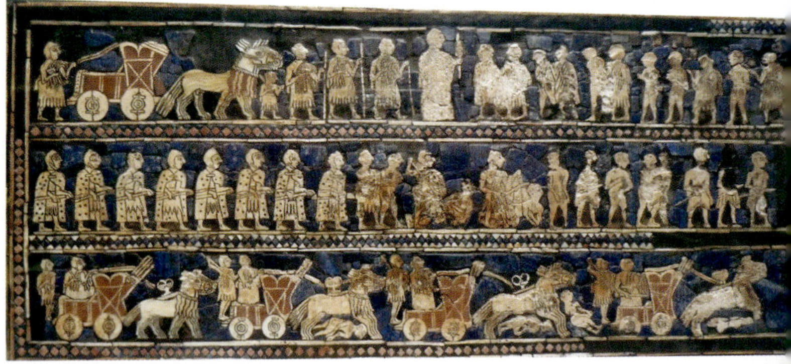

Above, below and inset: The Standard of Ur (WA 121201)— one of the earliest illustrations of an army in battle formation, below. Length: 48 cm . On the reverse side of the Standard musicians are depicted one of whom carries a lyre (inset) similar to the one found in the tomb. See WA 121199—see page 87

service in the next world—they were even accompanied by the oxen harnessed to their wagons. The bodies of six guards were found, together with the remains of sixty-four richly clothed attendant women. It illustrates the lavish use of gold leaf and beautiful jewellery at the time of Abraham and earlier.

War and peace

Behind you in *case 17* is the curious ***Ram in the thicket*** (ME *122200*). It predates Abraham and therefore cannot have any connection with the story of Isaac in Genesis 22:1–13. See picture page 74.

Beside it is the intricately carved ***Standard of Ur*** (ME *121201*) which depicts peace on

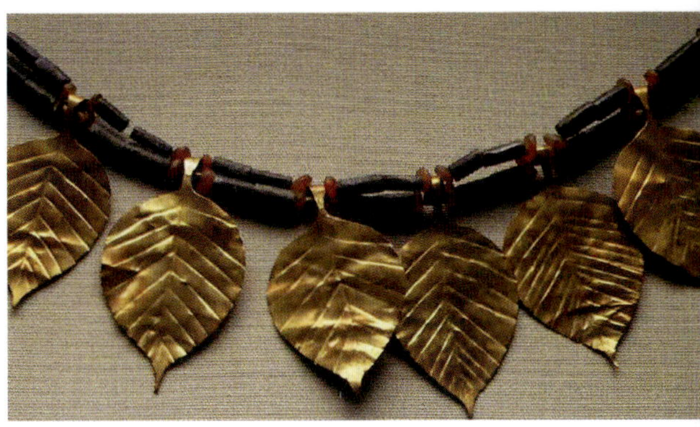

Right: The exquisite jewellery from Ur

one side—note the lyre at the top right (see *case 20* opposite)—and war on the other. This is one of the earliest known illustrations of an army in battle formation: light spearmen, charioteers, and elite guards flank the king. It is reminiscent of the battle recorded in Genesis 14. Both these items come from the royal tombs.

To your right in *case 21* is the **crushed skull** of one of the guards *(ME 121414)* who was buried with Queen Pu-Abi. The queen was buried beside the king, whose grave appears to have been partially robbed at the time of his wife's burial.

Cross over to *case 19* **The Queen's Lyre** and **Ancient Mesopotamian Music**. Both are typical of Abraham's time. We saw one of these illustrated in the Standard of Ur.

Below: A reconstruction by A Forester of the King's Grave from the Great Death Pit

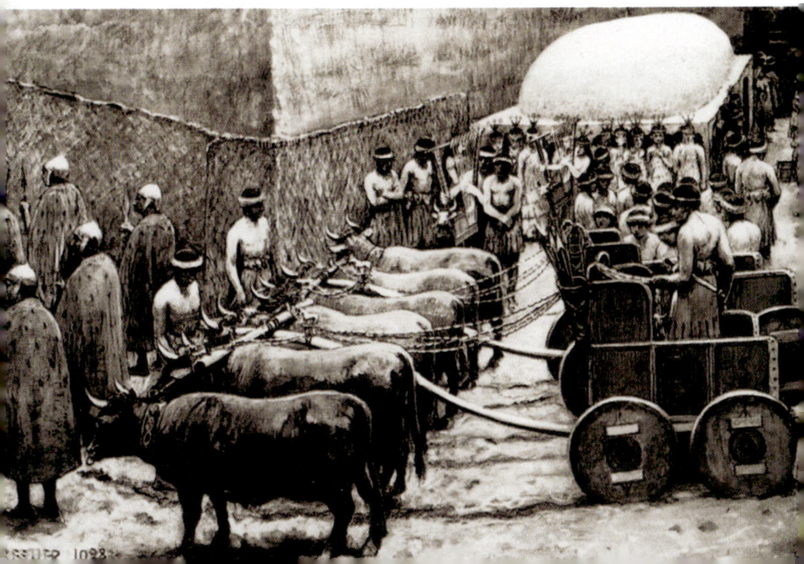

These instruments have been reconstructed from items found in the Royal Cemetery

In *case 18* **The Great Death Pit** illustrates the lavish use of gold leaf and beautiful jewellery at the time of Abraham and earlier. The **Reconstructed head of a Sumerian woman** (ME *122302*) from the items discovered in the tomb and beside it the skull of one of the young girl attendants 18 to 20 years of age.

To your left in *case 15* notice the exquisite **gold dagger** with its sheath (ME *119296 - see page 83*), possibly used for ceremonial occasions. This is an electrostatic replica. When it was first discovered, few believed that such intricate workmanship could be expected half a millennium before Abraham.

Cases 14 and 12 also contain items found in the royal tombs.

Cross the doorways and on the right hand wall in *case 3* note **The origins of writing from pictograms to cuneiform writing**, they are worth reading. A few minutes here will prove valuable as an introduction to much of the form of writing that we see in our tour. See Box: A short history of writing on page 20.

Cuneiform was impressed onto soft clay with a stylus and then baked or hardened in the sun; alternatively it was cut onto stone. These were heavy and cumbersome ways of storing

Below: *The beautiful headdress of a royal lady from the Great Death Pit (WA 122302 etc)*

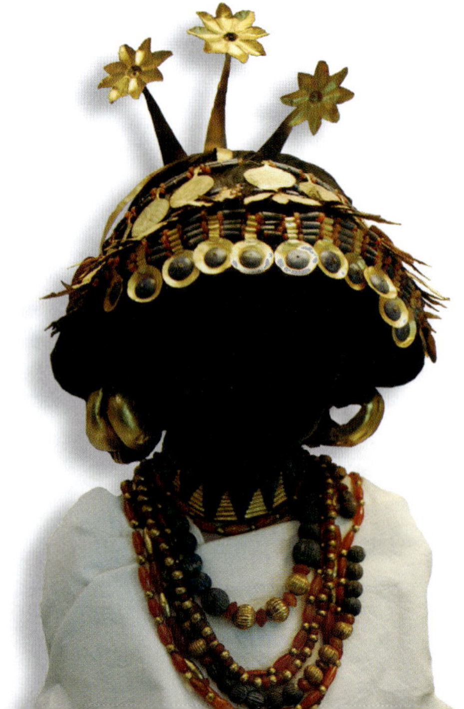

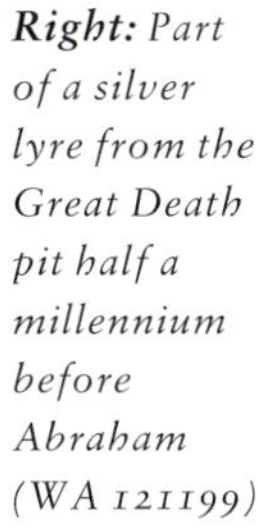
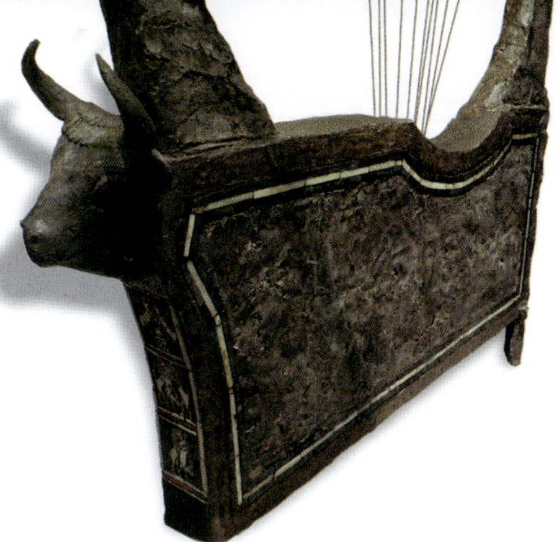

Right: *Part of a silver lyre from the Great Death pit half a millennium before Abraham (WA 121199)*

official documents—though excellent for the archaeologist as they were virtually indestructible. The recorded history of this region begins with the first evidence of writing about a thousand years before Abraham.

Start at the top left of *case 3* where you find early writing in the form of pictures around 3000 BC.

Opposite in *case 6* **The Temple of Ninhursag** are items from a temple close to the home of Abraham. Though 500 years before him, life changed only slowly in those days so they are still typical. As an illustration of the craftsmanship, notice the frieze of carved white stone on a bitumen background *(ME 116741–2)* and the artificial flowers *(ME 1919, 1011)*.

Continue into **Room 57 Ancient Levant.**

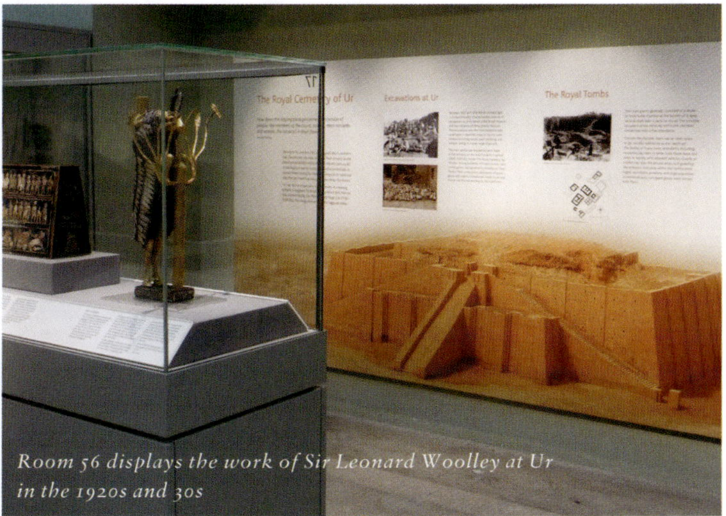

Room 56 displays the work of Sir Leonard Woolley at Ur in the 1920s and 30s

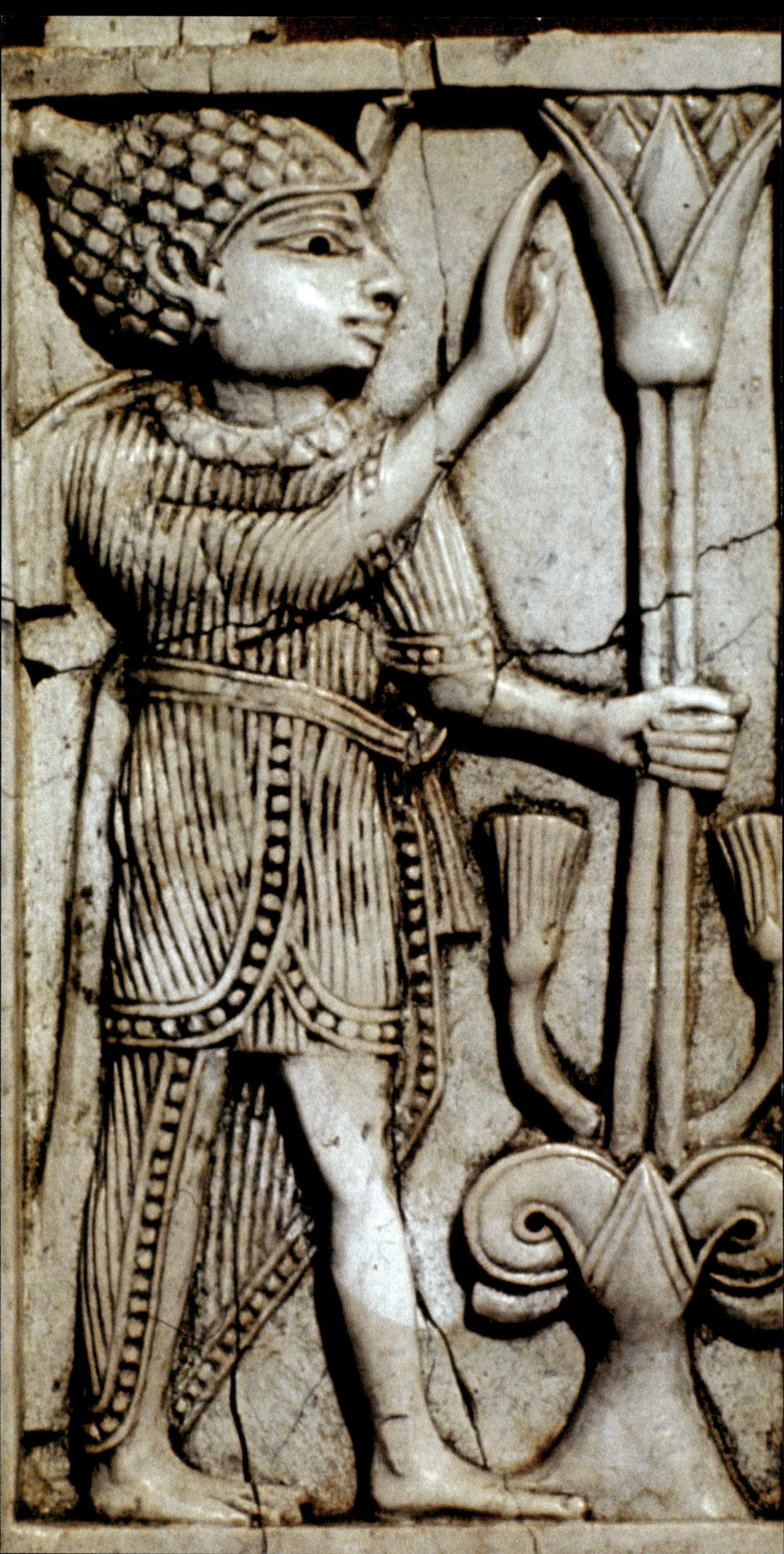

⑦ More troublesome neighbours

The Phoenicians were renowned for their trade and
beautiful ivory carving, though for much of Israel's history
it was the Philistines who were the aggressive neighbours
to the west, whilst the Syrians troubled her northern
borders

From the time of Abraham we move from Room 56 to Room 57 Ancient Levant and we are making a significant jump forward in time. This area is sometimes referred to as 'The Levant' and includes more of Israel's close neighbours.

Philistines—the neighbours next door

They came from the west and were the coastal people on the eastern seaboard of the Mediterranean; the modern name 'Palestine' derives from them. The biblical record identifies the Philistines as the descendants of Casluhim from the line of Ham (Genesis 10:14). Abraham and Isaac both confronted Abimelech of Philistia (Genesis 20 and 26) and throughout the history of Israel the Philistines were the aggressive next door neighbours, though they never managed to build an empire. Significantly Israel avoided the land of the Philistines when they journeyed out from Egypt (Exodus 13:17). It was during one of the many local conflicts with their neighbour that young David slew Goliath, a Philistine from Gath (1 Samuel 17:48–51).

The Phoenicians—the purple people

Covering some of the territory that we now know as Lebanon and part of Syria, they occupied much of the land that was known as Canaan in the Old Testament. The Phoenicians, known as 'the purple people' by the Greeks because of their skill with purple dye, were never a powerful people, frequently at the mercy of the ascendant nation; having little by way of agriculture or industry to offer to their world, they offered art (they became masters in ivory carving) and the skill of dyestuffs (their name is taken from the Greek word for purple). Lydia, whose story is recorded in Acts 16:11–15, traded in this expensive commodity. According to Pliny, by the first century AD there was a 'frantic passion for purple' across the Roman Empire. Throughout their history they

Facing page: A Phoenician ivory panel (ANE 118418) showing a figure wearing royal Egyptian-style garment. From the palace of Ashurnasirpal II. Height: 8cm

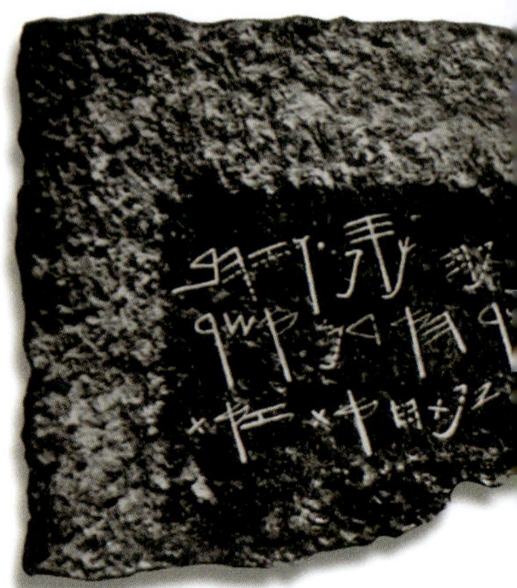

Right: Inscription
of a royal steward to
Hezekiah (WA 125205).
This is probably the
Shebna of Isaiah 22

were great seafarers and they became recognised sea traders. Their main ports were at Tyre and Sidon. King David traded with Hiram, their king (2 Samuel 5:11).

Syrians—the neighbours up north

The Syrians were Israel's immediate northern neighbours whose territory ran from the Euphrates down to the Sea of Galilee. The word 'Syrian' cannot be used of a political unit before the Seleucid kings of the 4th century BC; prior to that they were properly known as Aramaeans whose ancestry is traced back in Genesis 10:22 to Shem. It was from this line that Abraham was descended, giving rise to the reference in Deuteronomy 26:8 that when the Israelites entered Canaan they were to declare, 'A wandering Aramaean was my father.' King David married an Aramaean princess who gave birth to Absalom (2 Samuel 3:3). In the latter years of Solomon, a renegade, Rezon, established

himself at Damascus and this became the capital of southern Syria. From here on Syria was a troublesome northern neighbour who, after the division of the monarchy between Israel in the north and Judah in the south (in 931 BC) often either attacked or sided with Israel against Judah. See page 61 for a map of Israel's neighbours in the time of the kings of Israel and Judah

Room 57 Ancient Levant

Do not disturb

As you enter, on your right, above the board ***Ancient Levant*** look up to an ***inscribed lintel of a rock-cut tomb*** near Jerusalem (WA 125205). This is very likely part of the tomb of the royal steward referred to in Isaiah 22:15–19.

Shebna was in trouble because, as a steward in charge of the household of King Hezekiah of Judah, he was living above his station by 'chiselling your resting place in the rock'—he had carved out a tomb for himself in Jerusalem and inscribed it with

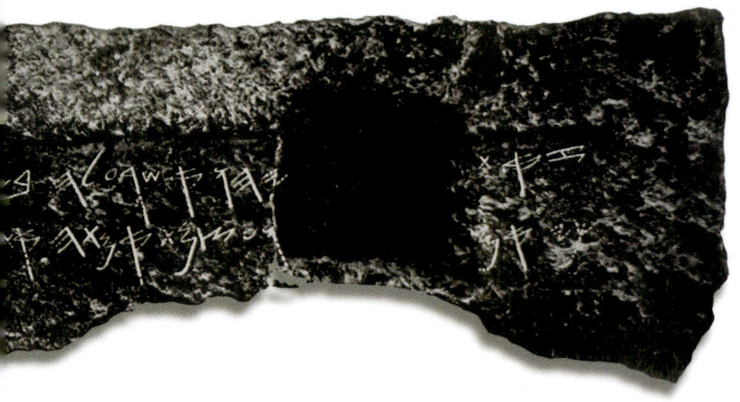

his own name. Isaiah declared that God was not pleased with his arrogance and that he would be deposed and 'ousted from your position'. By Isaiah 36:3 he appears to have been demoted to 'secretary' (or 'scribe'). The inscription tells us that there is nothing of value in his tomb except his bones and those of his maid-servant and he pronounces a curse on anyone who disturbs him. In the event he died in exile (Isaiah 22:18)

In *case 10* at the right hand end is a pink *limestone seal from Lachish* (*WA 12011*) 'belonging to Shebna, son of Ahab'. This may well be the Shebna of Isaiah's prophecy; in which case his father Ahab is not Ahab the King of Israel because Shebna is steward to the King of Judah! However, both names were fairly common.

Notice the *weights from Lachish* beside the Shebna seal (*WA 1980–12–14*). These weights from the time of Isaiah and Hezekiah are in shekels; before coins were minted, payments were made by weighing silver bullion.

(see page 109 'Message through money'). It is now known that the Hebrew word *payim* (1 Samuel 13:21) is one third of a shekel, because the word is engraved on one of the weights here.

Post-it notes

Above in *case 10,* the *Lachish Letters* are of interest. These messages, scrawled on scraps of broken pottery were written when Babylon was invading Judah in 587 BC. Such messages are known as *ostraca*—the equivalent of today's scrap paper. The prophet Jeremiah refers to the devastation caused by Nebuchadnezzar as his terrifying Babylonian army swept across Palestine in the time of King Zedekiah of Judah in 587 BC (2 Kings 25). Jeremiah refers to Lachish and Azekah as the only remaining fortified cities before Jerusalem itself is attacked (Jeremiah 34:7). Do not confuse this with the defeat of Lachish by Sennacherib in 701 BC that we saw in Room 10 (page 34–37).

One of these messages is particularly interesting. It is the

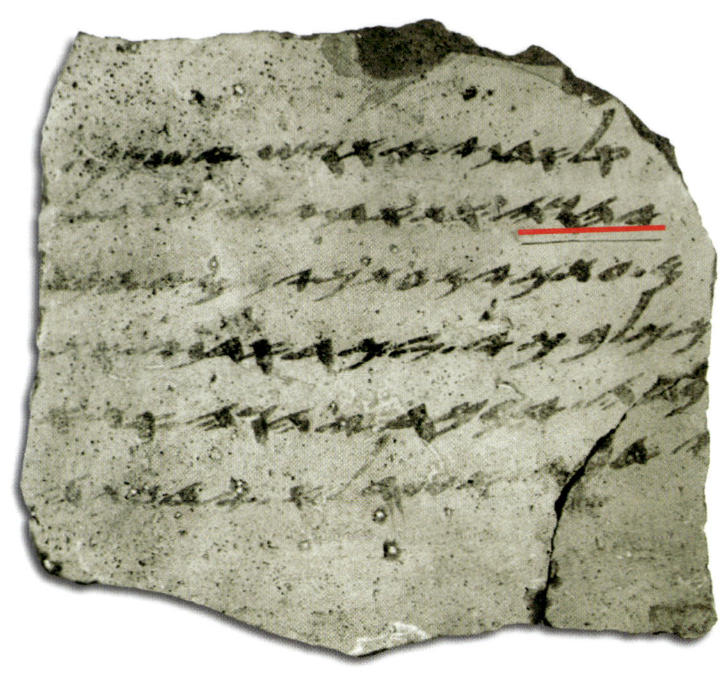

Above: *Lachish ostracon (WA125702). A hastily scribbled message as the Babylonian army advances on Jerusalem in the time of Zedekiah. Its particular significance is the presence of the special name for the God of the Jews 'Yahweh'. Height: 9 cm*

top right *ostracon* on the panel (WA 125702). This was found with the others in the shattered gatehouse of Lachish and is a note from an officer of an outpost to his commanding officer in Lachish (see Jeremiah 34:7). It contains the divine name Yahweh (LORD) when he wrote in haste: 'May Yahweh cause my lord to hear news of peace, even now, even now'. Yahweh is the first word at the right hand end of the third line down. Hebrew reads from right to left. The message includes the words: 'Who is your servant but a dog that my lord should remember his servant?'—this is an interesting echo of 2 Samuel 9:8; 16:9 and 2 Kings 8:13.

Another message closes with the ominous words: 'We are watching for the beacon from Lachish, following the signals you, sir, gave, but we do not see Azekah.' Azekah was 9 miles (15k) north of Lachish. It is a frantic and futile hope; the cities are falling and only these two are left before Jerusalem itself falls to the devastating armies of Nebuchadnezzar.

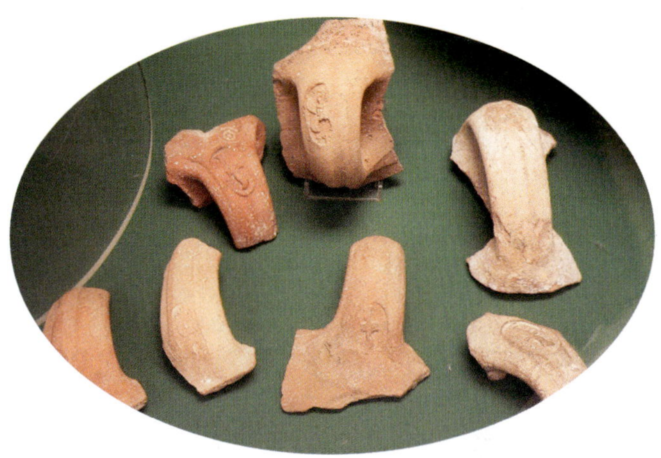

Taxes and more taxes

Also in *case 10* (below) notice the handles broken from storage jars *(WA132061 on)*. These come from Lachish possibly in the time of King Hezekiah (716–687 BC) and they are stamped 'Belonging to the King'. The cities of Hebron, Ziph, Socoh and Mamshit (Emmaeus ?) are each mentioned and these may have been administrative centres where taxes to the king were brought.

To the left in this case the *Bethlehem Tomb Group(WA 65–8–5,1–11)* includes an 'alabastron'. This is a stone (calcite) flask often containing perfume. Alabastron is the word used in Matthew 26, and we will meet one again later (see page 106).

The shelf above includes *Figurines and rattle from Lachish (WA 1980)*. Lachish was in Judean territory and clearly many were worshipping

Above: Handles from royal storage jars in the time of Hezekiah (WA132061 on)

Below: Philistine pottery and coffin lids with human features (android coffins) from the time of the biblical Judges. See page 94. Notice one figure has six digits on the left hand (22373). See 2 Samuel 21:20

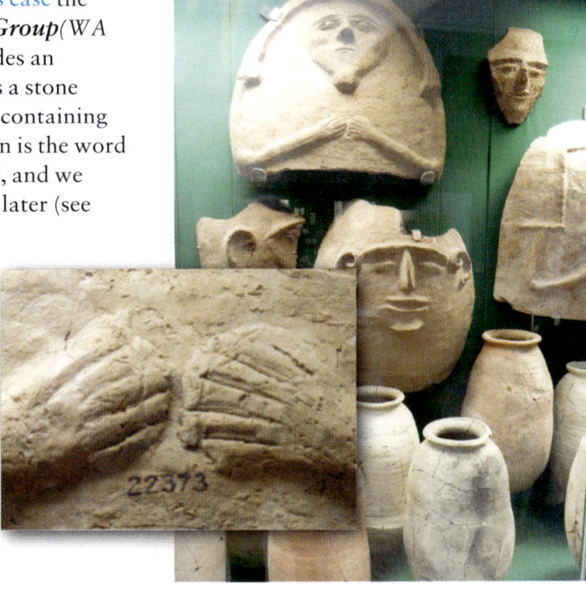

Canaanite gods in defiance of God's command (see also page 79).

Below, there are **Ivories from Samaria** (*WAL 31–48*) from the time of Ahab (1 Kings 22:39).

To the left in *case 9* **The Philistines**. Typically Philistine decorated pottery, stone jars and android coffin lids come from the time of the Judges.

In *case 8* **The Amarna letters** were written from Canaan to the Pharaoh of Egypt Akhenaten (Amenhotep IV) possibly when the Hebrews were still conquering the land in the time of Joshua. See timeline on page 77. Some refer to *Hapiru*, and this may be an early reference to the Hebrew invaders. See Box: Who are these Hapiru?

Who are these Hapiru?

The Amarna letters are part of a collection of 380 tablets that were discovered from 1887 at El-Amarna in Egypt. They are letters from various subject rulers to the Pharaohs of Egypt Amenhotep III and Amenhotep IV (later Akhenaten; see List of Egyptian Kings p 42) in the 14th century BC when Egyptian power was beginning to decline. The letters contain increasingly desperate pleas for assistance against the growing strength of homeless groups. Especially they refer to the *Hapiru*. The clay tablet *EA 29832* is from the ruler at Gezer and includes the plea: 'May the king, my lord, the sun in the sky, care for his land. Since the Hapiru are stronger than us, may the king, my lord, help me escape from the Hapiru, so that the Hapiru do not destroy us.' Just who these *Hapiru* were has been much debated. Some think that *Hapiru* was the name given to marauding bands generally, of which the Hebrews were part. However, if we accept an early date for the Exodus (see page 44), the appeal in the Amarna letters for help against these people would fit well the period of conquest under Joshua and the Judges.

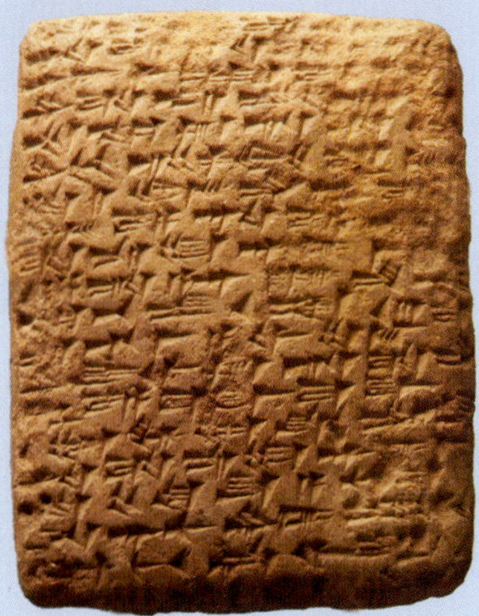

Left: A letter from Yapahu, King of Gezer, begging the Pharaoh of Egypt to defend him from the Hapiru (EA 29832)

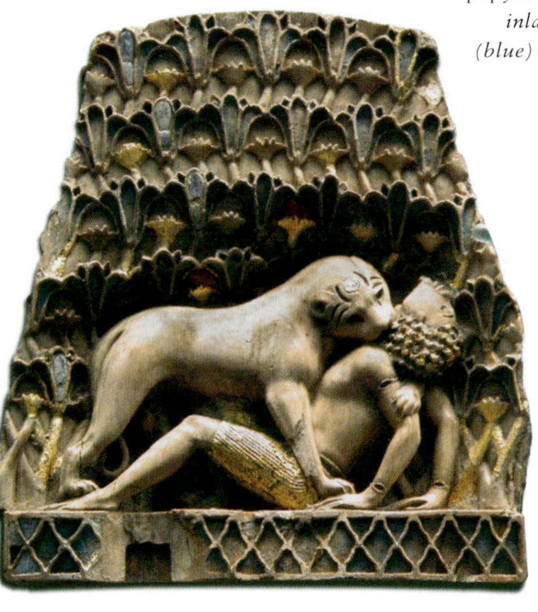

Below: *Phoenician ivory (WA 127412). A lioness killing a Nubian, against a background of lilies and papyrus flowers originally inlaid with lapis lazuli (blue) and carnelian (red) with gold foil*

Ivory houses and a crime writer

On the opposite wall, *case 12*
Nimrud Phoenician Ivory.

This is a sample of the way luxurious furniture was decorated by kings across the ancient Near East. From the time of King Solomon onwards ivory was a symbol of wealth in Israel (1 Kings 10:18 refers to an ivory throne overlaid with gold), and when the monarchy divided, both Israel and Judah squandered their riches in this way. The reference to Ahab's palace 'inlaid with ivory' in 1 Kings 22:39 was once a mystery to scholars—now all is clear. Ahab's wife, Jezebel, was a Phoenician princess and much of the ivory carving was done by Phoenician craftsmen copying Egyptian designs. The white of the ivory was enhanced by coloured glass inlays and gold foil plating. Excavations in the ruins of Israelite palaces at Samaria revealed hundreds of pieces of intricately carved ivory; it is possible that many of those you see here date from the time of Ahab about 860 BC.

However, a more likely dating would locate them in the mid 8th century in the time of Azariah (Uzziah) of Judah and Jeroboam II of Israel. It was this wasteful luxury that the prophet Amos vigorously condemned in his preaching at this time. Amos 3:15 records, 'The houses adorned with ivory will be destroyed', and 6:4 pronounces a woe on

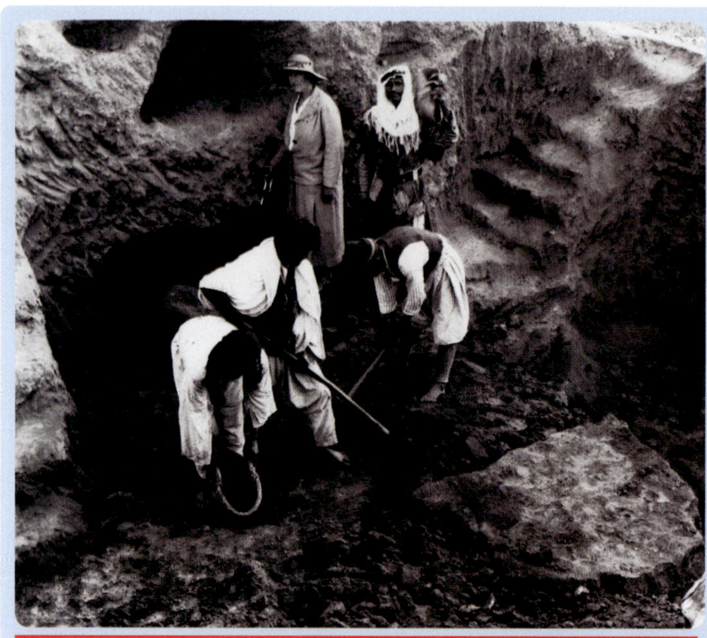

Agatha Christie and the ivories

Agatha Christie's second husband, Sir Max Mallowan, was a noted archaeologist, and the renowned crime writer herself travelled extensively with him. On some of the digs she helped clean a number of the ivories now on display in the Museum, including the ivory of a lioness killing a Nubian (Nubia is now Sudan) against a background of lilies and papyrus flowers (*No.7 WA127412*). The theme is Egyptian in origin and symbolises the king triumphing over his enemies. Max wrote about her work at Nimrud: 'Agatha's controlled imagination came to our aid. She instantly realized that objects which had lived under water for 2000 years had to be nursed back into a new and relatively arid climate.' Describing the cleaning process Agatha wrote: 'I had my own favourite tools, just as any professional would: an orange stick, possibly a very fine knitting needle—one season a dentist's tool which he lent, or rather gave me—and a jar of cosmetic face-cream, which I found more useful than anything else for gently coaxing the dirt out of crevices without harming the friable ivory. In fact there was such a run on my face cream that there was nothing left for my poor old face after a couple of weeks.'

Above: Agatha Christie at an archaeological dig in north-east Syria in the 1930s

those who 'lie on beds inlaid with ivory'. Even later than this, among the items of tribute that the Assyrian king Sennacherib claims Hezekiah sent to him at Nineveh are 'ivory-decorated beds and ivory-decorated armchairs, elephant hide and tusks...'

Note the **woman at the window** (*no.9 WA 118156*); Jezebel met her death in a scene reminiscent of this (2 Kings 9:30).

In the left corner just before you enter *Room 58* there is a large storage pot from Hazor (*WA 132309*), which dates from the time of Joshua, around 1400 BC (Joshua 11:10).

Bones and beans

Enter **Room 58** and on your left in *case 4* is a **burial chamber from Jericho** dated somewhere in the Middle Bronze Age (between 2000 and 1550 BC). This is laid out as it was found, and by the artefacts buried with the dead it was clearly owned by a wealthy family. The custom of burying members of a family together is reflected in the tomb of Abraham, Sarah and their descendants at Hebron (Genesis.23:17–20; 24:9,10; 49:29–32; 50:13).

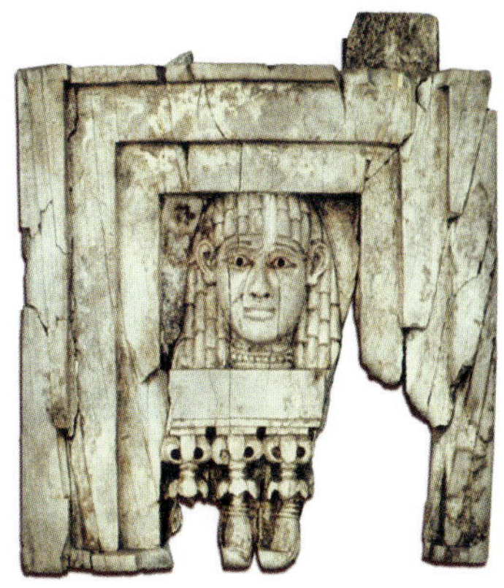

Above: An example of intricate Phoenician ivory (WA 118156) from the time of Ahab and Jezebel, or a century later in the time of Amos: 'Woman at the window'—reminiscent of Jezebel's death

Opposite in *case 3* is a collection of food discovered in the palace at Zarethan from about 2,700 BC. A sample of the food familiar to Abraham and his family.

As you exit this room, notice the case on your right **Early Farmers** and the reference to Bab edh-Drah identified as a possible site for the biblical Sodom.

To continue your tour, turn left through Room 73, 72, 71 into Room 70 The Roman Empire

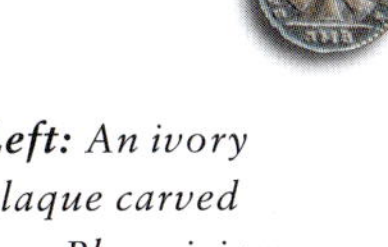

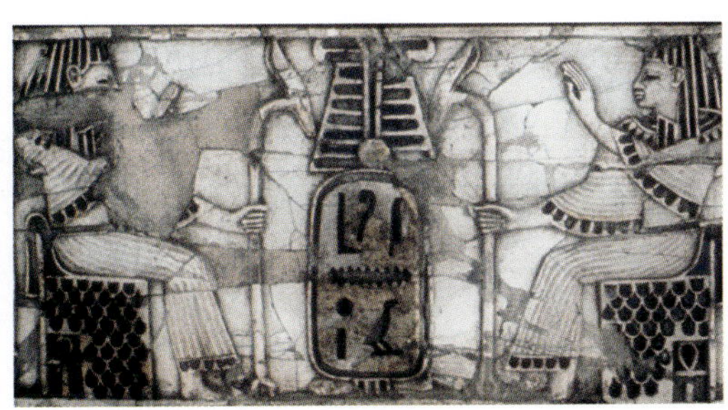

Left: An ivory plaque carved by a Phoenician craftsman imitating Egyptian style. 8th century BC (WA 118 120)

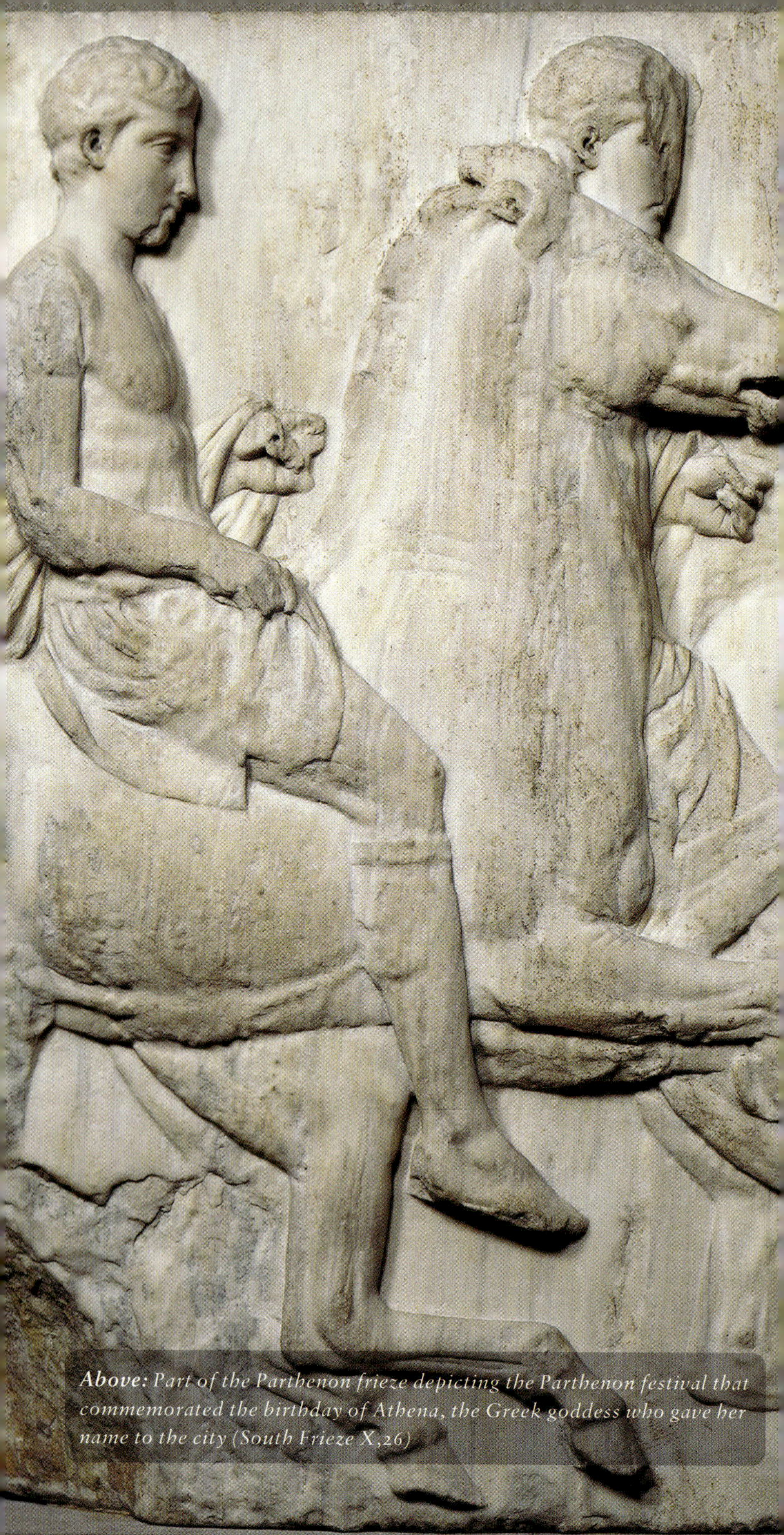

Above: *Part of the Parthenon frieze depicting the Parthenon festival that commemorated the birthday of Athena, the Greek goddess who gave her name to the city (South Frieze X,26)*

8 People of the Way

History dramatically changed for ever by the life, death and resurrection of Jesus of Nazareth. With the spread of the Greek language, a network of Roman roads and the Jewish expectation of the Messiah, the time was right for the spread of Christianity. The New Testament covers a period of only a century compared with at least 3500 years of the Old Testament.

Room 70 — The Wolfson Gallery Roman empire.

The first Emperor of Rome

Directly on your left is a bronze bust of *Caesar Augustus* (GR 1911.9–1.1). The first ruler to appoint himself the 'august' Emperor of Rome. This is the 'Caesar Augustus' at the time of the birth of Jesus and his childhood visit to the Temple in Jerusalem (Luke 2:1,41–52). He ruled from 27 BC to AD 4. As Octavian, his navy won a decisive victory at the Battle of Actium (off the coast of northern Greece) on 2 September 31 BC in consequence of which, Anthony and Cleopatra fled to Egypt where they committed suicide.

Behind the bust of Augustus, in *case 3*, you will find the story of this victory and items relating to it, including coins from the time of Octavian and later as Augustus (*nos. 9, 10 and 21, 22*), together with a lead glazed figurine of Cleopatra (*no. 20 MME 1897*).

A little further on the left is a marble bust of **Augustus** (*GR 1879.7–12.9*) and to the right of him is his wife *Livia*

(GR 1856.12–26.1722), the first empress of the Roman Empire. Notice her neat braided hair style: it was known as a *nodus* (knot), and it set a fashion trend in the first century. The style involved a top-knot or roll above

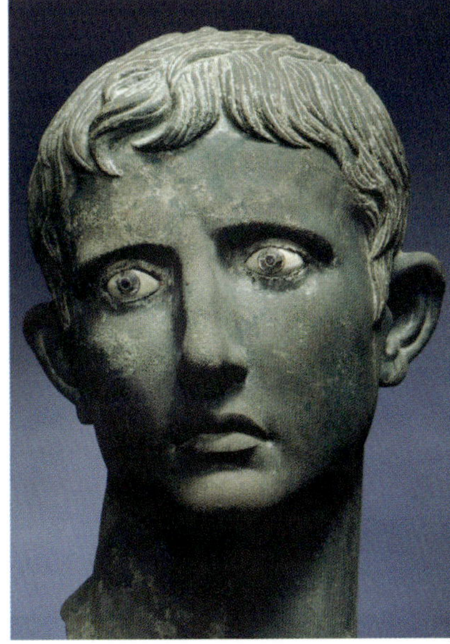

Below: *Caesar Augustus was the first Emperor of Rome and the emperor at the time of the birth of Jesus. This Bronze bust is in Room 70 as you enter (GR1911.9–1.1). Height 43cm*

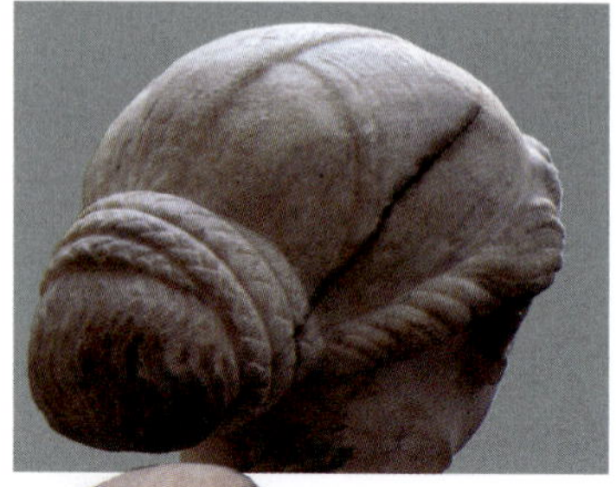

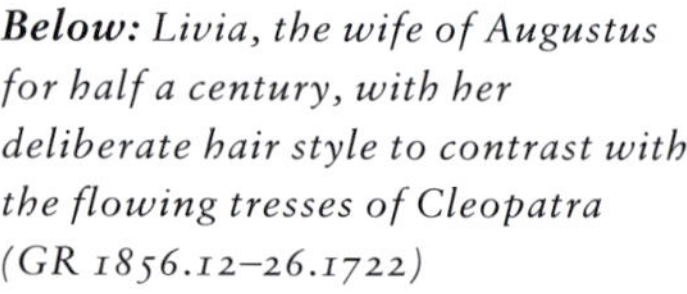

Below: Livia, the wife of Augustus for half a century, with her deliberate hair style to contrast with the flowing tresses of Cleopatra (GR 1856.12–26.1722)

Top: The nodus (knot) was connected to a bun at the back by a central braid

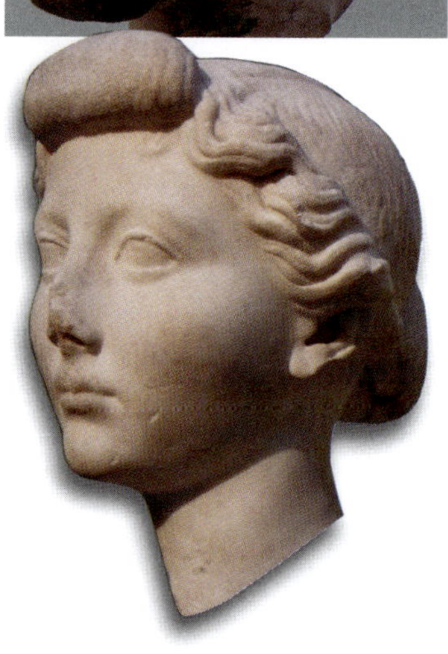

the forehead and connected by a central braid to a bun at the back of the head. Livia invented it to contrast with the beautiful long tresses made famous by Cleopatra. Paul in 1 Timothy 2:9, and Peter in 1 Peter 3:3–4, both insisted that a woman's true beauty comes not from 'braided hair', but 'good deeds' and 'a gentle and quiet spirit.' Surely they mean: 'Ladies, you do not have to follow the fashion.' Livia lived to the age of 86 years.

List of Roman Emperors

Augustus*	27 BC–AD 14	Birth and early life of Jesus Christ.
Tiberius*	14–37	The adult life and the death and resurrection of Jesus Christ.
Gaius (Caligula)	37–41	The conversion of Paul and the formation of the church.
Claudius*	41–54	Acts 11:28 and 18:2. Conquest of Britain.
Nero	54–68	Persecution of Christians, martyrdom of Peter and Paul. Some of his household converted (Philippians 4:22).
Vespasian	69–79	Jerusalem destroyed in AD 70 by his son Titus.
Titus	79–81	A short but popular reign. Eruption of Vesuvius.
Domitian	81–96	Possibly in his reign John was exiled on Patmos.

* These kings are mentioned by name in the Bible
Timelines: from Abraham to Solomon page 77. For list of Hebrew kings page 63. Egyptian kings page 42. Assyrian kings page26. Babylonian kings page 69. Persian kings page 54.

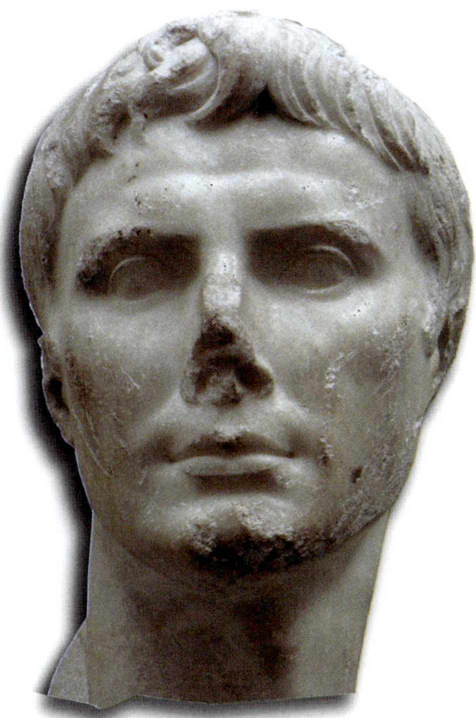

You may like to cross over to *case 7* (to the left of the door you entered). The right hand panel contains a terracotta lamp *(no.13. GR 1856.12)* showing a portrait, probably of Livia herself, with the same neat hair style.

Return to Livia, and beside her is **Tiberius** *(GR 1812.6–15.2)*, her son by her first marriage whom Augustus adopted as his heir, and he was emperor throughout the adult life of Jesus Christ.

Behind Livia, in *case 8*, there are interesting exhibits regarding the background of Augustus and Tiberius **The Emperor and the imperial family**. Note especially the second panel from the left no. 10 **An Aureus** (a gold coin) recording the decree of the Senate when Octavian was proclaimed Augustus *(CM 1864.11)*.

Cross over to the marble bust of Claudius, the emperor responsible for the conquest of Britain in AD 43. He is referred to in Acts 11:28; 18:2; 23:26.

To your left in *case 15* '**The sword of Tiberius**' *(GR 1866.8–61)*. Beside this, note the origin of the emperors honoured as a god; refusal to acknowledge this led to the persecution and martyrdom of many Christians. Also notice Livia, or Octavian's sister *(no.1)*, and other women *(no.5)* depicted as the goddess Diana; this demonstrates Diana's widespread influence.

See the information board to the right **The emperor and Roman religion**. Having deified his father, Julius Caesar, Augustus styled himself *divi filius* (the son of a god), thus ensuring that he was worshipped as a deity after his death. Tiberius was therefore also *divi filius*. The frequent reference to Jesus as the Son of God (eg Luke 1:35; John 5:25 and 20:31) would be clearly understood as a claim to deity.

On the reverse side of *case 15* note *no.2* the coin of Nero *(CM 1920.6–15.4)* also indicating his divinity and *no.7* a deified Augustus.

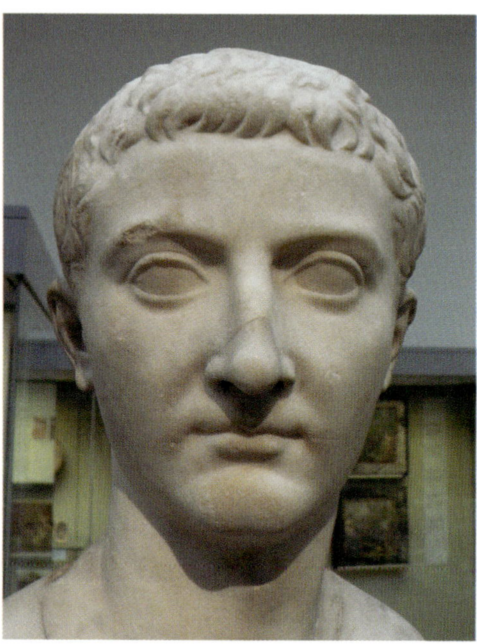

Left: The Emperor Tiberius (GR 1812.6–15.2) was the son of Livia and the adopted son of her husband Augustus. Tiberius was the Roman Emperor during the adult life of Jesus

Below: A bronze lepton of Pontius Pilate, Governor of Judea at the time of the trial of Jesus (CM 1908.1–10263). See page 111

Cross over the centre to a marble bust of **Vespasian** (GR 1850.3–4.35), the emperor responsible for the destruction of Jerusalem in AD 70, and beside him is his son **Titus** (GR 1909.6–10.1), who as general carried out the siege of Jerusalem; partly for this victory he was known as 'Rome's golden boy'. Titus became emperor from AD 79–81.

Pontius Pilate and Herod the Great

Continue and on the right is a marble bust of **Hadrian** (1805.7–3.94) the emperor responsible for the wall completed in AD 126 in Roman Britain to separate 'the Romans from the Barbarians'.

Behind this in the centre panel of *case 27* is an interesting coin collection from **Judaea.** Jewish kings were allowed to mint their own coins.

No.1 (CM 1908.0110.538) is a bronze coin of **Herod the Great.** This is the Judean king at the time of the birth of Jesus Christ and who ordered the death of the Bethlehem boys (Matthew 2:16).

No.2 (CM 1899.4–2.83) is a coin of **Philip**, the tetrarch of Iturea and Trachonitis and one of the sons of Herod the Great. Caesarea Philippi (Mark 8:27) was named after him and the Emperor. He married Salome, the daughter of Herodias, the wife of Herod Antipas; these three were responsible for the death of John the Baptist (Matthew 14:3–12).

Of particular interest is *no.3 (CM 1908.01–10–530)* a bronze coin of **Pontius Pilate** whilst he was Procurator of Judaea from AD 26–36. The obverse of the coin depicts a ladle and a staff which were Roman cultic symbols. The reverse carries the date of the seventeenth year of emperor Tiberius which would be AD 30/31(John Baptist began preaching two years earlier according to Luke 3:1) the seventeenth year may be the very year of the crucifixion of Jesus. Five years later Pilate was recalled to Rome to give an account to the imperial authorities of his harsh administration.

No.4 *(CM 1985.10–2.1)* is a coin of **Herod king of Chalcis** AD 41–48, showing Herod and his brother **King (Herod) Agrippa of Judea** as part of the ceremony crowning the emperor Claudius in AD 41 (Claudius is the emperor who ordered the Roman invasion of Britain in AD 43 and he is referred to in Acts 11:28 and 18:2). This is the Herod who ordered the execution of James and put Peter in prison (Acts 12).

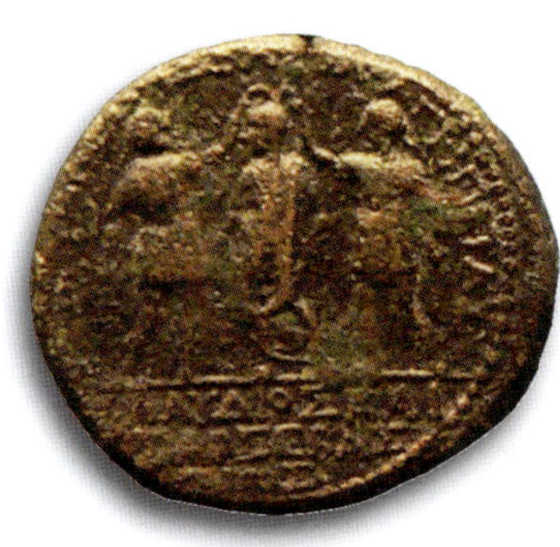

Above: A bronze coin of Herod of Chalcis with his brother Herod Agrippa at the crowning of the emperor Claudius in AD 41 (CM 1985.10–2.1)

Below: A bronze coin of Herod the Great (CM 1908.0110.538)

Other coins here commemorate the quelling of the Jewish rebellion and the destruction of Jerusalem in AD 70 *(nos.5 and 6)*.

Below these coins are small lamps. *No.12 (GR 1908.11–20.19)* is from Jerusalem in the time of Jesus. See picture page 104.

The panel on the right of *case 28* contains two coins of **Augustus** *(nos.3 and 4)*, one of **Tiberius** *(no.5)* and one of **Nero** *(no.6)*.

Behind you, in *case 25* you will find small bronze *(GR 1909.6–20.2)* and terracotta *(GR 1883.7.24.1)* statuettes of Artemis (Diana) from Ephesus in the first century, and below these a large first century lamp, clearly from a wealthy family, in the form of a

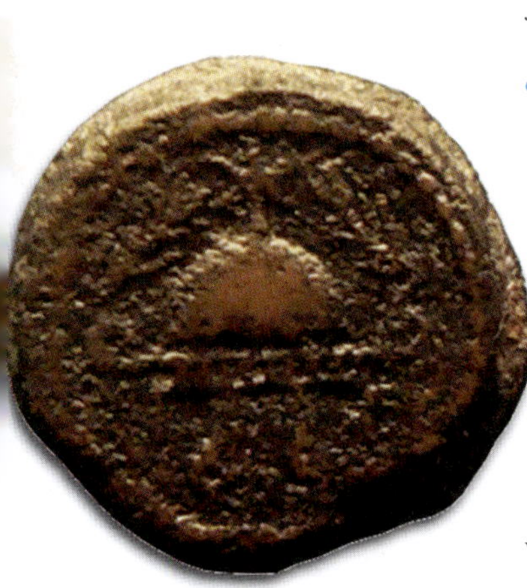

ship (*GR 1862.4–14.1*); among the figures of gods on it is that of Castor or Pollux (twin gods) which reflects the figureheads at the prow of the Alexandrian ship carrying Paul to Rome (Acts 28:11).

In *case 35* on the end wall of this room (right) there are coins from the time of Emperor Nero, under whose orders the apostles Paul and Peter were likely executed. *Nos 1–7* are all from the time of Nero, and include a silver denarius (*no 2*). *No.11* shows both Nero and his wife Poppaea, whom he later murdered; this is from Ephesus at the time Paul was there (*CM 1979–1-1–1712*).

To the right notice **Circulating the imperial image**. The emperor's image (statues, busts, coins etc) expressed his authority and power. Paul made use of this when he referred to Jesus Christ as 'the image of the invisible God' (Colossians 1:15).

Notice behind you as you leave this room a large statue of **Septimus Severus** (*GR 1802.7–10.2)* who was responsible for severe persecution of the Christians between AD 193–211.

Continue into **Room 69 Greek and Roman Life**

This room provides an excellent introduction to first century AD. It is worth browsing here. A few items to focus on.

Immediately in front of you (case 20) is a display of **Drama**. Jesus frequently referred to the Jewish leaders as 'hypocrites' (Matthew 6:2 for example). In the theatre, masks were used to portray the part of the actor. These were known as *hupocritai*, one who pretends with an outward show (two-faced). Our word 'hypocrite' is derived from this.

Turn left and go to case 26 **Potters and carpenters.** An excellent collection of first century oil lamps. Lamps have a long history, and the basic open bowl with a groove for the wick changed little over the millennia. By the Greek period, moulds were made to produce lamps for the mass market, and the Romans decorated their moulds. Christian symbols were being added by the third century AD. Because of its

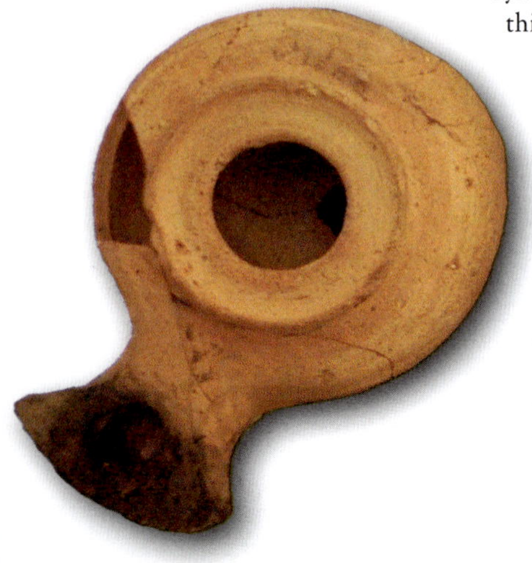

Left: An oil lamp of the type commonly in use in the time of Jesus. Sesame oil would be poured into the reservoir and a wick of flax placed in the end. Such lamps would be placed on a stand or in a niche in the wall. Length 12cm (GR 1908.11-20.19)

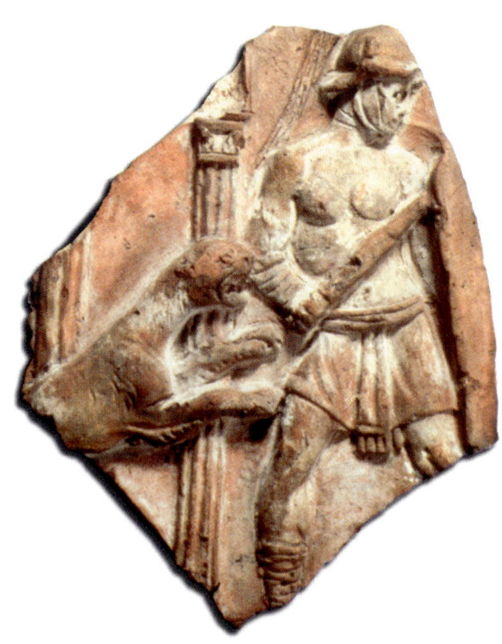

Left: Part of a plaque depicting a gladiator fighting lions (GR 1866.4–12.13)

widespread domestic use, the lamp also became a symbol of spiritual light and life (see Matthew 5:15 and John 1:7; 5:35 for example). The multiple lamps would be owned by wealthy families. Notice two moulds for making lamps with the Christian chi-rho motif (GR 1975.1–29.1)— the first two letters of 'Christ' in Greek. These are dated in the fourth or fifth centuries AD and were made in Tunisia though they come from Rome. The carpenters tools are reminiscent of the daily toil of Jesus as he grew up in his father's workshop.

Return to *case 20* depicting the **Gladiators**. In the second century BC one public contest lasted for 117 days and involved nearly 5,000 pairs of gladiators. Women also fought in the arena and this was especially popular. Christians became part of the contests as they were turned over to wild animals. In 1 Corinthians 15:32 Paul made a clear reference to this barbaric 'sport': 'If I fought wild beasts in Ephesus for merely human reasons, what have I gained?' By AD 400 gladiatorial fights were abolished, largely through Christian influence.

Continue on this side to *case 18* **Boxing and wrestling**. Paul alluded to the sport of boxing when he claimed: 'I do not fight like a man beating the air.' (1 Corinthians 9:26) and he also referred to wrestling in describing the prayers of Epaphras (Colossians 4:11).

On the end panel of this case is a relief of female gladiators— sadly a popular sport.

Go round to *case 23* **Roman music** for a pair of flutes and a bronze trumpet (GR 1844 and GR 1839). See Luke 9:23, 11:17, 1 Corinthians 14:7 for the flute, and Matthew 24:31, 1 Corinthians 14:18, Revelation 8 for the trumpet. The small **Bronze** *figure of pan with pan pipes* (*GR 1772.3*) is significant since Pan was worshipped at Caesarea Philippi at a shrine close by where Jesus was acknowledged by his disciples as the Christ (Matthew 16:13).

Return to *case 17* **The Roman Army.** In the centre is a **Terracotta panel** (*GR 1805, 0703.342*) showing part of a triumphant procession with prisoners in chains—did the apostle Paul have this in mind in Colossians 2:15 'having disarmed the powers and authorities, he made a public spectacle of them, triumphing over them by the cross'? Note also here the **Bronze parade masks** and the **Ivory sword hilt** from a *gladius* which was the small double-edged sword referred to in Hebrews 4:12. To the left of this are **Two bronze plates** (*GR 1930.4–19.1*) awarding citizenship for long service in the legions; here, Gemellus, served in the cavalry in Britain. The coveted Roman citizenship could be gained by birth, purchase or merit (see Acts 22:25–29).

Continue to *case 4* **Greek and Roman dress** notice the three scent bottles that illustrate Roman footwear. The swastika on the sole of one boot is an ancient religious symbol used by the Aryans some three millenniums before Christ and later by the Buddhists. It was adopted by the German Nazi party and became the symbol of the Third Reich.

Next, in *case 5* **Spinning and weaving**, note the silver distaff (*GR 1913.5*)—see Proverbs 31:19

Continue to *case 6* on your right **Women** and notice the small onyx scent bottle (*GR 1869.2–5.6*) and compare with the picture of an alabaster jar on page 107. This recalls the story in Matthew 26:6–13 where the word *alabastron* refers to a small jar like these rather than a box (see also Room 57 *case 10* page 93).

Behind you in *case 7* is an interesting display of **Reading and Writing.** Showing the various materials used. Luke 1:63 records that Zechariah, the father of John Baptist, asked for 'a writing tablet'. It was most probably a wooden board similar to the writing tablet seen here (*GR 1888.9–20.72*

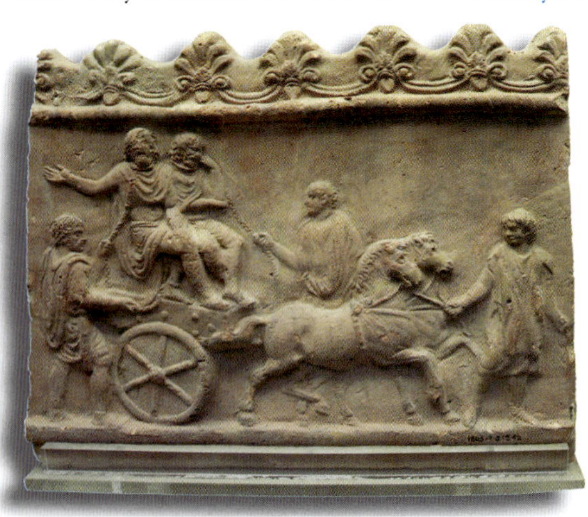

Above: A terracotta panel of Barbarian prisoners being led in chains as part of a Roman triumphal procession (GR 1805,0703.342)

to78). Notice the styli below it. Of particular interest is the **Four leaves of a wooden writing tablet** (GR *1888.9–20).* It is an early form of notebook and the Greeks borrowed the Latin word to describe it *membranae.* This is the word used in 2 Timothy 4:13 'When you come bring… my scrolls, especially the parchments (*membranae*).' Paul was using a notebook!

Behind *case 7* in *case 12* notice the **Lead tablet with a curse inscription** (GR *1934.11–21.1*). It was common for a curse to be written and nailed in order to 'fix it'. Paul's references in Galatians 3:13 and Colossians 2:14 would have a clear cultural resonance with his readers: 'Christ redeemed us from the curse of the law by becoming a curse for us …Having cancelled the written code, with its regulations, that was against us and that stood opposed to us; he took it away, nailing it to the cross.'

Left: An alabastron used for storing perfume or ointment. The top was sealed with mud or clay and the neck of the jar pinched so that it could be broken to pour out the contents. This example from Palestine in the time of Christ is from a private collection. Height:10cm

See also page 108. And Room 49 case 4 for a terrible curse tablet on Tretia Maria! To your right in *case 32* on the end wall **The gods of Olympus** notice a small bronze figurine of Artemis (Diana) of the Ephesians (Acts 19. GR *1951.6–6.14*) and the accumulation of gods in this case reminds us of Paul in Athens (Acts 17). See Box on Diana of the Ephesians page 115.

Return down the right hand side of the room to *case 3 on your left* **Medicine**. These medical instruments from the first century reflect those that would have been used by Luke, the writer of the Gospel and Acts. He was not only a careful historian but also a medical practitioner (Colossians 4:14). Surgical procedures were often performed without anaesthetics. The body parts were offered to the gods for healing.

Left: Bronze statuette of Artemis (Diana) possibly from Ephesus itself. Second to first century BC (GR 1951.6–6.14)

Enter into *Room 68* The Citi Money Gallery

Fascinating though this whole gallery is, we are concerned only with those exhibits that relate to the Bible and early Christian history. Walk to the last but one case on your left *case 6* **Money in daily life**

Top left *(Roman Offerings)* are coins found in the River Thames between 1824 and 1841 from the time of three Roman emperors: Domitian (AD 81–96), in whose reign John was possibly exiled to Patmos, Vespasian (AD 69–79), who ordered the destruction of Jerusalem in AD 70 and Antonius Pius who came to power in 138, long after the apostles.

To the right centre is a **curse tablet (1)**. See page 107. Below, *Contemporary copies*, is a **silver denarius** (1). See also page 109

Coin from biblical times

At the extreme bottom right corner of *case 6* is a large coin of the emperor Caracalla (AD 186–217) a cruel and extravagant emperor who was finally assassinated. This coin was minted in the Greek city of Cylices (now Belkis in northwest Turkey) somewhere between AD 214 and 217. Look carefully behind the head of the Emperor and you will see the Christian monogram chi-rho scratched there. The word *pax* (peace) has also been added. Was this an act of defiance or witness in a severe time of persecution? The bust of the Emperor is not defaced as that would be an act of treason. The torch on your mobile will enable you to identify the chi-rho more

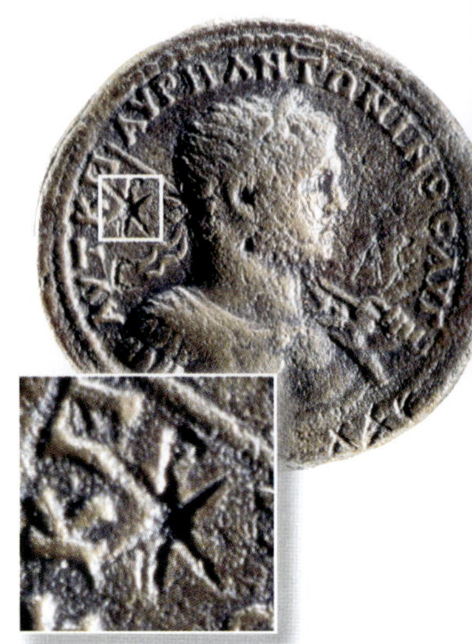

Above: A coin of the emperor Caracalla with the Christian chi rho emblem scratched on it

Below: A gold medallion of the Emperor Constantine

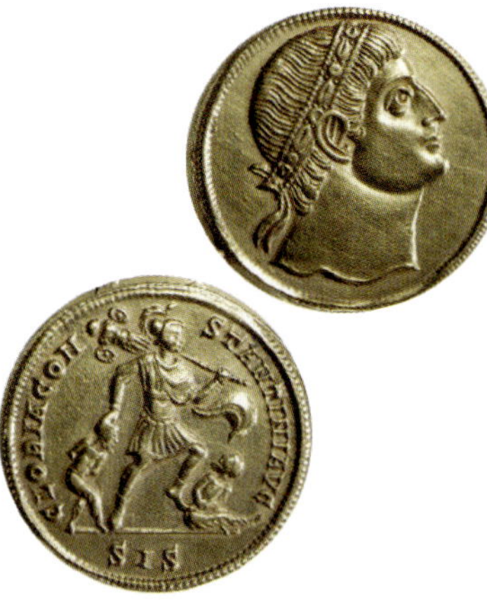

clearly. See page 122 and the Box on page 120 for an explanation of the chi-rho symbol.

Above the coin of Caracalla is a large **Medallion of Emperor Commodius**, December AD 192. However, he was assassinated in the same month and his image was chiselled off the coin; another

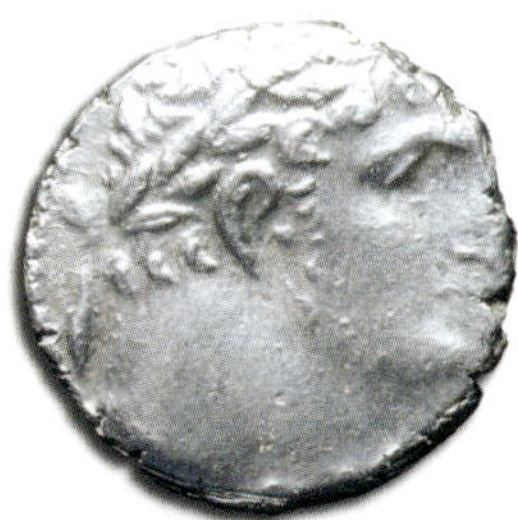

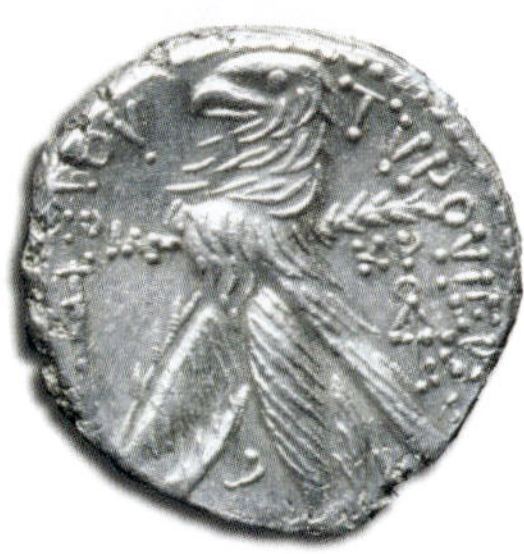

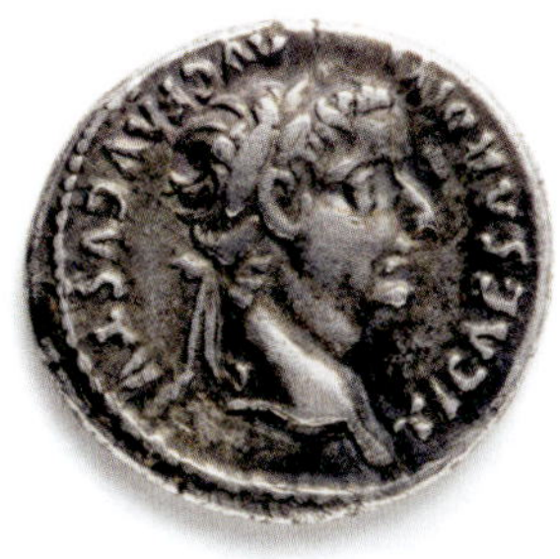

evidence of the damnation of memory (see page 117). Above this is a **gold medallion of Constantine the Great** from Thessalonica (no 3). It is dated AD 326 just two years after he became the sole ruler of the Roman empire. Medallions like this were worn as symbols of allegiance and were the gift of the emperor. See page 108, also see the Box on page 120 'The Emperor and the Cross' for Constantine.

Continue to *case 5* The beginnings of money.

In the first panel **Coins used in Jerusalem**. 1st century silver half-shekels from Tyre (no.1). These were the Temple tax which every male was required to pay. The shekel is not referred to in the New Testament, but the *didrachm* of Matthew 17:24 – the Temple tax – was equivalent to half a *shekel* hence some translations refer to it as the 'half shekel tax'. This was paid annually by every Jewish man and

the Temple authorities insisted on payment in coins from Tyre since these were of a higher quality silver. This is why the 'money changers' were involved in a lucrative trade in the Temple. The coin Peter found in the mouth of the fish was a *stater* (equivalent to four *drachm*) from Tyre and thus was sufficient for both him and Jesus.

No. 2 is a silver *tetradrachm* of Augustus minted in Antioch in 3 BC. This would be in circulation in the time of Jesus.

Coin from biblical times. Below no. 2 are two silver *denarius* from the time of **Tiberius** (AD 14–37). They are the size of a 5p piece. This was known as the 'Tribute Penny' and is referred to in the question and answer recorded in Matthew 22:19 between Christ and the Pharisees. Since Tiberius was Emperor for most of Christ's adult life, it would have been a coin just like this that was shown to him. Two things were offensive about this coin

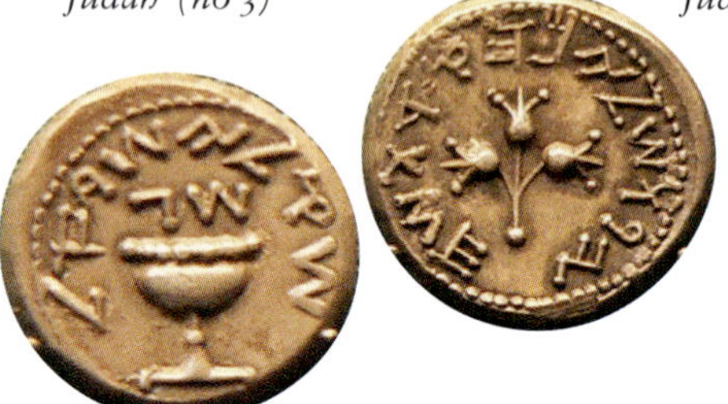

Below: Coins from the first Jewish revolt against the Romans from AD 66 declaring 'freedom for Judah' (no 3)'

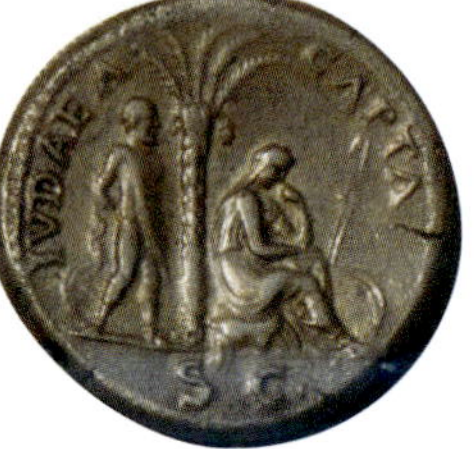

Below: The Roman response after AD 70 and the destruction of the Temple in Jerusalem declaring 'Judah Captured' (no 4)

to the Jews: the display of the Emperor's image on it, breaking the second commandment, and the title that Tiberius was the son of *Divus Augustus* — the divine Augustus. According to Matthew 20:2 the denarius was valued as a labourer's daily wage; it was also the daily pay of a rank and file Roman soldier. In the parable of the Good Samaritan, the merchant paid the landlord 'two denarii' (Luke 10:45), which presumably covered board and lodging until his return two or three days later.

Coins of revolution and oppression.

The Jews rebelled against the Roman oppression in AD 66 and minted their own *shekels* to assert their independence. These silver shekel coins (no.3) depict the Omer cup that was used for offering the firstfruits (Deuteronomy 26) and an almond tree in blossom (see Exodus 25:33). Their coins read 'Shekel Israel', 'Freedom of Zion' and 'Redemption of Israel'. It was a forlorn expression of independence because the city and temple were destroyed in AD 70. In response, a bronze

coin of emperor Vespasian (4) celebrating the destruction of Jerusalem in AD 70 declares *Judea capta* – 'Judah captured'. Coins were circulating in Rome to celebrate this triumph.

Although neither are on display here, the smallest coin in the Roman empire was a *quadron*, which in the time of Domitian would purchase three pints of beer! However, in Jerusalem the *lepta* was half this value. The Gospel writer Mark explains for his non-Jewish readers that the two *lepta* that the widow gave to the Temple were equal to one *quadron* (Mark 12:42).

Cross the room to *case 2*. The last panel on the right. **Projecting power.** Here there are six gold coins of the emperor Nero (AD 51–56), under whom Paul and Peter were most probably martyred. In these six Nero, who died at the age of thirty, is clearly gaining weight and aging! See the short video beside this panel 'The changing face of the emperor Nero'.

Below this, nos 6,7, are two bronze coins of Caesar Augustus, the emperor at the time of Jesus'

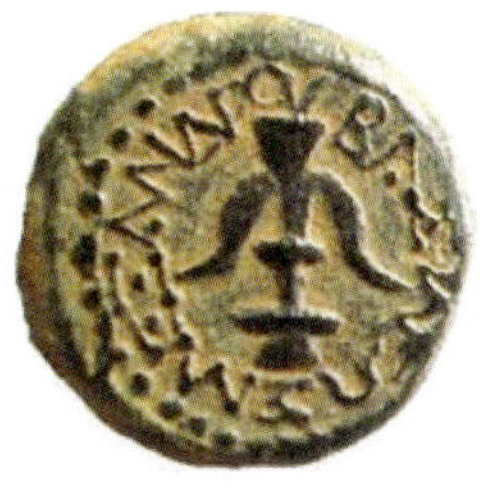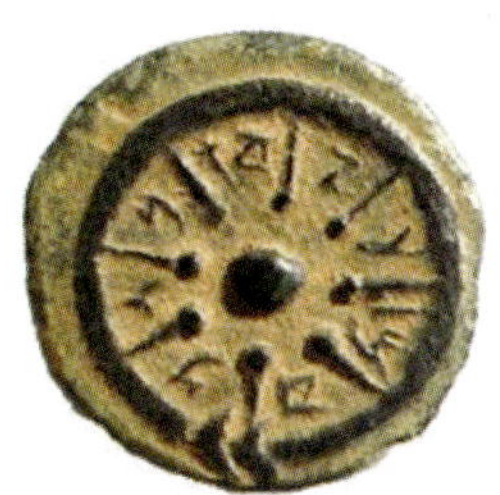

Above: A lepton was the coin of least value in Jerusalem and two of these were all that the widow in Mark 12:42 possessed. This coin is not currently on display

birth. As Octavian he was the stepson of Julius Caesar who, after his assassination, was deified as a god. Octavian proclaimed himself Caesar Augustus and to emphasise his role as 'son of the god' (DIVI F) imprinted his head alongside those of his stepfather. The title 'Son of God' that Jesus used (eg John 5:19–25) was well understood by both Jew and Roman.

The ***Roman military dagger*** (above right no.4) illustrates the weapon used by Brutus and his assassins in the murder of Julius Caesar on 15 March 44 BC. He received 23 wounds! Julius Caesar was the first ever to have his portrait on a coin. No. 5 two silver denarius coins with the image of Brutus.

While you are here, you may wish to turn to the next chapter and visit 'Christianity comes to Britain'.

If you earlier visited the Elgin marbles and the adjacent rooms downstairs, this brings you to the close of your tour through the British Museum with the Bible. Continue out of this room and take the South Stairs (or the lift) to the ground floor to return to the Great Court.

If you have not yet visited the Elgin marbles and the adjacent rooms, continue out of this room and take the South Stairs (or the lift) to the ground floor, through the Great Court and rooms 4, 8, 23 and into **Rooms 17 and 18 The Parthenon Galleries**. See the ground plan inside the back cover.

Pause in Room 17 on your right is the **Nereid Monument**. This is the façade of a Greek temple named after the daughters of the sea god Nereus (Neptune). Built around 390–380 BC it was the largest tomb found in the Lycaonian area of Turkey, an area visited by Paul and Barnabas (Acts 14:5–7). It is in the form of a Greek temple, illustrating the Hellenistic (Greek) influence across Asia Minor which was still prevalent in the time of the New Testament. See picture on page 114.

Paul and the Parthenon

The significance of the 'Elgin Marbles' for our purpose is that the apostle Paul would certainly have seen these sculptures high up on the magnificent Parthenon (meaning 'virgin', referring to the goddess Athena) whcn he visited the city around the year AD 50, a visit that is recorded in Acts 17. See Box: The Elgin Marbles page 112 The two side rooms have interesting displays on the Parthenon.

Exit back through rooms 18 and 17 into Room 23 and turn left up the stairs into **Room 22 The world of Alexander.** Continue to half way up the left hand wall to the busts of four Greek philosophers by the board *Philosophy.*

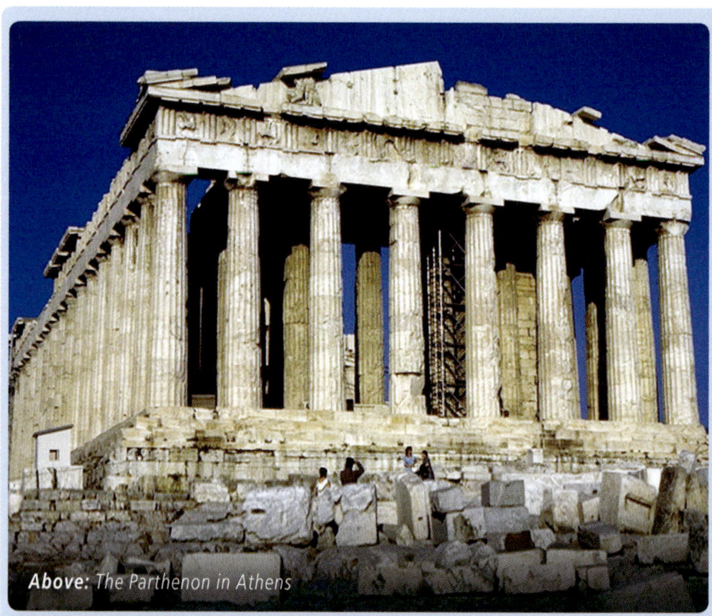

Above: *The Parthenon in Athens*

The Elgin Marbles—the sculptures from the Parthenon

The Parthenon, the central focus on the Acropolis ('High City') in Athens, was built between 447 and 438 BC and was dedicated to Athena, the goddess and patroness of the city—nearly 500 years before Paul arrived there. A thousand years after its construction, the building was converted to be used as a Christian church, and it was finally ruined in 1687 by an explosion during the Ottoman Empire—the Turks had used the Parthenon as a store for their gunpowder! From the ruins, Lord Elgin brought these sculptures to England and they came into the possession of the British Museum in 1816. Many of the sculptures you see here depict scenes from mythology, but the procession that makes up the frieze, illustrates the impressive Panathenaic festival commemorating the birthday of Athena. The frieze well illustrates how devoted the Athenians were to their deities (see Acts 17:22).

Acts 17:18 – Mars Hill

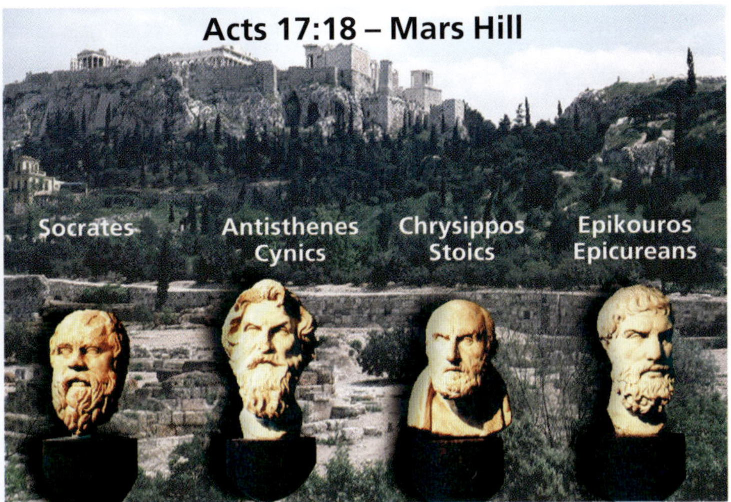

Above: The four philosophers representing the systems of belief that Paul confronted whilst in Athens: Epikouros, Chrysippos, Antisthenes and Socrates

'Vain philosophy'—four wise men?

Whilst Paul was in Athens, 'a group of Epicurean and Stoic philosophers began to dispute with him' (Acts 17:18). From right to left we have: Epikouros, Chrysippos, Antisthenes and Socrates. Epikouros *(GR 1873.8–20.726)* was the founder of the Epicurean philosophy, and Chrysippos *(GR 1824.2–1.2)* was the founder of the Stoic philosophy. Later, on hearing of the resurrection, 'some of them sneered' (v. 32); these may well have been the Cynics— Antisthenes *(GR 1873.8–20.724)* was the founder of the Cynics and a disciple of the Greek philosopher Socrates *(GR 1973.3– 27.16)*.

In Colossians 2:8 Paul, a master of clear thinking, warned against being taken captive: 'through hollow and deceptive philosophy, which depends on human tradition and the basic principles of this world rather than on Christ.' Luke is equally dismissive of those at Athens who spent all their time 'doing nothing but talking about and listening to the latest ideas' (Acts 17:21).

Diana—protectress of children

Now go to the large column base in the centre of the room *The Temple of Diana in Ephesus (GR 1872.8–3.9)*.

This is the huge base of one of the columns of the Temple of Diana in Ephesus. It is virtually all that has been discovered of the original thirty-six sculptured columns, and the apostle Paul would have seen them all. In this city, Paul's preaching threatened the business of the craftsmen who made small household

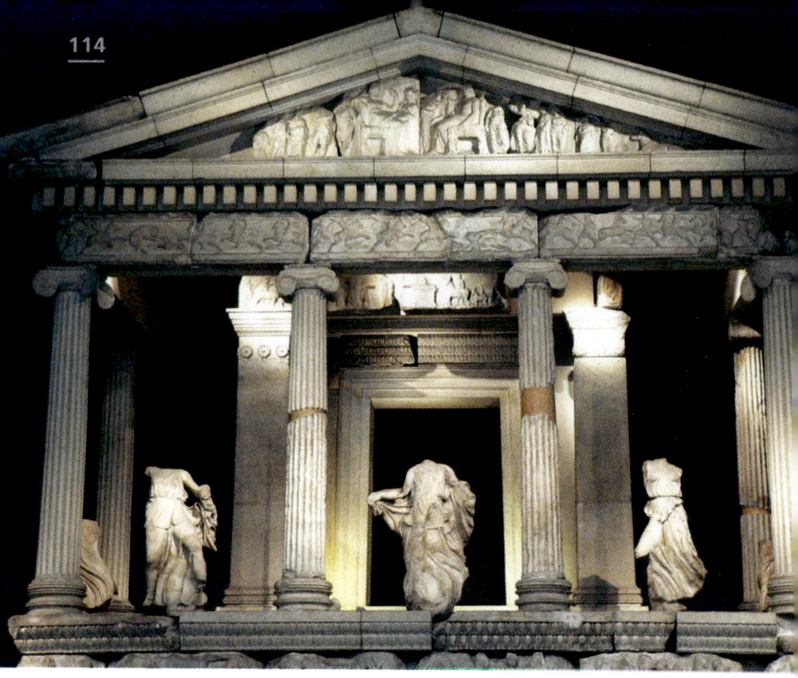

Above: The Nereid Monument from Xanthos in the region of southern Turkey through which Paul and Barnabas travelled. See page 111

idols of Diana such as we saw in Room 69 on page 108; the riot that followed is recorded in Acts 19:21–41. It is uncertain who the figures are here, but one is very likely Thanatos—the winged god of death, the other Hermes—the messenger of the gods and the one who leads souls to the underworld, and a woman, who has been variously identified. See Box 'Great is Diana of the Ephesians'.

Whilst all that remains of the Temple of Diana today in Ephesus is a lonely column in a pool of water, Paul's gospel is preached all over the world.

Alexander the goat

Continue to the opposite wall to the bust of *Alexander the Great* (GR 1872.5–15.1). This is the Macedonian who, in the fourth century BC, set out to conquer the world until the world ran out. Master of three million square miles of territory his military genius is legendary. He was depicted in Egypt as Pharaoh with ram's horns representing the god Amun (see page 46). Alexander was often referred to as 'the two-horned one'—a sign of deity, strength and virility. The book of Daniel used the figure of a goat to represent him (Daniel 8:3–8).

To your right in *case 2* are four coins with the head of Alexander on them (*nos. 4–7*), and one of his famous white horse Boukephalos (or Bucephalus), *no.14*. The name means ox-head.

No.35 is a coin of Octavian c. 30 BC, the Roman Caesar who later took the title of Augustus to become the first Roman Emperor (Luke 2:1).

'Great is Diana of the Ephesians'

Diana is the Latin name of the goddess known in Greek mythology as Artemis. She was the daughter of Zeus and Leto and twin sister of Apollo. She was the patroness of childbirth and the Amazons—a tribe of women who lived apart from men—and protectress of little children and all suckling animals. Artemis remained a perpetual virgin, though she symbolised fertility. Revered as the moon goddess, she was a great hunter and often she is portrayed with packs of hunting dogs around her. At Ephesus Artemis was worshipped as a Nymph, and legend told that her image fell from the sky and that a shrine was built around it, and eventually a temple was erected around this. The Ephesians were proud of their role as guardians of the image of Artemis (Acts 19:35), and she became the centre of a lucrative tourist industry. Inscriptions confirm that she was well known as 'Artemis the Great' (Acts 19:28). The first temple of Diana (referred to in the Museum as the 'archaic' temple), was built between 560 and 540 BC. It burned down in 356 BC and the building of a new temple began at once and lasted for 120 years. The temple roof was supported by 100 massive columns, 36 of which were sculptured. The marble temple became one of the seven wonders of the ancient world. It was finally destroyed by the Goths in AD 263. The temple of Artemis in Ephesus was a temple of refuge and anyone banished here was under the protection of the goddess; the Artemesian had its own government and protection. This did not hinder Cleopatra from having her younger sister Arsinawe IV dragged out from its precincts and murdered in 41 BC.

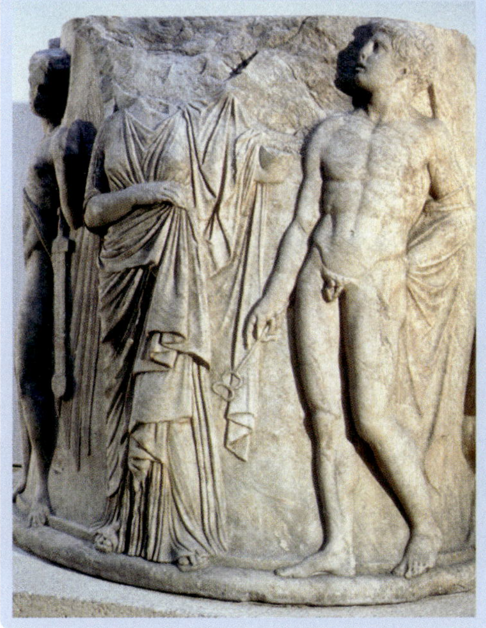

Left: The only remaining sculptured column base of the temple of Diana (GR1872.8–3.9)

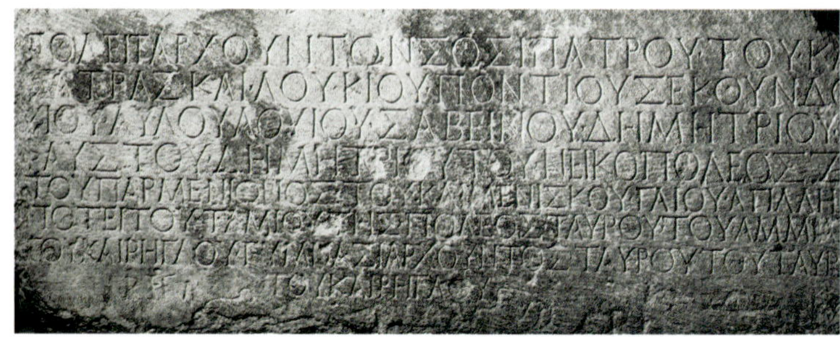

Above: *The Politarch Inscription reveals the careful accuracy of Luke as a historian (GR1877.5–11.1). The first word in the inscription is in Greek uncial (capitals) POLYTARCHOUNTON (below)*

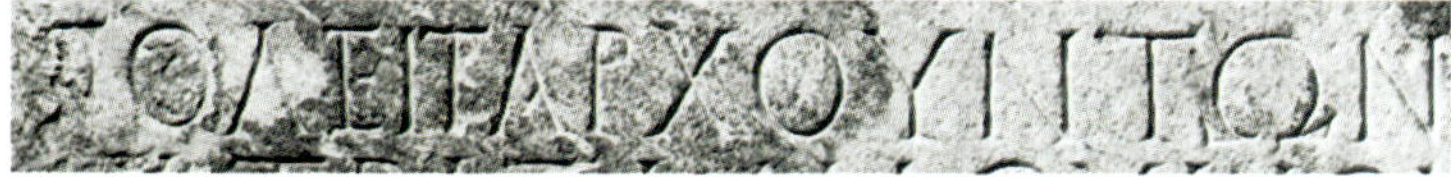

Continue to *case 4* **marble statuette of Artemis** as a hunter (*GR 1864.10–7.53*). Notice the evidence here that these statues were often originally colourful. See the note on page 23 at the Victorian Entrance Hall.

The following two items are an excursion into the basement if you have time and if the rooms are open. Return to the column base of the Diana temple and continue behind it and down the stairs into **Room 21 Mausoleum of Halikarnassos.** Cross to the stairs opposite and turn left down to **Room 77 Greek and Roman Architecture.**

Clinical analysis

This room includes relics of the first (archaic) temple of Diana. Turn right into **Room 78 Classical Inscriptions.** In the far right corner you will fine a stone inscription *The Politarchs and other Magistrates.* This is **The Politarch Inscription**

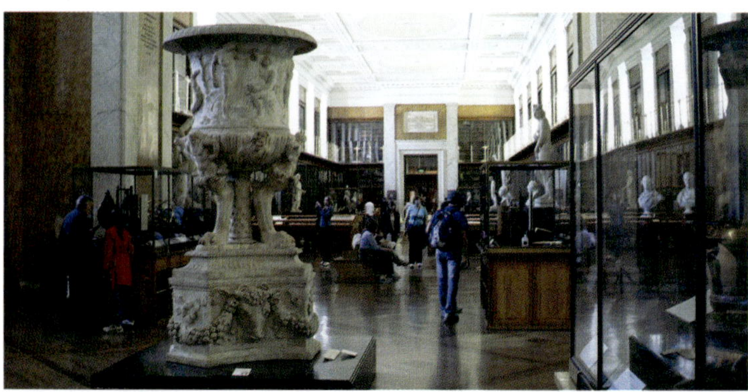

Above:The Enlightenment Gallery

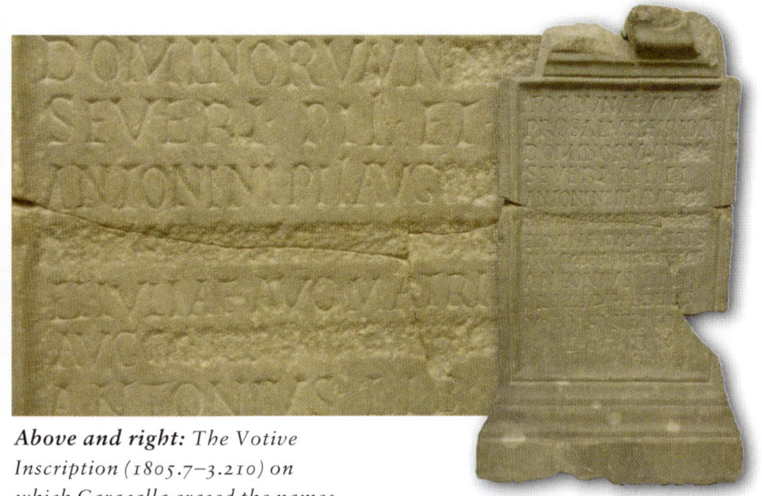

Above and right: The Votive Inscription (1805.7–3.210) on which Caracalla erased the names of his brother and his own wife after their murder—damnatio memoriae

(GR1877.5–11.1) and it confirms the accuracy of Luke (the compiler of the Acts of the Apostles) as a careful historian. It was originally part of a Roman gateway discovered at Thessalonica and dated to the 2nd century AD. Its significance is that at Thessalonica the word Luke uses to describe the 'city officials' (Acts 17:6) is *politarchas*. The first word in this inscription (which is written in Greek uncial—capital letters) is from the verb *politarcheo*, 'to act as a politarch'.

Luke was a physician by profession and was well acquainted with the political arrangements in the various provinces of Asia; his correct use of titles for the local dignitaries, unlikely to be known by a much later writer, reveals a clinical precision. Incidentally, four of the men listed in this inscription as politarchs bear the same names as men recorded in the New Testament: Sosipatros and Lucius (line 1 and 2 and see Romans 16:21) and Secundus (line 2 and see Acts 24:4) and Gaius (line 5 and see Acts 20:4). They are not the same men of course, but it shows that the names were common in Thessalonica at that time.

Continue back along this right hand wall to *Latin Inscriptions.* The *Votive Inscription* (1805.7–3.210) of Septimus Severus reveals that the names of Geta and Plautilla, the brother and wife of the Roman emperor Caracalla were erased after their murder by the brutal Caracalla. This was the damnation of memory in the ancient world that we have referred to elsewhere. See page 43.

If you broke your tour from page 39, please return to that page to continue your tour.
Otherwise, this brings you to the close of your tour through the British Museum with the Bible.

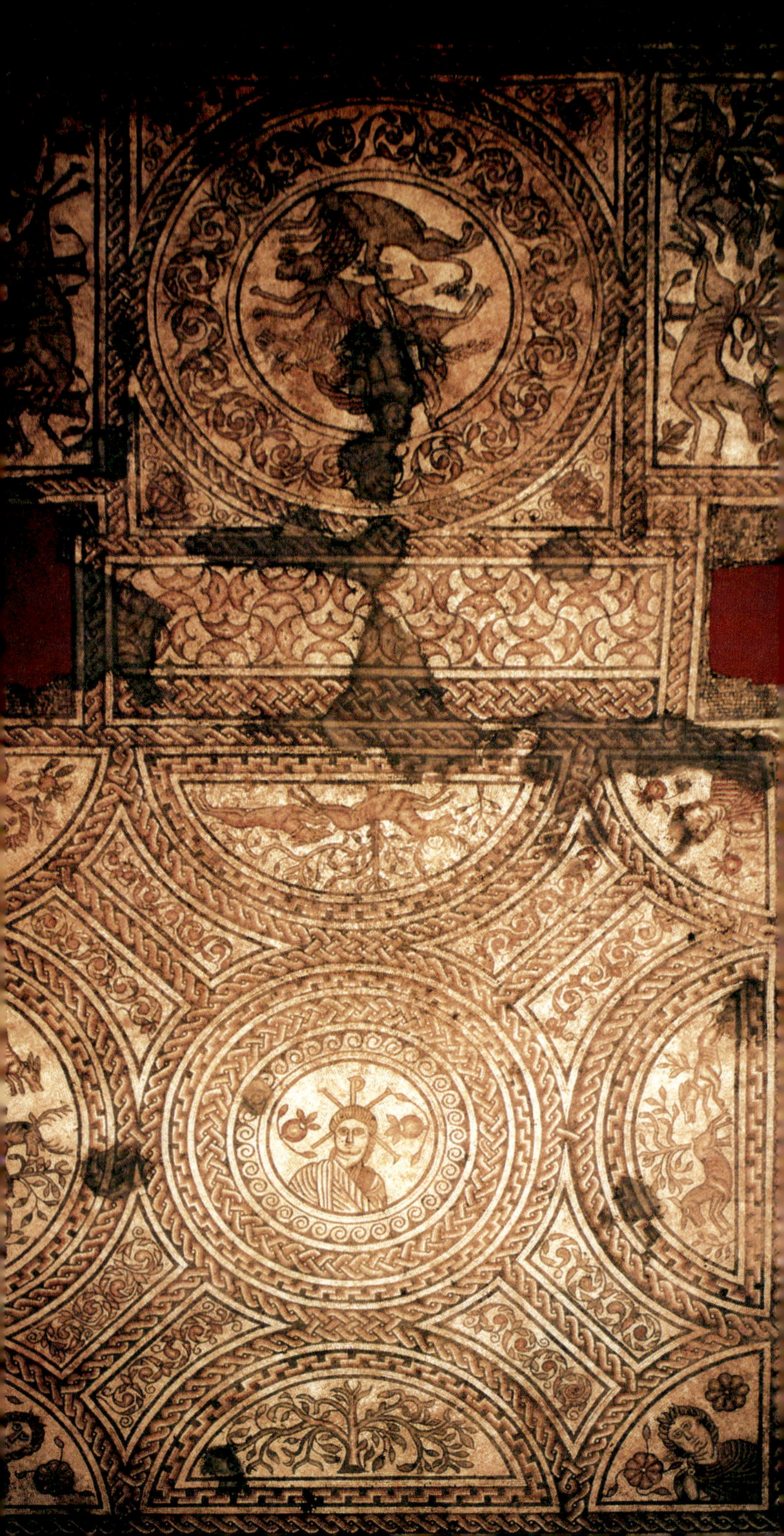

❾ Christianity comes to Britain

Far from the centre of Roman power was an inhospitable and wild island. Yet this outpost of the empire received Christianity. But how did it come to these shores and what effect did it have on the lives of the ordinary people? It was here at York, known to the Romans as Eboracum, that Constantine was hailed as Augustus after the death of his father Constantius in AD 305. He was the first Roman emperor to embrace the Christian faith

From **Room 68 The Citi Money Gallery** continue ahead into **Room 36** (Europe) and ahead into **Rooms 40 and 41**. Turn left into **Room 49 Roman Britain.**

Rule Britannia!

The Romans first came to Britain half a century before Jesus Christ was born. Julius Caesar landed with two legions in August 55 BC and again the following year, but he was forced to abandon his campaign more by the British weather than by the defenders! It was not until AD 43 in the time of the emperor Claudius that General Plautius forced a firm landing on the island. However, the Romans never subdued the whole of 'Britannia Romana', and the emperor Hadrian began his wall in AD 122 from Tyneside to Solway—a distance of just over 117 kilometres (73 miles)—to keep out the troublesome Picts and Scots in the north. By and large the newcomers integrated well with the local inhabitants and trade and intermarriage were established and the population of Britannia soon rose to around two million. The coveted Roman citizenship was a route to influence and wealth and the 4th century saw the expansion of the great Roman villas. The remains of many villas and military encampments have been discovered, and we confidently expect more archaeological finds in the future.

The Romans have landed

At first the Roman pantheon of gods intermingled with Celtic mythology and the paganism

Facing page: Part of the 4th century mosaic from Hinton St Mary in Dorset. The central figure of Christ is surrounded in the four corners by what is probably the four Gospel writers: Matthew, Mark, Luke and John

of the natives. Exactly when Christianity first arrived in Britain is not known. Almost certainly it came with merchants and Roman legionaries. Remember, in AD 43 Paul and his team were evangelising across Asia Minor (modern Turkey) and the Gospel was spreading fast. There is strong evidence that Pomponia, the wife of General Plautius was a Christian. But what firm evidence is there for the early arrival of Christianity?

It is certain that the message of Jesus Christ was here long before Patrick (a Welshman) preached to the Irish in the 5th century, or Columba (an Irishman) preached to the Scots a century later; and it was certainly well established before Illtud was preaching to the Welsh or Augustine and Aidan to the English in the 5th, 6th and 7th centuries.

Tertullian, the bishop of Carthage in North Africa, who died in AD 222, could boast that 'parts of Britain inaccessible to the Romans were indeed conquered by Christ'—though he does not specify which parts. What is also certain is that by the Council of Arles in August 314,

The Emperor and the Cross

There is an interesting story behind the chi-rho monogram (see page 113 for its meaning). In July 306 Constantine, whilst serving in Britain, was proclaimed Emperor at York. The following account was told by Constantine himself to Eusebius, an early Christian historian: In the year AD 312 Constantine was preparing for a battle with his rival Maxentius, when he saw a cross of light in the sky and the words 'In this sign conquer'. The following night he claimed that Christ appeared to him and commanded him to make a copy of what he had seen and use it as his standard. The result was his *Labarum* (pictured below on a coin of his realm; This small coin is not currently on display in the Museum. (1890.0804.11)—a tall pole with a cross-bar plated with gold; near the top was a wreath in gold and precious stones enclosing the chi-rho monogram. From the cross-bar hung a banner with his own portrait on it. From now on this always accompanied him in battle. The same monogram he ordered to be painted on the shields of his soldiers. Whatever the reality of his 'conversion' at this time, it is a fact that Constantine later embraced the Christian faith, ended the persecution of Christians, won all the battles he fought and became the sole Emperor of the Roman Empire. In AD 328 he enlarged the Greek city of Byzantium and renamed it Constantinople (modern Istanbul) making it the centre of Roman government above Rome itself. Probably Constantine was the first to use the chi-rho symbol officially— though we have seen it scratched on a coin possibly a century earlier in the time of Caracalla (see page 108).

five representatives of the church in Britain attended—including the bishops of York, Lincoln and London. The significance of this Council was that it was called and presided over by the Roman Emperor, Constantine. See Box: The Emperor and the Cross on page 120.

But there is other firm evidence for the early arrival of Christianity in Britain—and it lies in the discoveries you will find in this room.

By the end of the 4th century, with Rome's borders being squeezed throughout her empire, a weakened leadership and a steady withdrawal of her armies, it was time to abandon this wet and windy outpost. When the Romans left Britannia, life became more insecure. The decay of Roman law and order and increasing raids by fierce warriors from across the North Sea—the Anglo-Saxons—led many families to hide their treasures in the hope of returning to it in better days.

They never did return, and it was what some of these families left behind that is so valuable for us.

1. Carlisle

2. Newcastle-upon-Tyne

3. York

4. Lincoln

5. London

6. Water Newton
    (Cambridgeshire)

7. Mildenhall (Suffolk)

8. Icklingham (Suffolk)

9. Hoxne (Suffolk)

10. Risley Park (Derbyshire)

11. Hinton St Mary (Dorset)

12. Lullingstone (Kent)

13. Canterbury (Kent)

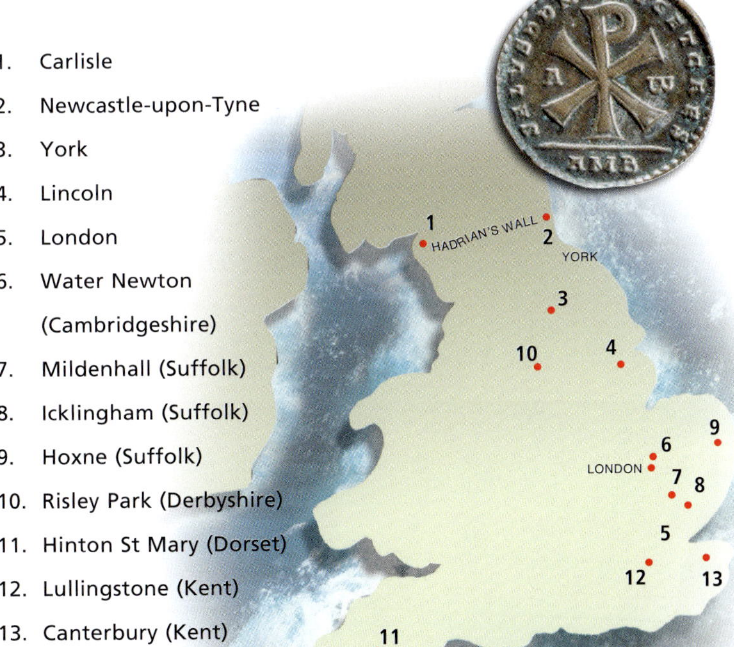

Map of England showing where the hoards of treasure were found

Above: *A coin of the Emperor Magnentius (AD 350–353). Possibly the earliest evidence of the Christian chi-rho monogram stamped on a coin. This item is currently not on display*

Early Christian symbols

For the first three hundred years of Christianity, bitter persecution was experienced by those who followed 'the way' (Acts 9:2; 19:9,23), and they developed symbols that would help to identify the faithful.

The earliest Christian symbol was not the cross—which for the Romans represented the cruel death of a degraded criminal—but the first and last letters of the Greek alphabet, *alpha* and *omega,* which were often used to refer to Christ as the beginning and the end. This was prompted by Revelation 22:13 in the New Testament: 'I am the alpha and the omega, the first and the last, the beginning and the end.'

Here is alpha and omega in Greek capitals (known as uncials): ΑΩ (sometimes written as A W) and in lower case (though this minuscule script did not come into use until the 7th century AD) α ω.

The early Christians also used the **symbol of a fish.** This was because the Greek word for 'fish' is *ichthus* (uncial: ΙΧΘΥΣ. minuscule: ιχθυς). The word forms an anagram for 'Jesus Christ God's Son Saviour':

I	Ιεσυς	Jesus
X	Χριστος	Christ
Θ	Θεου	God's
Υ	Υιος	Son
Σ	Σωτηρ	Saviour

A fish was a very appropriate symbol for Christians—see for example Matthew 4:19; 13:37; 14:17.

However, the symbol that became most widespread was the **chi-rho** monogram which was made up from the first two letters of the name 'Christ'. In Greek the word 'Christ' today looks like this: Χριστος.

These three symbols are represented by some of the exhibits you will see in this room.

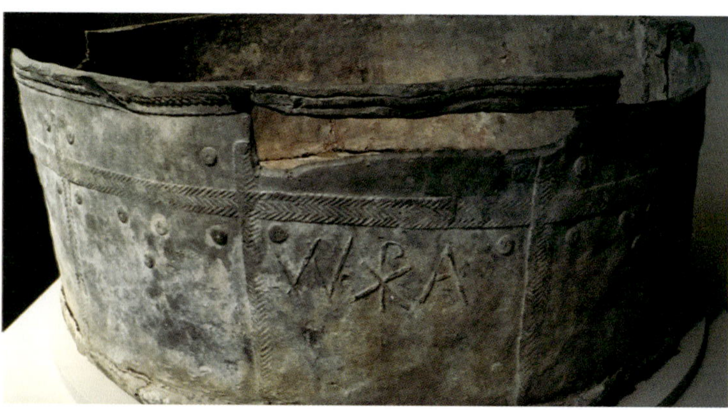

Above: A fourth century lead tank from Icklingham, Suffolk with the Christian chi-rho and the alpha and omega symbols (P&EE1946 2–4.1)

Immediately on entering **Room 49** look to your right and you will see a *lead tank* (*PRB 1946 2–4.1*) from an early Christian cemetery in Icklingham in Suffolk. Notice the chi-rho symbol with the omega placed before the alpha; perhaps the craftsman put the letters in the correct order in his mould so that the cast came out back to front; it is unlikely that he knew Greek but simply copied a drawing. The purpose of this tank is not known.

First, the tableware

Now for the treasures those families left behind under threat from the fierce Anglo-Saxons.

The Mildenhall Treasure in the case immediately in front of you as you enter the room. Go to the right side of this case.

In the centre of this case, some of this silverware is marked with the Christian chi-rho monogram and the alpha-omega letters.

In 1942, during the Second World War, a farmer, 'ploughing for victory' in his field in West Row, a small Suffolk hamlet near Mildenhall, turned up a hoard of buried treasure close by the remains of a 4th century Roman building. The thirty-four pieces of silverware were clearly 4th century in design and since the East Anglian coast was at the frontline of those Anglo-Saxon raids across the North Sea, it

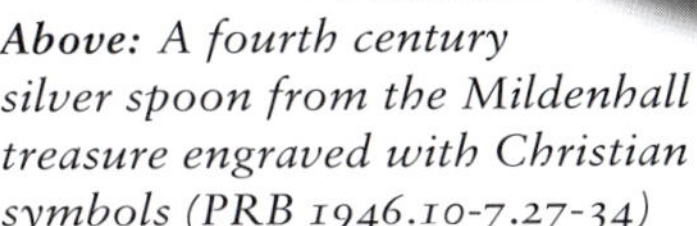

Above: A fourth century silver spoon from the Mildenhall treasure engraved with Christian symbols (PRB 1946.10-7.27-34)

is very likely that the family valuables were hidden in haste. The fate of the family may be imagined. The Mildenhall Treasure was acquired by the British Museum in 1946.

Whilst much of the treasure is decorated with Bacchus, the god of wine, three of the four spoons on the left have, in the centre of the bowl, the chi-rho with the alpha and omega on either side of it (*PRB 1946.10-7.15/17*).See text card *Spoons 4th century AD*.

Two other spoons have personal names: Papiltedo and Pascentia (husband and wife?) with *viva*— 'may you live'— inscribed. See the Museum text card and note the outstanding detail of this 4th century silverware. According to inscriptions found with this set of tableware, they belonged to Eutherios, an influential minister under the emperor Julian (AD 360–363). Julian was a nephew of the Emperor Constantine and was brought up as a Christian, but when he became emperor he revived pagan worship and was dubbed 'the apostate'.

In *case 23 behind you, we have* the **Hoxne Treasure** (Suffolk).

Some of this also displays the chi-rho symbol. The Hoxne (pronounced 'Hoxon') Treasure was discovered in 1992 and was thought to have been buried at around the same time as the Mildenhall Treasure. It included 15,000 gold and silver coins which confirm a burial after AD 407/8 (the Romans left in 410), plus 100 spoons and some beautiful jewelry.

Notice the set of five silver spoons (*See text card Spoons with Christian symbols and inscriptions. PRBP.1994.4-8,89-91,109,135*) with the chi-rho just below the bowl of four of them. Also, at the extreme left of this case there are five **Inscribed silver spoons**, one of which has the Christian symbols.

On the other side of this case, the **Thetford Treasure**, contain no Christian symbols.

Move left to *case 18*

Many of the lead and pewter items in the first two sections

contain Christian chi-rho emblems. Notice the small piece of **bronze sheet** from 4th century Gloucestershire

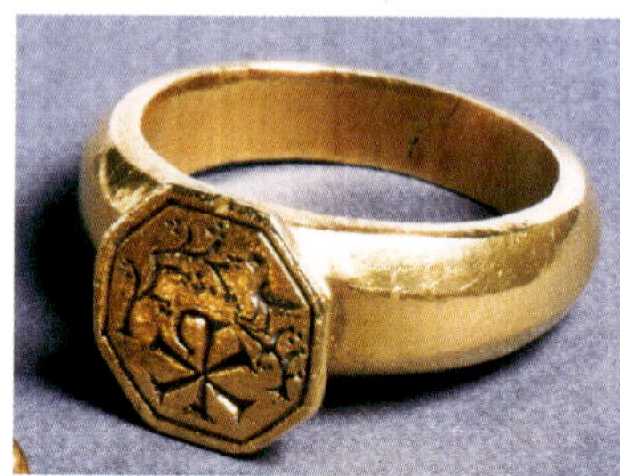

Above: A beautiful fourth century gold ring with the chi rho emblem reversed for the purpose of sealing (PRB P1983 10–3.1)

with Christian scenes (*P&E 1978,0102.70. See the text card*). Beside it is a silver spoon from Staffordshire with the chi-rho monogram engraved in the centre and with the alpha and omega on either side. Next to it are **two silver toothpicks** (*P&E1991 6-11*) each with the Christian chi-rho emblem. Then four **gold rings** (*PRB P1983 10–3.1 and 1984 10–1.1*) with Christian phrases or monograms, and a **silver fibula** (brooch. *PRB 1954.12–6.1*) with chi-rho. Above them is a large pewter (lead and tin) plate; can you discover Christian symbols in the rough pattern? See text card **Pewter plate**.

At the end of case 18 (**The Water Newton Treasure**) is a **silver strainer** with the chi-rho engraved on the handle. Beside this are communion bowls and votive offerings (in fulfillment

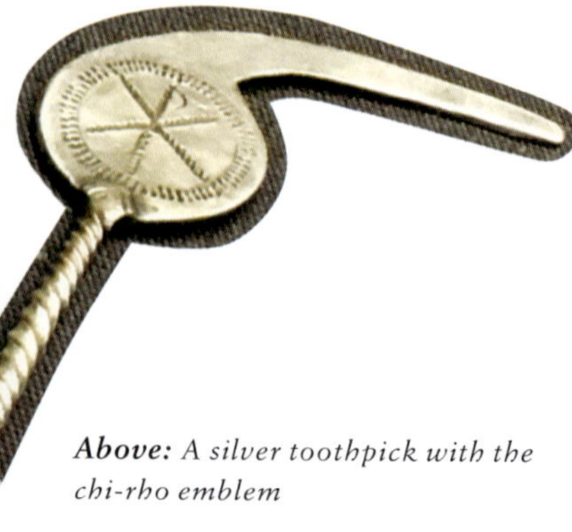

Above: A silver toothpick with the chi-rho emblem

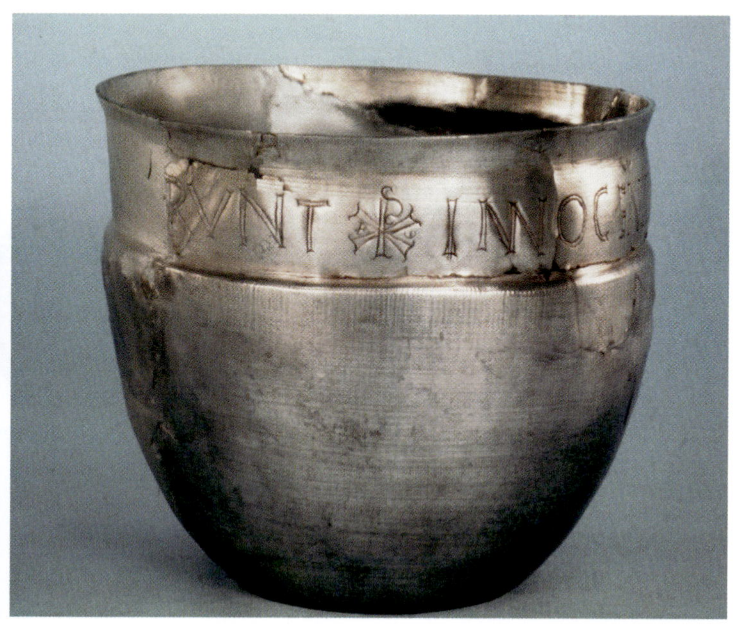

Above: *Water Newton silverware from the 4th century, used in Christian worship (P&E 1975 10-24). This bowl has the names of two women, Innocentia and Viventia on the rim*

of a vow). Discovered in 1975 at Water Newton near Peterborough in Cambridgeshire (Peterborough was the Roman town of Durobrivae), these items were intended for Christian ceremonies. Although they were badly damaged, they are the earliest Christian silverware from the Roman Empire.

The large dish *(PRBP.1975.10–2.7)* reveals the outline of the chi-rho which has been marked out presumably to be engraved later. Some of these items were dedicated by Publianus whose name is engraved round the larger bowl *(PRBP.1975.10-2.5)*. It includes also the words *sanctum altare tuum domine*

subnixus honoro. The true significance of the final two words is somewhat obscure but one translation of this inscription is: 'your holy altar, Lord, I am trusting, I honour'— it is uncertain whether the trust and honour is in the Lord (*domine*) or the altar. It also includes two chi-rho monograms. Other items were dedicated by three women: Amcilla, Innocentia and Viventia— perhaps members of the same congregation. In the centre is a silver communion cup.

Continue to the large **Mosaic from Hinton St Mary,** Dorset *(1965.0409.1).* In 1963 a blacksmith was digging new foundations for his smithy when he stumbled across the remains of what proved to be a large Roman building complex including a villa. Dated to the 4th century, this is one of the earliest known representations of Christ and the only mosaic of Christ found in Roman Europe; you will see the chi-rho motif behind the head of Christ. See page 118 for a full picture before, tragically, this centre piece was removed from the full mosaic when it was broken up. Around the edge are what may be the four Gospel writers.

Continue left to *case 14*

In *case 14* is a bronze head of what is thought to be the emperor Claudius or Nero (*PRB 1965 12–1.1*). Claudius conquered Britain in AD 43 (and see Acts 11:28 and 18:2). Paul and Peter were martyred in the time of Nero. The large head in the centre is of the Emperor Hadrian, discovered in the Thames at London Bridge in 1834, probably part of a larger-than-life statue placed in the forum in London. For the Romans, to see the image of the emperor was to be in his presence. Paul used this concept in Colossians 1:19 '[Jesus] is the image of the invisible God' and Jesus himself claimed 'Anyone who has seen me has seen the Father' (John 14:9).

Cross to the left side of *case 10* behind you. **Coinage in Roman Britain** discovered in Britain. Coins of the Emperor Caracalla (1–4, AD 198–217); see page 43 and page 108 for one of his coins with Christian graffiti

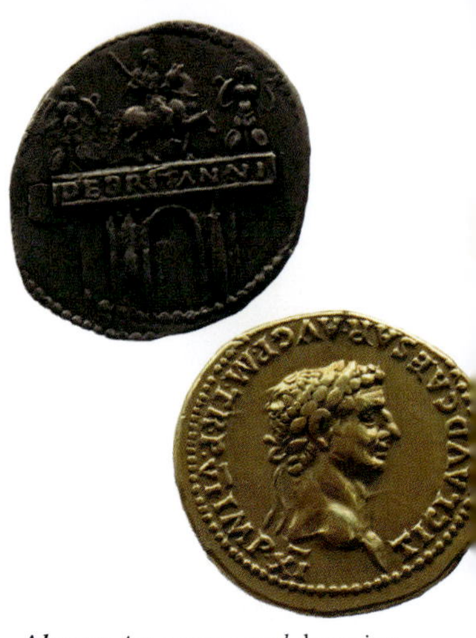

Above: An aureus *and* denarius *of the emperor Claudius minted AD 46. The reverse of the* denarius *commemorates his conquest of Britain in AD 43. De Britanni stamped across it is the earliest reference to the newly acquired Roman province of Britain. The triumphal arch depicted was later erected in Rome.*

Below: A gold solidi *of Constantine AD 326*

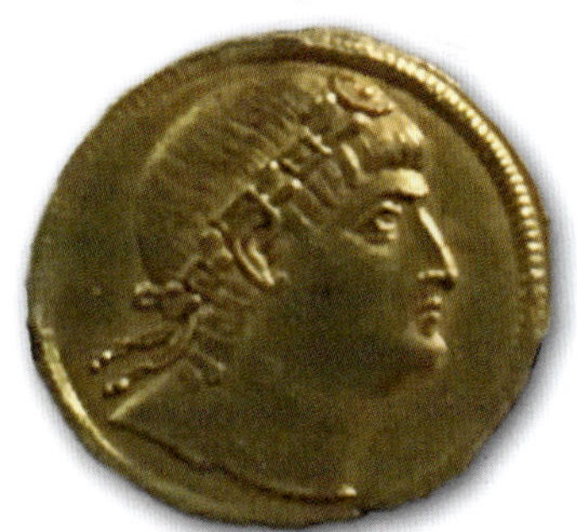

on it. Coins of Diocletian (7–9, AD 284–305) and gold *solidi* of Constantine (10) the first emperor to embrace the Christian faith (AD 306–337) and see Box on page 120. There are also coins of Maximus (32–33, AD 235–238) which may have been minted in London.

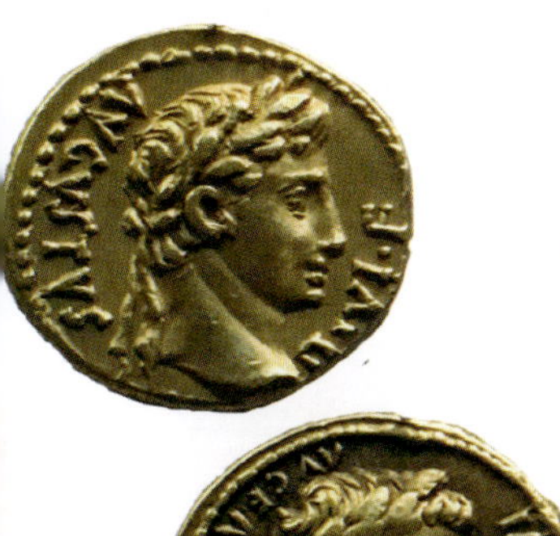

Left: Aurei *of the emperors Augustus and Tiberius*

Below: Compare the model in case 6 with this legionary in complete armour

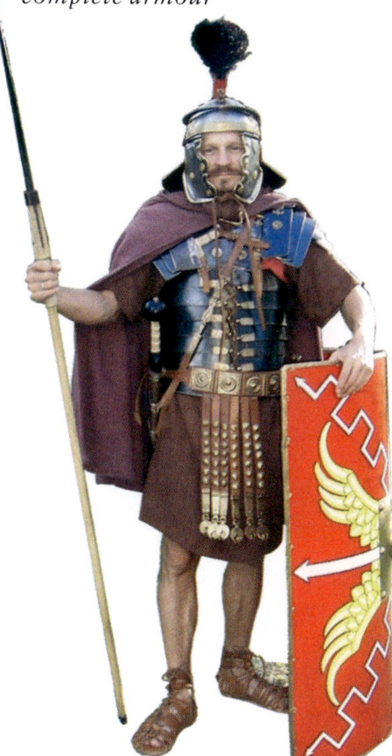

On the opposite side of case 10 there are *aurei* of Augustus and Tiberius (18,19). An *aureus* and and *denarius* (23,24) of Claudius with *De Britanni* stamped on it. See the coins and caption on page 126.

Behind you in the centre of *case 11* you will find a pile of silver coins from the time of Domitian (AD 81–96). These were discovered in 1985 at Snettisham in Norfolk and dated AD 154. There are no Christian symbols on them. It was very probable that it was Domitian who exiled the apostle John to Patmos (Revelation 1:9).

In the centre of this room is a model of Housesteads Fort on Hadrian's Wall.

In case 8 and on both sides of *case 6* is a display of Roman military armour found in England. Notice the pilum (javelin) designed to buckle when it hit its target. In Ephesians 6 Paul illustrates the Christian's armour from the belt, breastplate, footwear, shield, helmet and the short sword (gladius) of the Roman legionary. Surprisingly little has been discovered of Roman weapons and armour after three hundred years of occupation.

Return up this room and go towards the right-hand corner by the door you entered.

Painted walls from Lullingstone Roman Villa (PRB 1967 4-7.1) comes from a Roman villa in Kent. The room in which these were found was used

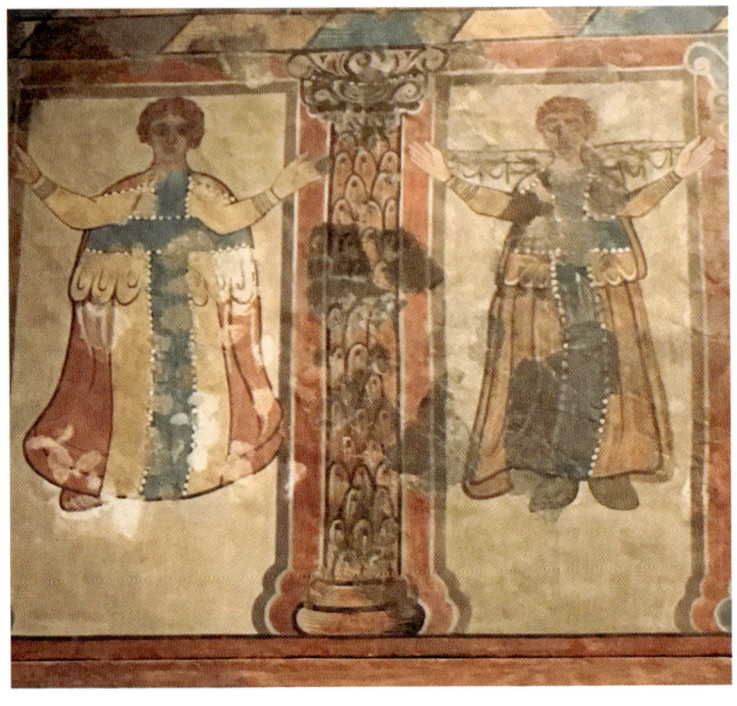

Above: Two wall paintings from the private chapel in the Roman villa at Lullingstone, Kent. One shows Christians at prayer

for Christian worship. It was excavated in 1949. The villa was built late in the 1st century but subsequently altered and pagan worship is evident. By the 4th century the owners had adopted Christianity and hence the chi-rho motif and the frieze of Christians at prayer (the large panel above). To the left of the frieze is a mosaic of the chi-rho with alpha and omega. This was probably a house church, or private chapel— only a few examples of house churches are known in the entire Roman Empire.

There is no certain evidence of Christian emblems found in Britain before the fourth century—yet!

When did merchants, soldiers and civil servants first bring the gospel to England? Hopefully the answers to this and many more questions may be revealed in a field or on a building site by an archaeologist or by some unsuspecting worker.

If you are interested in life in Britain before the Romans left in AD 410, it is worth browsing this room to admire the fine jewelry (case 11), glass (12, 13), pottery (21), medicare (4) and notice the curse tablet, and see page 107, literacy (2), military equipment (6,8), religion (15), ironwork and building materials (16).

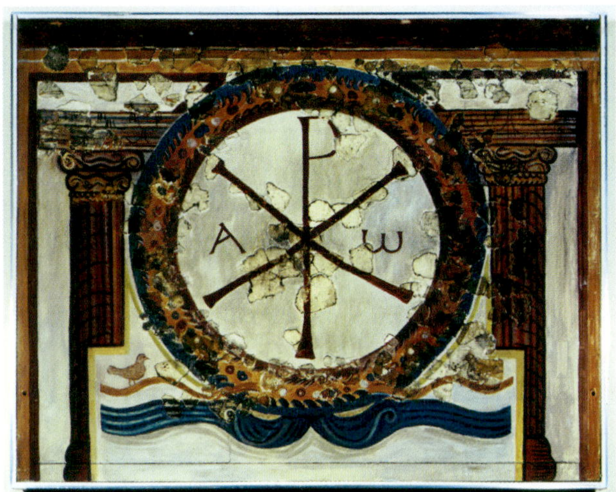

Your shortest route to the entrance hall from here is to leave this **Room 49 into Room 41** and turn right into **Room 40 and 39.** Here you will find lifts to your right. Straight ahead, the main Victorian staircase—which has been used by generations of visitors for almost 180 years—will take you to the entrance hall.

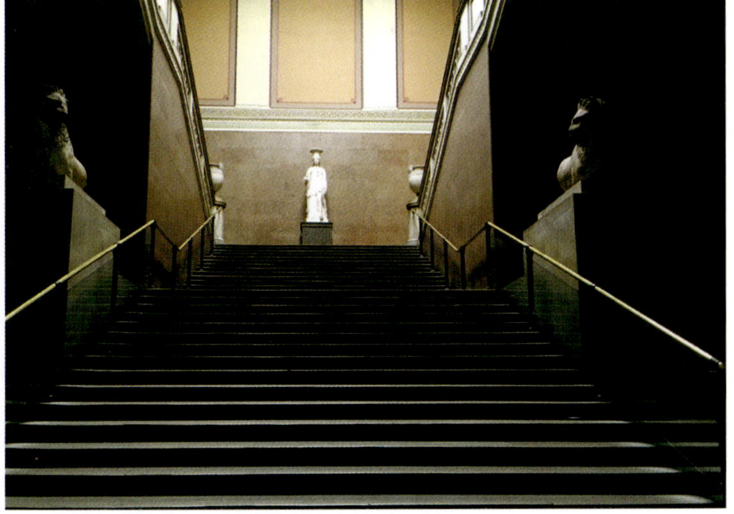

Top: *Fourth century Roman wall decoration from Lullingstone in Kent with the Christian chi rho and alpha and omega (PRB 1967 4–7.1)*

Above: *The grand Victorian staircase provides a fitting conclusion to your visit*

Words that are either used in this book or will be found in your tour of the Museum

Aureus
A gold coin of ancient Rome valued at 25 silver denarii. The aureus was regularly issued from the 1st century BC to the beginning of the 4th century AD.

Apostle
The word means 'a messenger' but is also the title given to those who were the close disciples of Jesus Christ.

Cartouche
A cartouche is an oblong enclosure with a horizontal line at one end, indicating that the text enclosed is a royal name. As time went on, many people hired an artist to create a cartouche for their own coffins.

Cuneiform
The wedge-shaped signs of Babylonian and Assyrian writing.

Cylinder
A memorial or record inscribed with cuneiform script onto clay (less often stone) in a barrel-shape.

Cylinder seal
The typical stone seal used in Babylonia and Assyria; up to 2 inches (5 cms) in length with a design engraved around the circumference.

Cursive
Letters of the alphabet that were joined together in writing. In Greek this joining took place around the 7th century AD.

Demotic script
The cursive form of Egyptian hieroglyphics used for ordinary documents in Egypt from around 650 BC to AD 500. The word means 'of the people' and refers to writing that was in a popular, commonly used form by ordinary people.

Dyad
A pair of statues often carved from the same block.

Dynasty
A line of rulers generally from the same family.

Fertile Crescent
The territory stretching from Egypt in the south through Palestine, Syria and Mesopotamia in the north and then down to the Persian Gulf. It forms a large crescent shape of the most fertile land. See page 76.

Hieratic script
A shortened form of Egyptian hieroglyphs for writing on papyrus.

Hieroglyphic
The earliest writing from Egypt and elsewhere that represents a word, syllable or sound in the form of pictures. From the Greek meaning 'a sacred carving'.

Ingot
A length of cast metal, usually gold or silver but also lead or iron.

Lapis lazuli
The mineral sodium aluminium silicate and sulphur in the form of a bright blue gemstone stone that was commonly used for jewellery. It was mined in Afghanistan.

Levant
The lands to the east of the Mediterranean where the sun rises; from French *lever* to rise.

Minuscule (var. miniscule)
Lower case letters that were later joined up into cursive writing in the 7th century. The opposite of uncial.

MS
The short form of 'manuscript', a handwritten document. The plural is MSS; lit. 'written by hand'.

Mummy	From Arabic *mummia* meaning bitumen or rock-like as mummies ended up being black and hard.
Obelisk	A four-sided, stone pillar tapering at the top; usually inscribed with texts as a monument or record.
Obverse	the side of a coin with the main image on it. The other side is known as the reverse.
Ostraca	Pieces of broken pottery on which messages were written. Singular 'ostracon'.
Ossuary	Small chest in which human bones were placed.
Pewter	A combination of tin and lead.
Pharaoh	The title of the kings of Egypt from around 14th century BC. The word comes from the Egyptian *per-aa* meaning 'a great house'.
Porphyry	A hard rock, largely composed of crystals, quarried in ancient Egypt.
Potsherd	A piece of broken pottery or glass. See also Shard.
Prism	A hollow or solid object with several parallel sides.
Pyramids	In Egypt, gigantic tombs: the shape may represent a theory of creation.
Relief	Raised relief: in which the objects stand out from the background.
Sunken relief:	In which the objects are let into the background.
Reverse	The side of the coin which has the secondary image on it. The principal side is known as the obverse.
Sarcophagus	A stone coffin often sculptured or inscribed. It comes from a Greek word meaning 'flesh-eating'.
Seal	The impression made on clay or wax by a stone seal or signet to mark ownership; it is also used of the tool that makes the impression. In Babylonia these were generally cylindrical, in Egypt the scarab was used, and in the Levant more commonly a single stamp.
Shard	See potsherd. A variant of 'sherd' a short form of potsherd.
Stele	(alt. stelee, stela) An upright pillar with an inscription and sometimes a sculpture. From the Greek meaning 'a standing block'.
Tell	The Semitic word for a ruin-mound that is made up from the successive layers of occupancy of a site.
Thebes	The ancient city of Upper Egypt on the banks of the Nile. By 1600 BC it became the capital of all Egypt.
Uncial	The early form of modern capital letters; the uncials, which are un-joined letters, are found in Greek manuscripts.
Votive offering	An offering made to the gods in fulfilment of a vow.
Ziggurat	A series of platforms each on top of and smaller than the previous one with a shrine on top and steps leading up to it. The usual form of the main temple in Mesopotamian cities. See page 83.

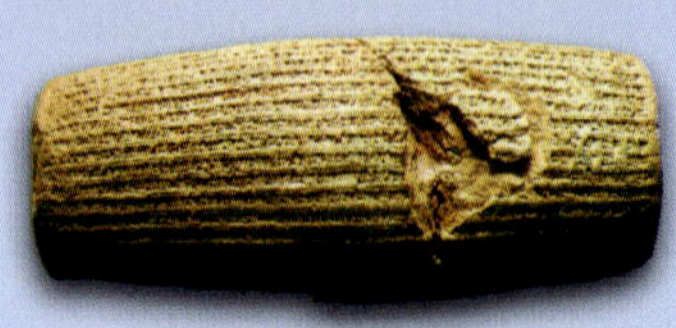 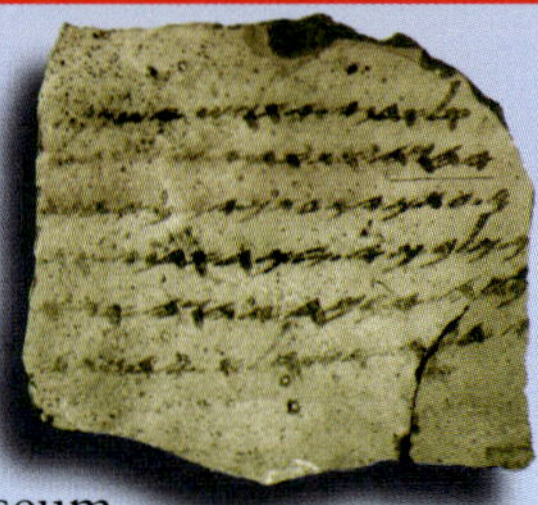

If you have limited time in the museum, you may find it worthwhile to visit just the items listed here.

Authors of this guide

Clive Anderson is a Christian minister who lives in Hampshire, England. He leads tours to the British Museum, Italy, Greece, Israel and Jordan and is the author of a number of books and articles. Clive is married to Amanda.

Brian Edwards is the author of more than twenty books including two historical biographies on John Newton and William Tyndale. He co-authored with Clive the popular *Evidence for the Bible*, which is available in the Museum bookroom. Brian is married to Rosie.

Day One (www.dayone.co.uk) organizes Bible-related tours round the British Museum. The authors would like to thank Ian Cooper, Glen Shotton, Mike Keeping and Ben Virgo for their help in this.

Acknowledgements

The authors would like to express their appreciation to the many people who have assisted in the preparation of this guide: in particular Professor Alan Millard and the late Professor Donald Wiseman for their invaluable help, encouragement and advice. We are grateful also for the cooperation of the various departments in the British Museum.

Recommended reading list

For those who would like to read more fully on the Bible and archaeology in the British Museum we recommend.

Alan Millard, *Discoveries from Bible Times: archaeological treasures throw light on the Bible* (Oxford: Lion Publishing, 1997), ISBN: 978 0 7459 3740 3. 352pp. hardback. A magnificent illustrated exploration of ancient civilizations and biblical history.

T.C. Mitchell, *The Bible in the British Museum: Interpreting the Evidence* (London: British Museum Press, 2004) ISBN-10: 0714111554 (Paperback)

A more technical book for those who want to 'dig deeper'.

Evidence for the Bible by Clive Anderson and Brian Edwards. See page 137 for the details of this popular book.

Picture credits

All pictures of items in the British Museum are by courtesy of the Trustees of the British Museum.

British Museum Friends

Becoming a Friend of the British Museum enables you to support the collection and enjoy exclusive benefits including special events and unlimited free entry to exhibitions. Details online or in the British Museum.

DAY ONE TRAVEL GUIDES

This series is unique: each book combines biography and history with a travel guide.
128 pages

- **PLACES OF INTEREST**
- **PACKED WITH COLOUR PHOTOS**
- **CLEAR ILLUSTRATED MAPS**
- **GREAT GIFT IDEA**

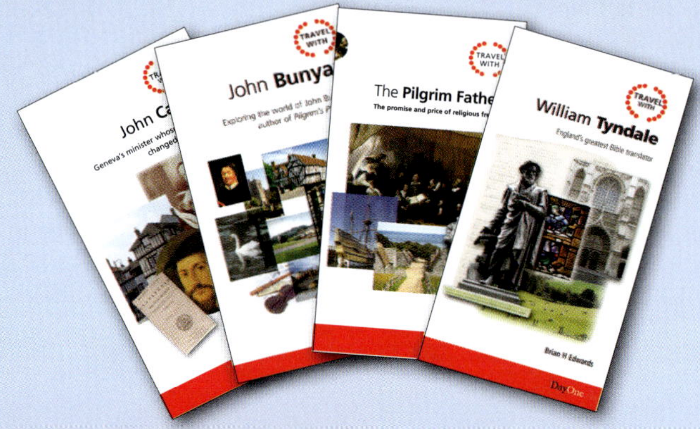

CURRENT TITLES IN THE SERIES

People travel with…

John Blanchard

William Booth

John Bunyan

John Calvin

William Carey

William Cowper

Jonathan Edwards

Billy Graham

William Grimshaw

John Knox

C S Lewis

Martyn Lloyd-Jones

The Martyrs of Mary Tudor

Robert Murray McCheyne

The Pilgrim Fathers

Frances Ridley-Havergal

JC Ryle

C S Spurgeon

William Tyndale

William Wilberforce

Places travel through…

The British Museum

Cambridge

Oxford

Egypt

Israel

Jordan

Parliament

Rome

Wales

ORDER TODAY

For more information visit our web site: www.dayone.co.uk   email— sales@dayone.co.uk

Day One Publications Ryelands Road Leominster HR6 8NZ Tel: 01568 613 740

In Europe call: ++ 44 1568 613 740   **In North America,** call toll-free 888-329-6630

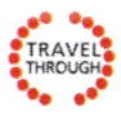

Oxford

City of Saints, Scholars and Dreaming Spires

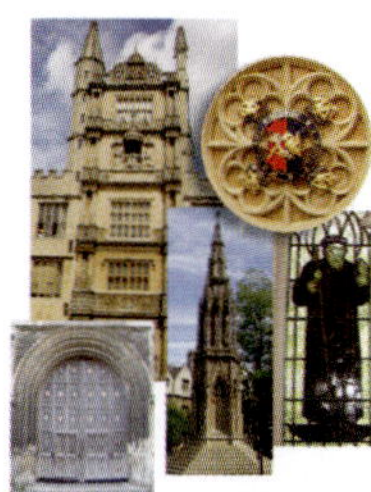

Andrew Atherstone

DayOne

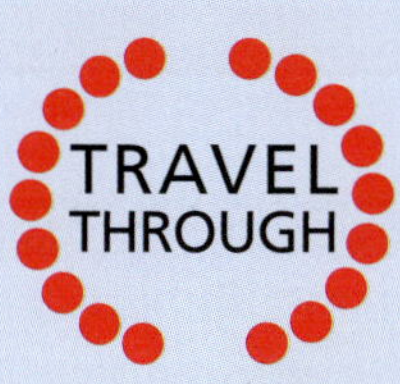

TRAVEL THROUGH

The Houses of Parliament

Cradle of democracy

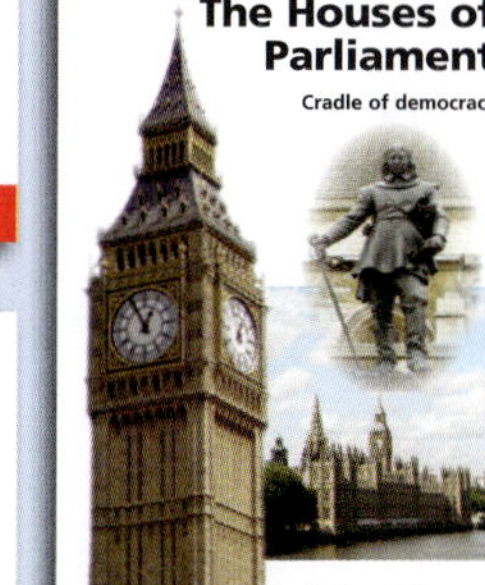

Andrew Atherstone

DayOne

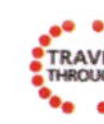

Cambridge

City of Beauty, Reformation and Pioneering Research

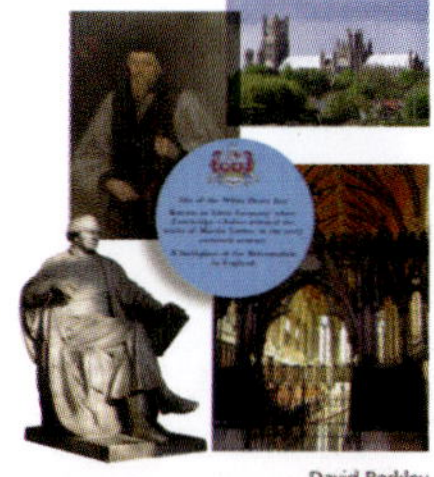

David Berkley

DayOne

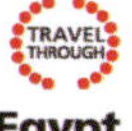

Egypt

Land of Moses, monuments and mummies

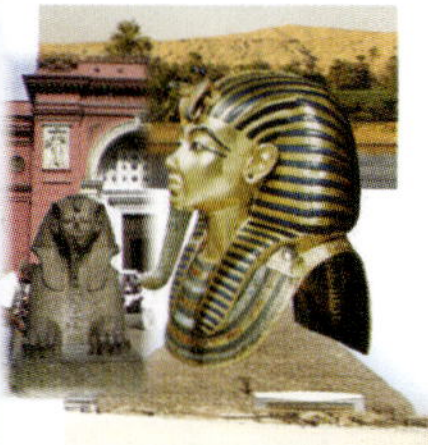

Clive and Amanda Anderson

DayOne

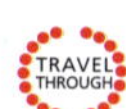

Rome

City of Empire, Christendom and Culture

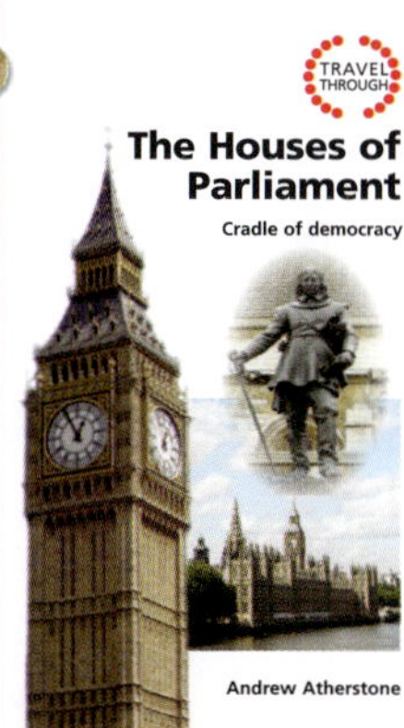

Nigel Scotland

DayOne

TRAVEL WITH

William **Tyndale**

England's greatest Bible translator

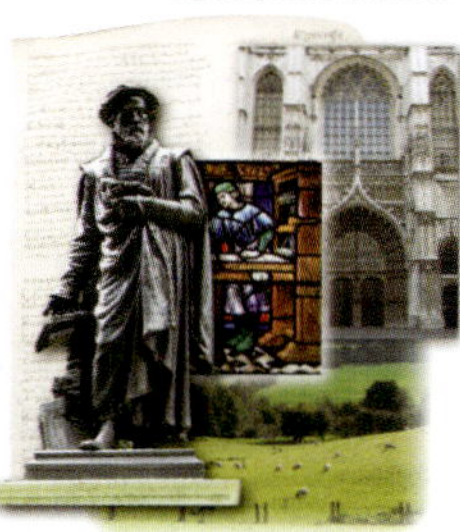

Brian H Edwards

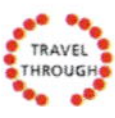

Wales

Land of beauty and blessing

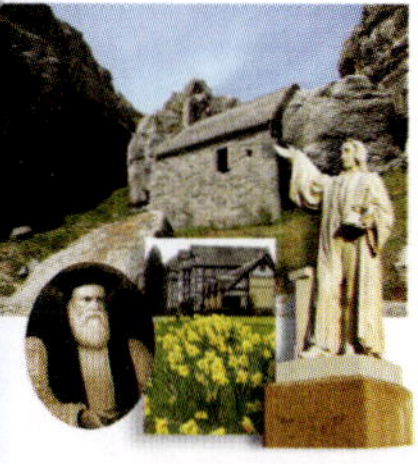

John Aaron and Gwyn Davies

DayOne

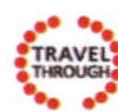

Israel

Land of promise, faith and beauty

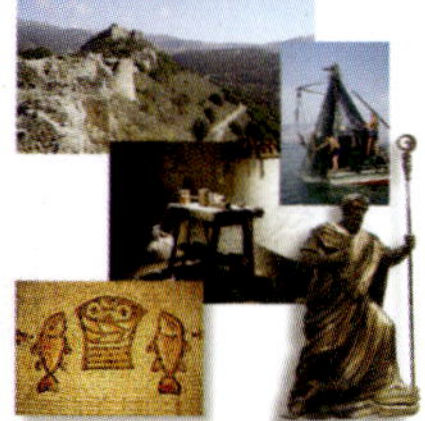

Paul Williams and Clive Anderson

DayOne

DAY ONE GROUP TOURS OF THE BRITISH MUSEUM

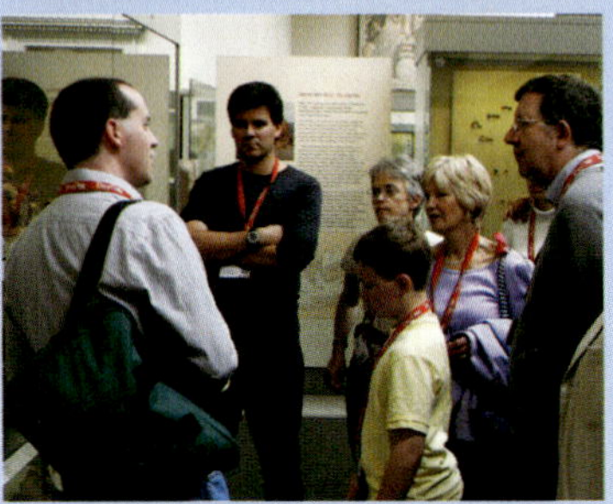

The authors of this guide and their colleagues conduct tours of the Museum to take in many of the Bible related items. To see when tours are planned, go to the Day One website and click on British Museum Tours. Email us with your dates of preference. To arrange a group tour, email us and Day One will contact you.

DAY ONE TOURS OF BIBLE RELATED COUNTRIES

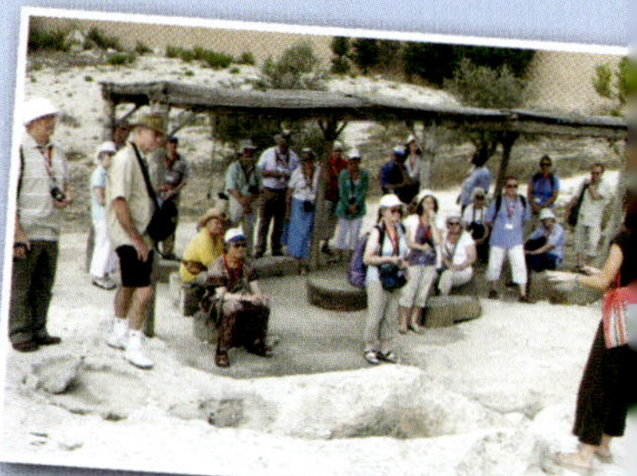

The Travel Guide series began by covering the lives of people who made a significant contribution to the Christian faith. The series has now expanded further by including places of biblical and historical interest, both within the United Kingdom and overseas.

To accompany these guides, DayOne recommend some tours to give tourists an experience that will never be forgotten. Tours include Israel, Egypt, Turkey and Greece. The series also includes Cambridge, Oxford and Rome. Further information on the tours can be obtained online (https://www.dayone.co.uk/pages/overseas-tours) or by contacting Day One Christian Ministries at the address on the back of this book.

Above: Day One tour group at the Nazareth Village, Israel

Right: A Day One tour at Karnak Temple, Egypt

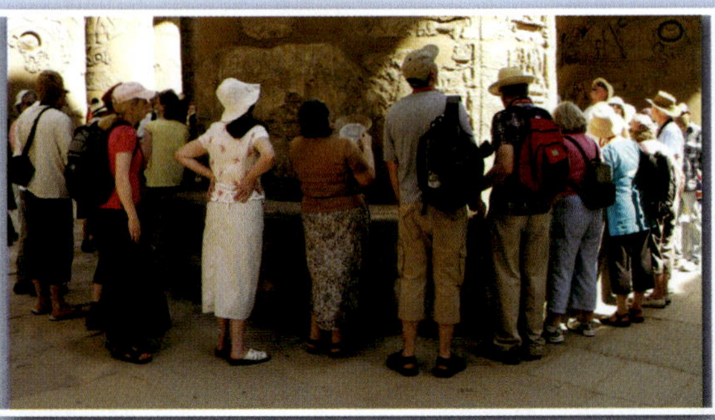

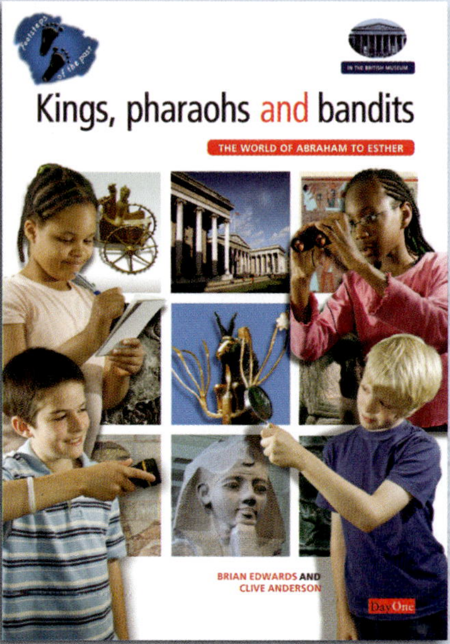

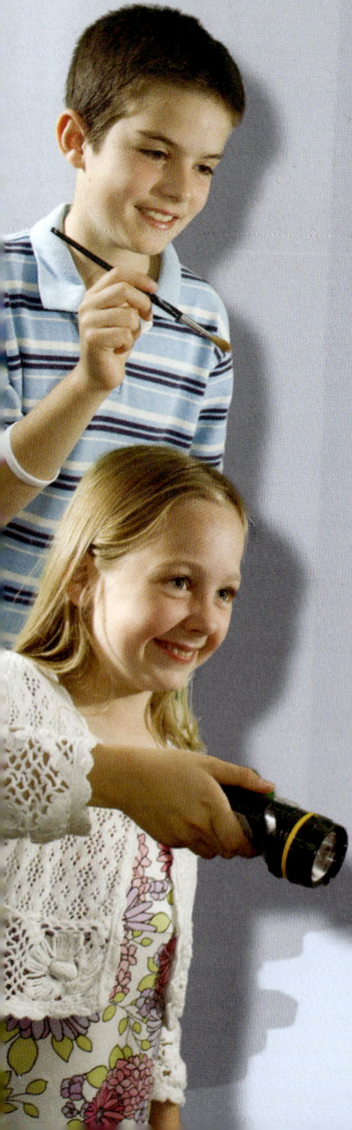

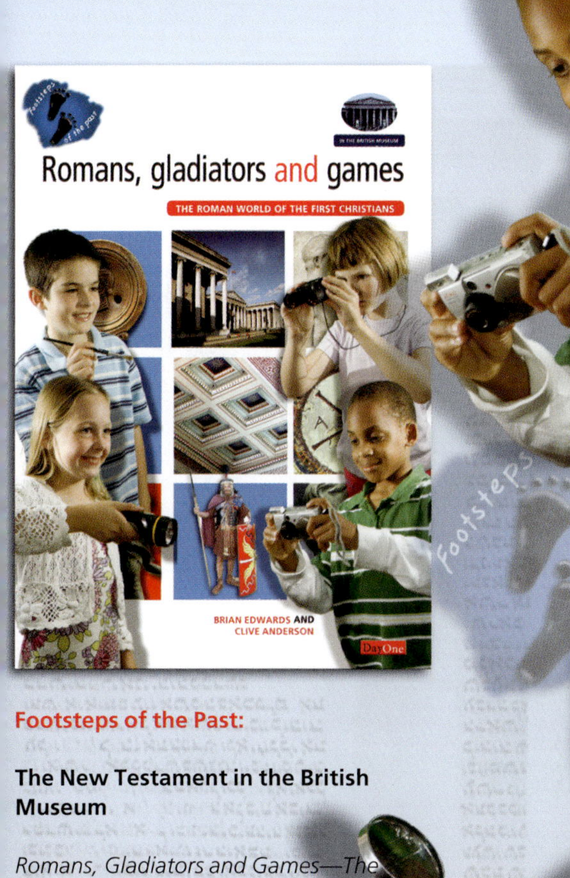

Footsteps of the Past:

The New Testament in the British Museum

Romans, Gladiators and Games—The Roman world of the first Christians

Authors: Brian H Edwards and Clive Anderson

Gladiators fighting to the death, cruel emperors who control the lives of millions and marbles you cannot roll—all waiting for you to discover. Step into the exciting world of the first century, see how people lived, worked, played and died. Into this world a new religion was born. See what marks the Christian faith left on the lives of people, and wonder at the change it made to history. Colour in a centurion, find out the size of Diana, discover the lights that people used in the evenings and many more fascinating activities.
978-1-84625-036-1

For more information
visit our web site:
www.dayone.co.uk
email— sales@dayone.co.uk
Day One Publications
Ryelands Road Leominster HR6 8NZ
Tel: 01568 613 740
In Europe call:
++ 44 1568 613 740
In North America, call toll-free
888-329-6630

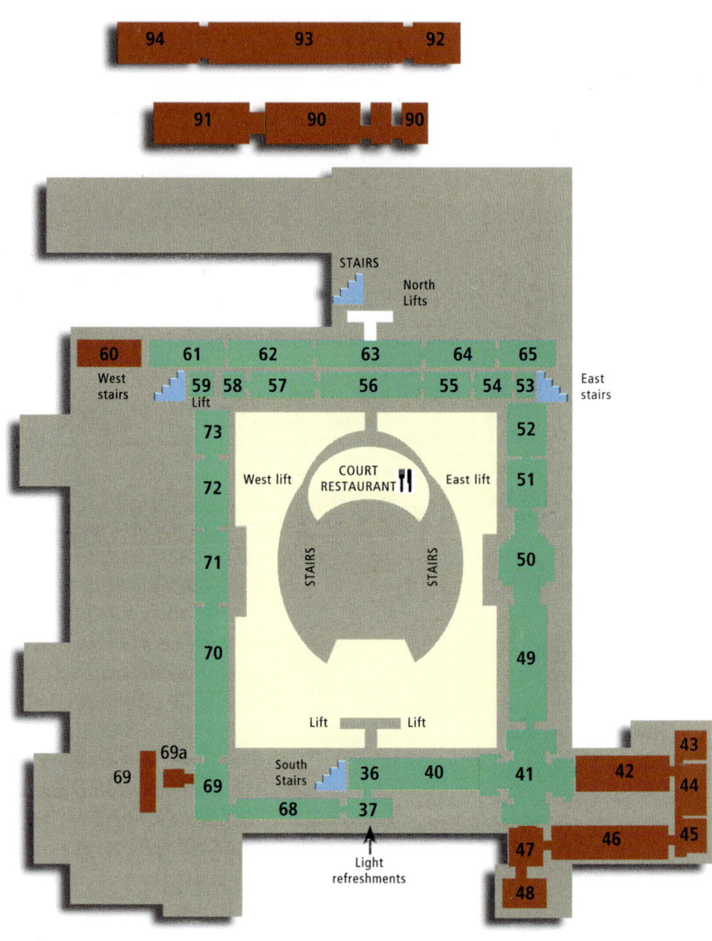

Upper floor Rooms 36–73